PRAISE FOR *A VERY PUBLIC OFFERING*

“Stephan Paternot, former CEO of theglobe.com and world-famous instant millionaire, offers up an engaging memoir that documents the dramatic rise and precipitous fall of the online company he founded. Although Paternot generously shares his personal experiences and struggles, his book also serves as a capsule history of a particular moment in American culture, a moment in which Wall Street’s mania for Internet ventures allowed capital to be invested with a seeming disregard for consequences or common sense . . . The next chapter in Stephan Paternot’s life is bound to be interesting, and probably successful as well.”

Barnes & Noble Review

“Part morality tale, part fairy tale, and part college diary . . . The book is hard not to like. Mr. Paternot ably captures one of life’s rare moments, when the spotlight is shining on you and you haven’t figured out yet that it will soon go dark.”

Wall Street Journal

“It’s a first-person account [illegible]mebody who lived through the roller coaster.’

[illegible]ly

"In this giddy, fast-moving memoir, [Paternot] wisely focuses on the day-to-day mania of the mid and late 90s Internet Revolution, vividly showing what it felt like to run a brand-new company racing headlong across unknown terrain."

Publishers Weekly

"It was the greatest Cinderella story in Silicon Alley history."

New York Post

A VERY PUBLIC OFFERING

A VERY PUBLIC OFFERING

The Story of **theglobe.com**
and the First Internet Revolution

STEPHAN PATERNOT

Published by Actarus Press, New York, NY

Edited and designed by Girl Friday Productions
www.girlfridayproductions.com

Cover design: Joanna Price
Editorial: Alexander Rigby, Monique Vescia
Image Credits: cover © By The_Pixel/Shutterstock;
© By Yevgenij_D/Shutterstock
ISBN (paperback): 978-1-7329324-0-1
ISBN (ebook): 978-1-7329324-1-8

Thanks to Andrew Essex for help with the original 2001 version of the book and Jeremy Blachman for help with the updated 2018 edition.

To Todd (Waddi)—this journey could never have been made without you. Ready for the next one?

CONTENTS

PART 2: The Reality

A VERY PUBLIC OFFERING

PREFACE

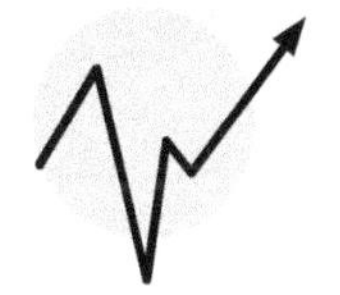

to the Updated Edition

I started writing this book in the fall of 2000, when just a few months had passed after leaving theglobe.com, the company I co-created, built, and shepherded through an IPO; the company that, for a little while, made me feel like I had made a lasting mark on the world (as well as made me rich beyond my wildest dreams, though only on paper); the company that I still thought, at the time I wrote this book, would find a way to survive the bursting of the dot-com bubble and come back to life.

As I rerelease this memoir, almost twenty years have now passed since I walked away, and I've gone on to new pursuits, personal and professional, and have reinvented my career no fewer than a handful of times. With time, I see the world differently than I did as a twenty-seven-year-old who had jumped right from college to leading what was at one point one of the most valuable technology businesses in the world. I read some of these pages now and I cringe just a bit at how naïve I was, and especially how naïve I was about the impossible challenges that every successful business inevitably faces, the tension between long-term vision and short-term profits, between satisfying investors and satisfying customers, between staying ahead of the curve and merely managing, day by day, to stay afloat. (I also can't believe I ever wore plastic pants—you'll find that story later in the book.)

Looking back at it today, I'm incredibly proud of what my friend and cofounder, Todd Krizelman, and I built and of the job we did navigating a brand-new-at-the-time industry and too-early-to-even-understand internet landscape. Our choices (and our company's ultimate fate) may very well have been different a few years, or certainly a decade, later; the highs may not have been quite so high, but the lows would have almost surely not been nearly as low.

This is a first-person, insider account of an exciting time and place in internet history, and I've preserved in this updated edition my thoughts and feelings as they were back when I wrote it—notwithstanding a few typos corrected. At the end, I've added some new perspective, an update as to my life and career after I walked away, and a few thoughts about the tech industry, where it's been and where it's going, that I hope I've earned the right to share.

I was convinced, back when I first wrote these pages, that this chapter in my life was closed, and that I had learned what I needed to learn from my experience. I couldn't have been more wrong. What I didn't fully realize at the time is that as we grow and mature, we're never completely done with our past—our past shapes and informs everything that comes after, and theglobe.com, for better or worse, has certainly influenced every aspect of these past two decades of my life.

I hope you enjoy this trip all the way back to the dawn of the internet era, and I'll see you at the end for an update.

PROLOGUE

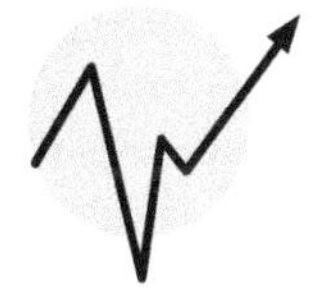

A Good Day to Go Public

When I think about it now, I guess I should have been more concerned that we were going public on Friday the thirteenth.

But sometimes you realize these things too late.

Not that it would have mattered: we didn't have much control over the timing.

I can still picture that morning in 1998. It was a cold, gray November day in New York City, and the last leaves had fallen from the trees near my apartment just off Union Square. This was the Friday that my partner, Todd, and I were supposed to head over to the midtown offices of Bear Stearns, the investment bank that was taking us public. The night before, we'd established an opening price of $9, and just in time, because our S-1 (the detailed SEC registration document) would go stale the coming Monday. Friday was the last possible day to file before everything crapped out. Another delay would be a death sentence. If it didn't happen, we'd run out of money. In other words: game over. The sky was threatening to fall, and our mission was to keep it propped up.

I hadn't slept the night before, spending most of that time watching CNN and the White House announcement that five American aircraft carriers were heading for Iraq. War talk. Todd and I knew that a declaration of war, among other problems, could really disrupt the market. I was up until 3:00 or 4:00 in the morning, tossing and turning, thinking about all the things that could possibly go wrong. You don't get many chances to go public, and for a moment, it seemed like the stars were aligned against us.

At the time, I had a unique way of dealing with stress: Theraflu, straight up, no chaser. Yet, even with an inordinate amount of over-the-counter medication in my system, the eve of the IPO was a long, restless night. At the time, my personal life was in as much tumultuous uncertainty as the market. That Friday evening, after the IPO, I was supposed to go out on a first date with a beautiful girl I'd recently met who was the greatest thing that had happened to me in a long time. So I was doubly anxious. My biggest fear was, of course, that everything would go wrong. With possibilities of war, romance, and some serious banking all dancing in my head, I was scared shitless.

So, on Friday the thirteenth, I got out of bed at 7:00 a.m., showered, and dressed for a 9:30 meeting at Bear Stearns. My first thought was CNN. I switched it on and called Todd. "You watch the news?" The ships were on their way, but a declaration of war, at least for that day, was now considered unlikely.

I couldn't eat breakfast due to the jitters and walked out of the apartment with an empty, quaking stomach.

Breakfast aside, what does one wear to an IPO? We'd thought for a moment about suits, but I deliberately remember thinking, *No, I will not put on a suit.* Todd and I always dressed casually. There's nothing greater than standing amid all those bankers in suits while people wonder, *Who are those two college boys in khakis and leather jackets?* In reality (and in pictures), we were just two scruffy college kids in ratty sweaters.

By 9:00, the sky had turned blue, and it was a beautiful day. My nerves were calmed a little when I met Todd at the northeast corner of Union Square. We grabbed a cab straight up Park Avenue, through the underground passageway beneath Murray Hill, and up and around Grand Central, hurtling down the switchback. The cabby was speeding, but I wanted him to go faster. I remember we both had huge bags under our eyes. We looked like hell. Note to self: if you're going to look like crap, the day of your IPO is not the best day to do so.

We arrived at Bear Stearns at 9:15 with plenty of time to spare and passed quickly through the lobby. By then, we'd been there so many times they knew exactly who we were. Still, the interminable security check-in made us anxious as we headed into the elevator to meet the Bear Stearns people on the *thirteenth floor*—another telling sign I missed at the time—where there were endless conference rooms, all marked alphabetically. We'd always met in conference rooms assigned boring, unsymbolic letters like *H* or *M* or *L*, and we wondered constantly what power plays occurred behind door *A*.

This time they ushered us into an even smaller and stuffier room than usual. Shortly thereafter, Ed Cespedes met us. Ed did mergers and acquisitions (M&A) for Dancing Bear, the VC (venture capital) outfit formed by Michael Egan, the former Alamo Rent A Car president who'd ultimately sink $20 million into our company, theglobe.com. Ed was one of those guys who loved the job, loved the action of growing and creating companies. He'd been instrumental in setting this whole thing up, and we had a special bond with him. He'd turn out to be one of the few genuine good guys in this story.

Around 9:30, a few Stearns muckety-mucks swung by to make sure we had the important tools: croissants, bagels, and gallons of coffee. I had a bagel with cream cheese, even though I still didn't have much of an appetite. (Whenever we went to a banking deal at a law firm, they always had all this food lying around, so I'd end up stuffing my face. What I didn't know at the time is that I'd become lactose intolerant, which was why I continually suffered from big-time stomachaches.) As we sat around, pounding bagels with cream cheese and smiling vacantly at each other for what seemed an eternity, the stress started peaking. The closer we got to showtime, the more we felt that something was amiss, and the more my stomach hurt.

Then the bankers came in. I won't bother mentioning their names, since all the Bear Stearns people who worked with us are gone now—there's no one left for me to feel bitter toward anymore. Anyway, one of them came in and I couldn't contain myself anymore. "Are we going to *price*?" I blurted. "Is this thing going through, or what?"

"Yes, yes, yes," the banker said casually.

"Oh, and by the way," he added with a grin, "word is it's going to open somewhere between $20 and $30 a share."

Here's what you should know. Forty-eight hours earlier, we'd struggled just to raise the price up to $8 a share. The best that Bear Stearns had been able to do was raise our price by a dollar.

Naturally, Todd and I were flabbergasted by this new amount. I'd assumed we'd price at $9, and if the stock went up, it would happen later in the process. But that's not the way it goes down. In actuality, there's a buildup in the price as a stock goes on to the market. But somewhere between $20 to $30? That's 200 percent higher than we thought! This was absolutely insane. Despite the stomachache, both Todd and I were in giddy hysterics.

Meanwhile, we were still sitting there in that room, waiting, waiting, waiting. Waiting, waiting, waiting, waiting. Then, finally, at around 10:15, a few more bankers came to take us down to the second floor—the trading floor—a huge cavernous space with four hundred traders, all eyeballs glued to their consoles and monitors, all screaming—like a scene out of *Wall Street.*

They led us through a narrow passageway that cut through the middle of the floor to the edge of the room, along this tiny walkway, like a prison catwalk above the inmates. At the end of the hall was a big corner office where Ace Greenberg sat.

Ace Greenberg was the chairman of Bear Stearns and a legend in the finance world. He'd been there for some ungodly number of years, and everyone knew him. I remember thinking that if we were being handled by the chairman, it must mean we were part of an omnipotent inner circle and would be well taken care of.

Ace was well known for doing card tricks. While we were sitting there, going insane from the anxiety, Ace did card tricks for us. Cards vanished out of his hands and then reappeared. He was so good at it, we actually wondered, *How the hell did he do that?*

About 10:35, another banker came in with an update. "Any minute now," he said. Ace's office was all glass windows. We could see the traders out in the middle of the floor; off in a pit, there was another pod of traders who would represent our deal. This particular banker kept shuffling back and forth between the two rooms like a gopher.

A few minutes later, he returned. He looked right at me and said, "By the way, the deal's not going to open at $20 to $30." He had this strange expression on his face, and I actually felt my heart beginning to break. Then he said, "It may hit between $50 and $60." I jumped out of my chair and said to no one in particular, "What the fuck?"

Everyone burst out laughing. Even Ace.

At 10:50, the banker came back again. "All right, guys," he said, "let's go." We all walked down that little aisle, single file, like prisoners marching toward the gallows.

Down in the pit, I could see a few people eyeing us. Now remember, IPOs happen—at most—a few times a month at any given bank. So the pit people always make an effort to check and see who the lucky bastards are. Since we weren't in suits and we'd just been screaming, the people in the pit must have thought something really bizarre was going on. I'm sure someone said, "Who are those two kids? What the hell is this?"

Once past the pit, we were taken to a wall of computer screens set in a room that looked like an extension of the *Millennium Falcon* with all these monitors and triggers just ready to fire away. Three or four guys sat behind the screens, and there was one main guy behind them—the head pit boss for our trade.

This guy was too busy to talk to us. He was fiddling with papers, whispering numbers. I still had no idea what was going on. I checked out the screen, trying to understand something, but it was all completely unfamiliar. In other words, more waiting. Then I realized we were starting a countdown. The thing was going to happen exactly at the stroke of 11:00. All of a sudden, the main guy was counting, "Ten, nine, eight, seven . . ." It was almost too much; Todd and I were in disbelief.

Do you want to know what an IPO feels like? Honestly? You feel like you're about to die. You're standing at heaven's gate, your whole life is flashing before you, and there's a judgment coming. We'd never done this before. We weren't bankers. We didn't know what it all meant. In my head, I'd worked out all these grossly exaggerated animated scenes, but then I was standing there actually mumbling stupid things like a Warner Bros. cartoon character.

Then it hits. "Three, two, one . . ." *Boom.*

The main trader yelled out, "Eighty-seven!" He was frenetically writing down numbers on some papers, and the whole room—bankers and everybody—was yelling and screaming. The whole room was one giant *"Waaaaa!"* Everyone started howling; a few guys threw their phones down. All these heads popped up like prairie dogs; everyone was looking. It was total primal chaos.

They were all looking at me.

My first reaction was, "What the hell is eighty-seven?! Eighty-seven pesos?" Everyone laughed at me. They said, "No, eighty-seven dollars."

Then, five seconds later, someone screamed out, "Ninety-seven!" Todd and I could only stare at each other, incredulous. The day before, we were at $9 and the deal was nearly dead. Now we were at $97. It took me a moment to realize we'd just become a $1 billion company.

Sweat was dripping off me, and my shirt was soaked. I could feel my body temperature soaring, the pressure building up to my head, and everyone was still yelling.

That was when the phones started ringing. A friend called to say, "*OhmyGod,* you guys are on CNN *right now.* Wait! You're on CNBC, too—it's breaking news." Everyone in the room was talking at once, and I heard myself becoming hoarse. My throat was beginning to kill me. The stock kept fluctuating. It flew between $97 and $60 within seconds. *Boom, boom! Boom, boom!* Up and down, thirty points up and down equaled a $300 million swing in market cap. It was a wild fluctuation. All the institutions that had gone into the stock were dumping it like crazy. As soon as the stock would dip, somebody would buy in. To get a sense of how much action we generated, think about this: theglobe.com IPO was a three-million-share deal. But sixteen million shares traded hands that day; each share was traded on average more than five times over.

People we'd never met made millions because of us. Anyone who put a hundred grand down made $1 million. Even the traders at Bear Stearns were dumbfounded. We'd just set worldwide stock market history; no one had ever seen anything like this before. And we were twenty-four years old!

As we were heading over to the NASDAQ office for a press conference, an older trader, a gentleman in his nineties, started tugging at my jacket. "Are you the guys who caused such a ruckus here today?" he asked. I nodded. "In my forty years on Wall Street," he said, "I have never seen anything like this before."

Today, those words mean a lot to me.

Still, at the time, I wasn't thinking about making history or that I was about to be running a billion-dollar company. I was thinking that I'd just extended our lease on life. Everything Todd and I had worked toward for four years wasn't exploding into a fiery ball. I didn't have to find a "normal" job.

I remember Mike turning to me and saying, "Well, enjoy it, boys. This is a really unsustainable number. It can't last."

Was *that* ever an understatement.

Now, three years later, when I meet people, a lot of them say, "Hey, I know you. I saw you on CNN. You're the kid who took that company public and set stock market history. You're the guy who was running a billion-dollar company at twenty-four. You're the one who was worth $97 million dollars before your twenty-fifth birthday." Then they smile and say, "You're the guy who lost it all."

They're right, and this is my story.

My name is Stephan Paternot. Between 1994 and 2000, I was the cofounder and co-CEO of theglobe.com, an online community that I started with my former college buddy Todd Krizelman when we were both twenty. On that fateful Friday the thirteenth in 1998, after four years of preparation—an adventure that began in the labs of Cornell University and culminated at the nexus of Wall Street and Silicon Alley—theglobe.com went public at up to $97 a share. I held a million shares. You do the math.

Fourteen months later, I watched in horror as the stock plummeted to $7, erasing my fortune almost as quickly as I'd managed to amass it. In August 2000, with the stock at $2, I formally stepped down as the chief executive of the company I cofounded.

The company's rise and fall, and the crazy era in American business history that theglobe.com ostensibly embodied, has never been properly documented.

Until now. Enjoy the ride.

PART 1

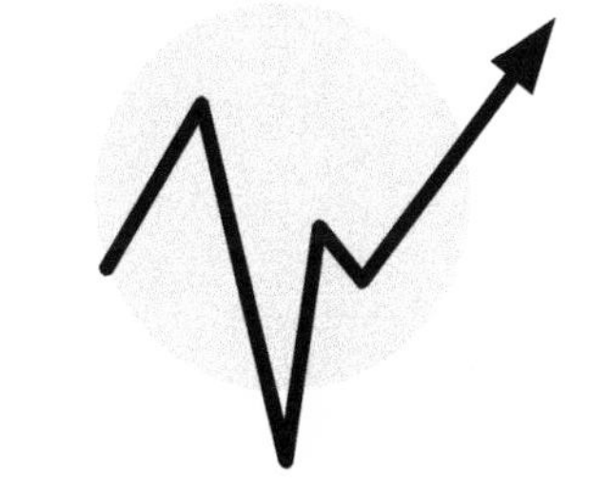

The Dream

1

It All Began with Snails

Growing Up Around the Globe

My first memory took place in our backyard in San Francisco where my mom would sprinkle snails on the hedges near the front lawn to churn the earth. Before I could even talk, I played in the mud with these slow-moving, slimy creatures. Playing with snails probably made me think I moved pretty fast.

I was born in San Francisco in 1974. Beyond the snails, I don't remember much more about the American phase of my childhood. There's a photo of me on the beach from that time, and I'm the little kid with a head three times too big for his body. And I'm completely blond. The little kid in that picture seems like an imposter in part since my hair went to a very dark brown as I grew up.

After San Francisco, we moved to Switzerland, but getting there requires a brief detour. My dad is Yves Paternot, a Swiss citizen who graduated from Harvard Business School and helped launch the US branch of Adia (now The Adecco Group, the largest temp staffing firm in the world), and who later served as CEO of the company.

While he attended Harvard Business School, my mom—Mia Heineman—was at Boston University. After they met and fell in love, my mom dropped out; she never formally finished her degree. Once married, they moved to California after Dad was hired by the founder of Adia to expand the company into the US. Shortly thereafter, Maddy, my sister, was born. Two years later, in 1974, I came along.

When I was four, my dad was transferred back to Switzerland, to the headquarters of Adia, and so we moved to Lausanne. This wasn't such a bad move for my dad since he'd be closer to his parents, who lived in Europe, but my whole American background was essentially erased overnight.

I was enrolled in Mont Olivet, a Catholic school in Lausanne. My teachers were nuns—and with nuns came rules. We had to follow the rules, like studying catechism every day, or else.

Lausanne is in the French-speaking region of Switzerland. Since I was only four (I'd stay until I was age nine), I essentially forgot whatever English I'd learned. French quickly became my preferred means of communication.

The entire Swiss population is less than six million people, and Lausanne is a relatively small city near a large lake, surrounded by the Alps. Just over 100,00 people live there;

everything is classic village life. Don't get me wrong. People love to vacation there. It's a beautiful little country. But the key word is *little.*

My problem with provincial life is the provincial mentality that comes with it. I'm sure that some Swiss people will be pissed at me when they read this, but here's the bottom line: it's a great place to retire (think Florida with mountains), but it's strange to grow up there. Even the presidential system is bizarre. One of the first things I realized about the society I grew up in was that they have six presidents who rotate into office every two years. So, if you ask Swiss citizens, especially young ones, who their president is, they rarely know. They actually don't know who their president is. I find this especially ironic since Europeans have such a good time making fun of Americans.

When I was eight years old, my mom and dad divorced after eleven years of marriage. This was during my fourth year in Switzerland, and at the risk of overstating the obvious, I'll say it was a tremendous event in my life. I remember crying, but for some reason thinking they weren't actual tears. I went through the motions of grief because that's what I thought I was supposed to do. But I actually felt happy about the fact that I was going to live with my mom. I would be the man now.

My mom is a very liberated American woman. My dad is more of an old school European. I think my mom went into the relationship loving my father, but hoping to turn him into the man she always wanted him to be. Of course, my dad entered the relationship never wanting to change anything.

After my parents split up, my mom, Maddy, and I moved to a small apartment. We'd been living in Lausanne in a nice house with a garage and a large garden. Thinking about it now, I don't think my mom had much money. She was supporting us with whatever money she'd inherited from her parents. We may not have been rich, but I enjoyed plenty of entertainment. I remember watching movies like *Condorman* and *Raiders of the Lost Ark* in the local little Swiss theater. Even at that age, I was particularly drawn to film. Meanwhile, my dad would visit as much as he could, bringing us gifts, new Walkmans, and other electronics that he picked up on business trips to Japan.

After living in Switzerland for five years, just as I was fully adjusting to speaking French, my mom told us we were moving back to the States. My dad, however, stayed in Switzerland and married my stepmother, Monica; shortly thereafter, Eric and Sophie, my half brother and half sister, were born.

We moved to Greenwich, Connecticut, to a place called Lyon Farm, near where my mother grew up. In Switzerland, we'd been speaking Franglais, a kind of pidgin French combined with English. In Connecticut, I had to start all over and learn actual English.

Around this time, my mom started dating. She briefly dated two chumps, and then she met Anders Bergendahl, a London-based Merrill Lynch banker who she's been married to now for nearly twenty years. Of course, I had no idea at the time that they'd end up together for so long. All I knew was that this guy lived in London, and that was a long way away. Mostly, I was pleased that she'd finally met a man she could love. But I was a lot less pleased that we were moving again, this time to London.

And so, a year and a half after arriving in Connecticut from Switzerland from San Francisco, we picked up and moved to England. By this time, my English was a half-French, half-American hybrid-cum-disaster.

We lived in a narrow, dimly lit house in Kensington, right off Victoria Road. It was a cool house that looked like a run-down East Village walk-up in New York City, with a tiny garden. Not long after settling in, it was my mom and Anders's turn to procreate—soon David and Alexander, my next two half brothers, were born.

My first few months in London were so scary. I went to a school called Hill House, which was an international school with a distinctly British flavor. The guy who ran it was an old British colonel. Everything was "Discipline! Righto, everyone!" I received cadet training with actual rifles. My fellow students had a lot of fun mimicking my American-French accent. (When people are making fun of me, I prefer that they not be armed!)

I quickly noticed the major distinction between the American and European school systems. In England, everything is handed to you on a platter but then force-fed down your throat. It's easy, since you don't have to make any decisions. But the reality is that you don't have any choices.

Hill House was famous for making kids wear knickerbockers—little, red, puffy pants. You're just asking to be beaten up in the street. Then they add in a bright rust-orange sweater. We looked like we'd been rudely yanked from the pages of a Dickens novel. Every day we'd walk from the school, which was in Knightsbridge, up to Kensington Gardens in the most spastic uniforms ever seen. There we'd play soccer and rugby until our knees and feet were lacquered in mud—there were no gym outfits—and then come back to class all dirty and sweaty for the rest of the day.

The food was standard British crap. After a while, I began to get over the culture shock and started excelling at math. I was still very poor at writing, however. I'd never read the standard schoolbooks like *Catcher in the Rye, Animal Farm,* all the classics. So I had never developed any idiomatic ease or analytical skills in English, and now they wanted me to read Shakespeare.

At thirteen, I was admitted to the City of London School, an all-boys British school where I'd stay till sixteen. My tenure at CLS wasn't helped by my unfortunate foot problem: flat feet. I'd had an operation to fix my right foot, and because of my bad feet, I couldn't wear regular shoes. I always had to wear sneakers. So I was in this British school where everyone's in dark uniforms, and, God, did I stand out in the crowd! I became known as "the kid with the white sneakers." Half the kids hated me because I had them, and the other half thought I was cool—the only kid who'd managed to break the rules.

At CLS, we had a choice of community service or combined cadet force. I opted for combined cadet force. What a moron! For two years, I did full military training. Not only did we practice during the week, but there were sessions during the year when we'd head to the countryside and suffer the indignity of nocturnal, self-reliance military training.

They used to drop us off twenty miles from our tents. We'd have twenty-four hours to get back to base camp. We had to carry fifty-pound packs while wearing full military gear. Since I had to wear rigid military boots, my feet were bloody stumps.

In the sense that a British school is all about education at the expense of socialization, the City of London School was the worst of the worst. They forgot that we needed to mature as human beings, too. Maybe these particular boys were so cruel and socially inept because they had no training in how to interact with females. We were sixteen and completely clueless! I had to adapt—and fast.

It so happened that my sister was going to the American School in London, which sounded like a dream. First of all, it was coed. Plus, it was international, there were no uniforms, and you picked the classes that interested you. What a concept!

So, at sixteen, I tested into the American School. It was 1990. Since my sister is a year and a half older than me, we were at that stage when brothers and sisters don't get along all that well. She and her friends were into older men, and I was the drooling younger brother. Inevitably, that awkward period began to pass.

Meanwhile, in school I discovered computer science. Programming was particularly interesting to me. Until then, the only computer I ever had was a Commodore 64 with 64K RAM, and I used it to play some primitive cassette games. (There was one called "Chopper Command" that I was very fond of.)

Now, all of a sudden, I'm sitting in front of these computers called Apples and I'm thinking, *What the hell are these?* At City of London School, I'd used these Brit computers like Acorn and Spectrum, but they were just pathetic pieces of equipment in comparison.

In the American School, I discovered the Macintosh—and what a hard drive was. Then they started showing us something called a BBS (Electronic Bulletin Board), where you could call up America and "download" things. I got my first 300-baud modem; one night, I hooked up to the phone line for eight hours straight on a long-distance call to download a half-meg game. The phone bill was astronomical. My parents were not pleased.

I was fascinated by the whole concept of the BBS. Back then, half the fun was trying to find the phone numbers to these exclusive clubs. There were ultra-elite ones, and you had to know someone who could get you in. And, of course, you couldn't download unless you uploaded something. You had to earn credits. As I slowly turned into a geek, I started spending an alarming amount of time playing computer games.

During my first semester, I took Intro to Computer Science with Professor John Servente. This guy was incredibly quirky; you either loved him or you hated him. And if you loved computers, he loved you. Remember, we had just come out of the late 1980s when people were still asking, "Why the hell should I have to take a computer science class? I'm never going to use a computer."

While I was discovering Apples, I also discovered girls. Even better, I'd been told that a girl or two in school was actually convinced I was cute. I ended up dating Elayna—popular, attractive, and someone whose attention made me the envy of my peers. We wound up going out for two and a half years, two of which would be long-distance.

When I think about the pride I had—Stephan Paternot, a computer geek who'd never even known how to speak to a girl, walking around with Elayna on my arm—I think, *How pathetic.* But back then, it caused a change in my whole perspective on life: it was the first indication that I could pursue what I wanted, but not be locked in as just a geeky, lonely engineer.

As my computer science education evolved, I decided to push things further and take a programming class. From there, I moved into advanced programming—almost all in the Pascal computer language. The more I took, the more into it I got.

Back then, the visuals of computer programming were primarily a black screen with text scrolling up and down. It was exactly like DOS, a long time before pointing and clicking.

Programming for me quickly became all about identifying a problem and deciding what to do about it. What did I want the machine to do? I'd backtrack my way from there. I sometimes worked on accounting systems; other times it was drawing. Sometimes it was just mathematical problems—extremely complex mathematical problems that required a computer to execute.

Programming for me just felt *good.* I liked being up at 4:00 in the morning, in my own little world where there were no limits as to what I could do. I could make the machine change what it could do, do it faster, more efficiently, figure out these problems . . . problem *solving.* With physics, something I'd briefly considered, I could figure stuff out on paper, but there was nothing especially tangible to make. With a computer, I could get a glimpse of the future. In retrospect, I realize we were just coming out of the Dark Ages of computing and I was watching it all unfurl.

Aside from computer science, my only other interest, or skill I should say, came from my history and psychology classes. Initially, unbeknownst to me, my teachers thought that my communication skills were strong. I discovered this one day when my history teacher asked if I'd like to join the debate team. I was surprised, considering I had changed languages and cultures so many times. I had become accustomed to living a somewhat shy and introverted life, and communicating or debating were the last things I was interested in. Although I didn't join the debate team, I did decide to join the Model United Nations program in which students from all over the world flew to The Hague in Holland to represent countries in mock debates. On my first occasion, I represented Russia and passed my resolution for nonproliferation of nuclear weapons around the world. Presenting in front of three thousand students was no piece of cake, but it was the first sign that I could speak well in public—and I loved it. This was the first inkling that there might be more to my life than just programming.

As I approached the end of high school, my next move—college—became a huge issue. I'd taken the SAT and scored 720 in math and 540 in verbal. Clearly, my math was stronger. My dad had always wanted me to study in Switzerland to be near him. He wanted me to go to the Federal Polytechnic School of Lausanne, a pure engineering program in a small town. I was opposed to this idea, but Dad was adamant. He said, "Steph, I pay my taxes, which automatically gets you free university in Switzerland." For him, it was an opportunity to save a large amount of money. It was a good engineering school—prepaid—and he definitely thought engineering was my thing. But I wasn't convinced. For the first time, I was discovering new horizons. I'd seen *Animal House* and all those other crazy stories about college life in America, and I wanted to have that experience. I wanted to be thousands of miles away from my family, be alone to discover and experience life in an entirely different world (of course, not realizing the downsides—20/20 hindsight and all).

I was always reluctant to confront my dad. (I would oppose my mom, but not my father.) When and if I had to challenge him, my hands would be shaking with fear at the prospect. When he came to visit me in London my final year of high school, we had another debate about my future, and I burst into tears, hating him for making it so difficult to tell him what I really wanted. I recall being in a restaurant with my dad and my stepmother, Monica, and her saying, "Yves, let the kid speak." She understood that it wasn't always about winning. It was about whether he wanted to be loved for the rest of his life, whether he wanted his kids to look up to him or to hate him. I was in tears from frustration and nerves, and I felt betrayed not being able to express myself openly.

I wanted to curse at him so badly. Do something that would insult him. But the last time I had done that, it had resulted in a terrible scene for both of us. I was much younger and had let a curse slip in the course of a conversation I was having with my dad. Out of reflex, he slapped me in the mouth, hard enough that my lip split. I started bleeding all over myself. I began crying, feeling humiliated from the slap, and my father was embarrassed by what he'd done. My father was not a bad man who liked to beat me, far from it. But a thing like that has a fundamental impact on you, especially when you're young. After that, I was never really comfortable speaking my mind around him.

So the argument about college continued; I wanted to go to the States and my mom supported my decision to leave. I'd applied to Penn, Cornell, Tufts, and a few backup schools, and was admitted to most of them. I didn't get into Brown, which was my first choice. And so it came down to Penn and

Cornell. I decided to attend Cornell because it was the better school for what I thought I wanted to pursue.

My dad remained steadfast: "You're going to Switzerland." I said, "No. This time I'm doing what I want."

I was on my way to Ithaca.

2

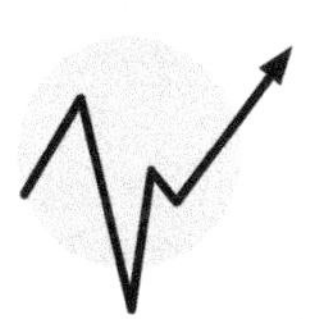

The World Wide What?

The Origin of the Internet and How Two Cornell Freshmen Glimpsed the Future

I arrived at Cornell in the fall of 1992. I was eighteen, freshly back from a one-month internship at the International Olympic Committee in Switzerland.

I remember wearing my standard British garb—a long leather jacket, a beanie (the hat, not the furry toy) that my sister gave me from a trip she'd taken to Morocco, and dark leather shoes with funky buckles. Everything about me sort of reeked of London, to the point where people asked if I was "the guy from the UK."

This was right when the United States was embracing grunge, and everyone seemed to be swathed in flannel. Coming from London, I had no idea what grunge was. To make matters worse, I'd begun growing my hair long. By the time I hit Ithaca, it was like some crazy weed that I arranged in a topknot with a rubber band.

Ithaca has always been known for its gray skies. Simply put, eleven months of the year, it's gray—if it doesn't happen to be blizzarding.

I remember my first day: all these people running around in red Cornell T-shirts, orientation counselors, people to welcome you, greet you, help carry your luggage to your dorm room. I quickly learned that there was a west campus and a north campus. West was considered the cooler area; north campus was geekier. I opted for a single-bedroom dorm on west campus (as opposed to sharing with a roommate) so that Elayna could visit me.

I found myself isolated in a dorm called McFaddin, a sinister old stone building. To get to my room, I had to climb this dark stone staircase to the third floor. My place had ancient little windows. Even when they were shut, a draft came in from the outside—it was always freezing. My windows overlooked the tennis courts. Someone was always playing tennis. All day and night, *dink, dink, dink.* My bed consisted of a mattress on the floor; there was one minuscule closet. (I was now experiencing the downside of American college life!)

This was back in the day when having your own computer was just starting to become standard procedure. This was something of a surprise for a kid from the technological backwaters of London. I felt left out and isolated without a machine of my own.

So one of the first things I did was hunt around for a computer; I remember searching everywhere for something that was functional yet economical. The coolest computer at the time was the PowerBook, so I ended up with a 20-MHz PowerBook 145. I shelled out the extra cash so I could have a 40-megabyte hard drive—that's 40 megs, not gigs. Even then, memory was everything. When you look back now, 4 megs of RAM and a 40-meg hard drive is a joke. But it did have a cute little black-and-white screen.

I didn't know about Moore's law at the time, but I quickly saw it in action when only six months later my fellow students had newer and far superior computers. To keep up, I convinced my dad to shell out $1,000 so I could buy myself a Centris 610, which had a 25-MHz chip. This was infinitely superior and came with 16 megs of RAM. It was a speed demon, and I became the envy of a couple of new friends who'd bought their computers just before me.

The good computer helped me feel more comfortable, but those first few weeks were still unnerving. Then there was the nagging question of what classes I should be taking. In my first semester, I planned to major in environmental engineering. I'd seen a lot of television programs about the environment going to hell, and I felt a minor calling, or at least I thought I did.

In my first environmental engineering class, we had to set up computerized flowcharts. We had to figure out, depending on the rate of river runoff and pollutants going in, how fast we could get rid of the pollution. Interesting in theory, but not for me.

It took just one semester for me to realize that I didn't want to pursue environmental engineering. Meanwhile, I was required to take freshman English, which meant Shakespeare. At this point, as I still wrote much better in French, I did terribly.

Slowly but surely, I made a few friends. While sitting in my friend's dorm room one day, in walks this little guy who looked like he couldn't have been older than fourteen or fifteen. I didn't know who he was, but he was certainly interesting looking: about five foot four, with short curly brown hair, brown eyes, and arms and legs hairy enough to match Robin Williams. I shook hands with the guy and he introduced himself as Todd Krizelman. Then he let out this killer smile, a sort of Jack-Nicholson-as-the-Joker grin from ear to ear. It was a funny visage to my cartoonish brain, but you could tell this guy had real warmth of character, even a sort of perpetual happiness about him. But although I knew he was a college student, and therefore must have been about eighteen or nineteen, I couldn't get over how young he looked.

Todd went over to his desk, and switched on his computer. My jaw dropped. Todd was probably the first guy in Cornell history to own a PowerBook 180. I mean, this piece of gear was an order of magnitude superior to what I had. (And it wasn't even the only screen he had. He'd already hooked his active matrix laptop with sixteen shades of gray to an external color monitor.)

Right away I started asking Todd about his gear, but he was pretty tight-lipped. He granted me twenty minutes to play one of his games. He seemed very organized, and it was clear he didn't like people messing with his stuff. Todd had this amazing flight game, a really smooth World War II fighter pilot simulator. I rapidly became addicted.

One evening, I was sitting in Todd's dorm room, playing with the flight simulator, when I noticed him take out a little pack from his desk drawer. This was nothing out of the ordinary, until he opened the pack and pulled out a syringe right in front of me. Two seconds later, he jabbed the syringe into a small vial, drew out some liquid, and stabbed himself in the waist with the needle. Then he turned to me with the needle in the air and said, "Now it's your turn." You should have seen my face. Then he smiled and said, "Only kidding. I'm a diabetic. I do this every day."

Because I'd never known anyone with diabetes, I spent the next few hours receiving a detailed lesson on what the disease entailed. By this time, Todd was a biogenetics major; he lived to give long-winded presentations of this stuff. What I found most fascinating—aside from the fact that he had to inject insulin several times a day—was this: if he didn't inject regularly or maintain body sugar at just the right level, he could end up in a coma, or even die. Todd also enjoyed telling me how easily insulin could kill an innocent bystander—and that there'd be no trace of what caused his death (think *Reversal of Fortune* with Jeremy Irons). Todd loved running up to me, syringe in hand, pretending to stab me. I didn't find this as amusing as Todd did! Of course, diabetes is nothing to laugh at.

Todd had taken a few computer science classes but very quickly discovered that he hated it. He couldn't program to save his life. Meanwhile, programming came so naturally to me that I ended up trading tutoring for more game time. Todd had one Pascal assignment in which he had to create an on-screen menu of different shapes—a triangle, a square, a star. Not only did he have to draw those elements, but he had to be able to point and click on the screen where he wanted it to draw the shapes. It seemed pretty basic to me, so we cut a deal. I would come and play his games, and then I'd help him with his programming. Todd made it through the class with a C-plus.

By the end of our freshman year, Todd and I were working in his dorm room so much that we might as well have been roommates. In time I'd learn that he'd come from California, near San Francisco. He'd practically grown up with the Mac (which might explain his difficulty with programming), and computers were in his blood. Even with his love for computers, Todd couldn't quite get the concept of industry out of his mind. He once had his own printing business as a teenager and had even run his own magic show. He understood money. He was very frugal and already into investing. In fact, he'd made some good money with Microsoft. Todd understood the business of computers; I understood programming. I saw the potential for synergy. "Wouldn't it be amazing if we started our own technology company?" We both sort of laughed at the suggestion and left it at that.

In 1993, the United States was just beginning to come out of a recession. Bush had lost; Clinton was taking over. Living abroad, I'd only cared about the United States in terms of its impact on international politics. A US student now, I noticed that my classmates were groaning about their work prospects after college. The talk was very dispiriting: it wasn't about picking the one thing you wanted—it was about finding anything.

This had a major impact on me. I'd have to start thinking about a career. I thought the obvious answer was to enroll in business school. Then I recalled something my father had told me: You can always become a businessman. If you want to be a Harvard MBA, great, but most companies like guys who've done some real-world engineering before, guys who have actual experience.

With this in mind, I backed away from business school during my second semester and stayed in engineering. But now, I would focus on computer science engineering. I plunged in full force and signed up for every available class. Besides, I'd been inspired by Cornell's job bulletin boards. Goldman Sachs and Merrill Lynch were looking for people in their information systems departments, and you could earn $53,000 a year. I remember that when I saw this I yelled out, "Fifty-three thousand dollars? That's huge!"

In the summer of 1994, I moved into a dilapidated apartment on Catherine Street that had a massive ant infestation. In addition, the doors were lopsided and the stove was faulty—it exploded in my face one day when I was cooking. The apartment was a death trap.

Literally.

I began noticing I was always ill, and I couldn't figure out why. One day I came home and discovered the heating was busted. When the gas company inspected the ancient heating system, they found that it was spewing ten times the legal level of carbon monoxide. And this had been the case for six months!

Engineering at Cornell was a tough major. Engineering used to be a five-year program; now they packed it into four. It helped if you did extracurricular study. I ended up spending all four summers at Cornell, taking extra classes just to stay ahead.

To simultaneously gain some so-called real-world experience while in school, I looked for an internship. I considered a sock company in New York that needed a computer network set up. Then there was a videoconferencing company called Datapoint, based in San Antonio, Texas. Videoconferencing sounded better than socks, so I decided to go to Texas. Plus, it wasn't so cold there.

Talk about feeling out of place. Here I was in cowboy country, still in my British-style clunky clothing, long hair, with a shoulder-length ponytail. After six months of working on software, I realized how much I absolutely did not want to be an engineer. When you're an engineer, you're sure that management is stupid because you have all these brilliant ideas. (Of course, management isn't completely stupid; they only see the dollar signs in what the engineers tell them.) I simply didn't want to be obsessing over minutiae late at night in my tiny cubicle and missing the big picture. I wanted to be in technology. But I wanted a place where I could see it from ten thousand feet up—from a vantage point where I could look down and see how things were really progressing.

So . . . adios, Texas.

I bought a beat-up Toyota Corolla (my mom lent me the money) and drove all the way from Texas at 112 miles an hour—the fastest the car could go—with a radar jammer I'd built myself. I raced over to New Orleans, took a quick detour down to Miami, and then up the coast to the dreaded Ithaca and somehow never got a ticket.

By this time, Elayna and I had been going out for two and a half years; the whole time we'd sustained this crazy long-distance relationship. Originally, she'd enrolled at Smith College, a few hundred miles away. After eight months, I finally convinced her to transfer to Cornell for a semester.

At the beginning of my junior year, Elayna arrived in Ithaca. But after two and a half years of living in separate worlds, we got together and things promptly started falling apart.

I was miserable. I couldn't pull myself together. Elayna was my first major love, and now she became my first major breakup. I needed to get my mind off her and focus my energies on something productive, something big.

At the time, my sister, Maddy, had just graduated from Vassar. I used to go down to her place to hang out (and try to meet her friends). Liz, one of Maddy's best friends in NYC, had just received her first *Vassar Quarterly,* the school's alumni magazine. One afternoon, when I was sprawled on Liz's couch feeling sorry for myself, I picked up the *Quarterly* and started distractedly reading.

That's where I saw a tiny column about this guy. I can't even remember his name. Actually, it wasn't even a column. It was just a blurb about a former student, letting people know what he was up to. The guy was selling T-shirts for the Helsinki Winter Games, shirts that more or less said, "Break a leg, Nancy," and other brainless slogans. Apparently, the shirts had sold so well that he'd received a call from a guy who ran a website called Cybersight. They were going to sell the shirts on the site.

At the time, nobody knew what a website was. Cybersight was supposed to be some sort of "online internet community," but there was no explanation. All it said was that the shirt guy and Cybersight were working together.

Here's all I knew about the internet in the fall of 1994: it was this cryptic geeky arena in which anyone who could type "reverse back slash, forward slash, colon" ruled the world. And anyone who didn't understand Unix could forget it.

Let me explain what was going on in the online universe at this point. AOL, CompuServe, and Prodigy already existed. They were the three commercial companies providing online access, but they weren't exactly burning up the marketplace. This was back when they all charged $4.95 an hour. AOL in particular was having massive troubles; their stock had plummeted. No one knew where it was all going. A few players were struggling to set up an electronic world, but no one was really buying it. The companies had maybe a few hundred thousand subscribers. In the grand scheme of things, no one thought it was viable.

I'd been reading about these companies and knew the huge battles they were having with hourly rates. I knew how Steve Case had been struggling to raise money for his baby, and the trouble he'd had doing it. As a Mac person, I also knew that Apple had decided it was going to jump into this online fracas with something called eWorld.

So when I picked up the *Quarterly* and I read about this site, all of a sudden something clicked: this theoretical universe called the internet—which was a completely separate universe from AOL at the time—was partnering with old-fashioned marketing. I thought to myself, *Wait a second.* Is the internet suddenly a viable medium for marketing? What does that mean? Is it going to instantly become user-friendly? Next to the blurb, there was a photo of two guys standing together, and for the oddest reason, I thought of Todd. I suddenly got so incredibly excited. I hopped into my car and hightailed it back up to Cornell.

I found Todd, and we plunged right in. I knew he was the guy to start a business with. We'd joked once about doing something in technology. Now we were serious.

Todd liked to draw schematics. Even years later, he'd walk up to a board with some markers when we discussed things. He started drawing templates right away to see what our business would look like. Then we decided to download Mosaic. Mosaic was the first program to marshal actual web graphics (the word *browser* wasn't even being used yet). With Mosaic, we'd heard, there was no such thing as background graphics. You literally had a gray screen with text on it, on which you could stick a picture at the top of the screen, left justified (you couldn't even center it). There was something called an image map, where you could make pictures clickable, and you could actually get an image to take you to another link.

But this was before all these terms existed. Nobody knew what a URL was. Nobody knew anything. We didn't even know how to type in an address. Finding an address, finding a site to browse—it was virtually impossible. There were no directories. We found this thing called Yahoo, a tiny directory at Stanford. When we found it, it was still at akebono.stanford.edu.

But it took so long. Downloading was an ordeal. We used my lame Zoom 14.4 kilobit modem, and Todd's 19.2 kilobit modem, which was the best that existed at the time. We started exploring these FTP download sites, like at the University of Michigan, where they had a massive site for Macintosh users. (We were Mac all the way; Windows was such a cryptic environment. We were always laughing at their little C:> and those crazy paths to link software.)

So we went to the UMich Macintosh site and downloaded Mosaic. It was a 0.8 beta version. We didn't know how to use it; we just started screwing around. Finally, after we got a tiny handle on things, we went to Cybersight.

We couldn't find the dumb T-shirts, but we stumbled upon one of the first experiences Todd and I had with something called a chat room. We went to this chat room, figured out how to use it, and then Todd hooked up his portable computer. We both logged into the same chat room, sitting right next to each other, and "talked" with each other—and with the thirty other people in the room.

It was primitive stuff. Basically, you'd write a message and hit Post. To see the message posted, you'd have to refresh the screen, refresh the screen, refresh the screen. You'd see other posts scrolling past. There wasn't much to look at. Just a blank screen with a line of text and then a space, a line of text and a space, a line of text, and so on. Each line was attached to somebody's name, or handle, or whatever that was called. That was it. Then it was post and reload, post and reload, post and reload.

Still, it was addictive. We were corresponding with all these strangers, random people from around the world pretending to be someone else. We must have spent four hours on our first session. The experience was so exhilarating. For an instant I could glimpse the world ahead, the future, everything. It freaked me out.

But before I could utter a word to describe what I thought, that inkling was gone—the sense was so fleeting. I'd seen it, and now it was gone . . . but I knew that something was there. Todd and I were just giddy. It was insane. We didn't know where this was going, but we knew with complete certainty that it was the absolute beginning. Seeing the effect it had on us, we knew that when the world discovered this, there would be mania, absolute mania.

As the initial excitement faded, Todd and I looked at each other and realized we had to scramble. People were going to find this stuff. This was going to take on a life of its own. If we were not in the game, we would be out of it. We realized that if we wanted to do something, make a chat site of our own, it would have to be now.

From that day, we began working together nonstop.

First, we had to figure out what the internet was, what its capabilities were, and what the hell HTML was.

Every college kid likes to think he knows more than his professors. In a weird way, we did. Or at least we soon would. As recently as 1994, Cornell, that bastion of Ivy League education, offered no courses in HTML. It simply wasn't taught. No one studied Mosaic; you couldn't learn it in school (my adviser would later end up teaching HTML and Java based on what we'd built with our company). We had to hunt for online sites with HTML resources.

We downloaded all sorts of documentation about HTML and how to use it. We quickly discovered that it was the language that web pages were made of. We both started trying to get a feel for its capabilities. We tried to design our own chat room and created a hack version. It was bad, but you could really see the makings of something commercial, something that didn't exist yet but which someone might theoretically pay for.

Ah, money. We didn't know in what shape or form profit would happen (there was no such thing as web-based advertising or commerce), but we knew there would be money to be made eventually—if eWorld and AOL were able to charge access fees, we knew at least there was the potential for something. We just had to figure out what that something might be. But at this point there were no standards, no rules.

We found out about Hot Wired, *Wired* magazine's website, but that didn't seem relevant. It was literally just a magazine online; we didn't have a magazine, and we couldn't start publishing or creating content. We had to think of something else. Chat was at least a starting point. The addiction potential with chat was awesome, and we were increasingly certain that we could pursue a business in that space, some new sort of community, something.

We didn't even have a name for the company yet. We decided to call it Global Solutions, which later evolved into WebGenesis. Over the next couple of years, we would eventually turn that into theglobe.com.

It was just the two of us for a long time. We had to figure everything out. One of the first things we realized was that we'd need seed money to get something off the ground, which meant we'd have to write a business plan. We had no experience writing a business plan. We had no experience with business classes. We knew nothing. Nothing. Don't forget: we were two twenty-year-old guys.

Ironically, one of the first things we discovered almost sunk us. The owner of Cybersight had published a decree in which he wrote, "The internet? Come on! That's never going to be commercial—an online mall will *never* happen." But we didn't give up.

Since we had no one to ask for advice, we called some guy in Boston who'd been writing and selling software. We thought maybe we could get some info from him about software for the internet. We must have sounded so amateurish; this guy must have thought, *Why on earth are these kids calling me?*

We didn't know how to speak like professionals. I mean, we sounded like two students trying to latch onto someone. People were probably just as wary of us as we were of them. We decided we'd just have to do this ourselves.

So we started working on a business plan. Like any good business, we needed a motto. During the summer, Todd had been interning at a biotech company whose motto was "To Please and to Satisfy." So that became our motto, too. "To Please and to Satisfy." It sounded brilliant, so we put it in our business plan. Why not, right?

We wrote a fourteen-page business plan, the most important part of which was the cream-colored paper with a nice font, a good cover, and a great binding. Todd and I were so proud of the way it looked (never mind the substance).

We had snapshots of what our site would look like. Since Todd and I were such Mac fans, we decided it would look like eWorld, Apple's pride and joy. We decided that you'd click on different areas and get little zoom diagrams. There'd be a newsstand where you could get news, and there'd be a little cafe.

That was the thing for us. If we created virtual cafes where people from around the world could get together, they could talk and have virtual coffee. So we described that, and that was the business model. We were so naïve.

As we continued our work, Todd did the graphics, and I worried about programming and the technical aspects.

There was still no such thing as page impressions; the only term that had vaguely begun to exist was *hits.* "How many hits are you getting?" Slowly, we learned about the growing interest in advertising, so we added all sorts of research about ad rates based on how traditional media worked. That would be the way we'd make money.

Around this time, my dad happened to be coming to the States. When he arrived, I showed him our magnificent business plan. He opened it up, and the whole binding fell apart. It was pathetic. Not a great first impression. Then he read the motto, "To Please and to Satisfy."

"*Hmmm.* Did you come up with that, Steph?"

The good part was that he read it and was actually supportive. But he didn't seem overly excited. And who could blame him? He'd never heard of the internet. There was no real business behind this business plan. He must have thought, *That's nice, Steph, but make sure you get your degree and don't lose focus on your studies.* As I mentioned, when I was growing up in Europe, I barely used a computer. My parents *never* used computers. They didn't even know where the on/off switch was, and there I was trying to talk to them about a virtual online community. It was total blind faith.

The proposition for theglobe.com, which Todd and I slowly got better at explaining, was the concept of community. It wasn't just a directory of sites, like Yahoo. We were all about being a destination site. That's the term we used. We wanted to be a destination. We'd be one of the places people would click to from a search engine to visit and stay and spend time there.

Our families would ask, "How do you get people to spend time?" We explained, "We'll have them read comics or download software and games. We'll have them hang out in the chat rooms. Most important, we're going to get people to meet other people. Because if they meet at our place, the common bond becomes each other. Then we don't have to worry about spending tons of money to keep people interested with other bells and whistles."

They had no clue what we were talking about.

But they went with it. If anything, they must have thought it would make for an interesting experience. My mom, dad, and Anders each put in $500. My grandfather put in $500. Other people I talked to put in a little bit of money, and it added up to $7,500. Todd raised the same figure. We returned from Christmas vacation early and headed straight back to the dorm. Now we had $15,000, enough to get started.

In the beginning of 1995, we first heard that Jim Clark and Marc Andreessen had rechristened Mosaic Communications as Netscape Communications. From that day on, we felt the first sense of real heated pressure. This web thing was starting to generate genuine companies. If there was one, there'd soon be a hundred.

The time came for us to come up with a budget. "Okay," we said, "we'll need a color scanner. We'll need another computer. We'll need all this gear." It looked like that $15,000 might not be enough.

Todd and I started looking in the backs of magazines for those tiny used-gear ads. We called everybody. We became master negotiators. "How much for this 8-meg SIMM of RAM? One hundred fifty bucks? How 'bout one forty-five?"

Ultimately, we got the gear we needed to start our baby up.

Meanwhile, we were still taking classes. Every time we had a free second, we'd rush back to the dorm to meet up and talk. It was hard to excel as a student. Even when we were sitting in class, we weren't really paying attention. Our minds were flying with the possibilities. My grades started suffering. I'd never been a really heavy studier, but this was ridiculous. To get by, I started engaging in that all-too-common college habit of, *um,* copying. Once, in Econ 101, a lecture hall class with three thousand students, I walked over and took several assignments out of an inbox up front to "borrow." Even so, I ended up falling to a B average.

As I was eking by in my classes, I was building the tools to understand a barely born technology, making up stuff as I went along. What I was doing seemed like a combination of computer science and electrical engineering. I was teaching myself about bandwidth, and bit rates, and all these other things that, until then, I would have never understood.

The time came for Todd and me to stop working out of a dorm room, but what were we going to do about the way we were desperately falling behind in our classes? What could we do? Then we had a brainstorm. And, like a miracle, one of my advisers accepted our idea. We'd create an independent project—something that we could get actual credit for. All we had to do was come up with a thesis our adviser would accept. Now, while we were secretly laying the groundwork for a new business, we'd also officially be studying the benchmarks of hard drive performance. In other words, we would test to see how hard you could push a computer before it exploded (which was kind of fun). And thus was born Independent Research CS490. Four credits per semester. Praise the Lord.

Now we were free to set up an on-campus office. We found this fourth-floor storage room, a cramped dust trap where the university stored all sorts of boxes and old stuff, and in March 1995, we convinced them to let us turn that into WebGenesis (the corporate name we still went by) World HQ.

The storage room was completely windowless. There would be days when we would go in there at 9:00 a.m. and leave at 3:00 a.m., and suddenly there'd be a foot of snow outside. To make the place more palatable, we moved the boxes aside, brought in some filing cabinets, and divided the room in half. The place always smelled very . . . stale.

Maintaining secrecy was a major issue. We were risk averse to the point of paranoia. Even if the university didn't care what we were doing, Todd and I had heard stories about schools belatedly taking credit for intellectual property created on their turf. So we kept our mouths shut and continued faux testing those hard drives.

In January 1995, Todd and I came to the conclusion that we could no longer build this company by ourselves. Shortly after we moved out of Todd's dorm room and into the windowless storage room, we decided to hire our first few employees. Of course, we didn't have a human resources (HR) department or a recruiting office, so we decided to do the most logical thing we could: place ads in the Cornell campus papers.

At the time, Todd and I were twenty-year-old juniors. It seemed practical to hire people with experience. We put out several ads that read, "Looking for seasoned management, must be at least Junior or Senior."

Shortly after running the ads we received dozens and dozens of responses. There was just one problem—we didn't know where to interview these candidates. We didn't think it would make a good impression to bring prospective employees for a first meeting in a windowless closet, so we opted for the more elegant campus space called Willard Straight Hall. This Cornell landmark is an ornate hall with a fifty-foot ceiling, beautiful stained-glass windows, plush red fabric, and a grand piano at one end.

Todd and I brought in three folding chairs and plopped them down in this great empty hall and called in our interviewees one at a time. Every twenty minutes, we'd call in the next person and go through a checklist: what year, what's your degree, do you use a computer, have you heard of the web, what do you like to do on the web, and so on. The best candidates were the ones who spoke about how they loved to go online and download stuff in their spare time, people who did this stuff for fun and liked the idea of getting paid to do it. The last thing we cared about was good grades. At this stage of the game, it was less about IQ and more about EQ, emotional quotient. We wanted people with character, people who were motivated, people who would want to work lots of late nights for nothing more than minimum wage because they enjoyed what we were doing.

Looking back now, given the HR department we set up years later, these first interviews seem like a joke. But at the time, Todd and I took them very seriously. Most of our questions could probably barely be heard above the clamor of whoever was banging away on the piano. Still, we managed to hire our first half dozen employees this way, even if they became deaf in the process.

Our first employee was Philip Karlson, one of my computer science buddies. Philip had long, long blond hair down to his butt; he had a Thor's hammer as a necklace; he made funny goat noises and drank massive pitchers of beer. He was also a great programmer.

Philip began setting up the servers, programming in AppleScript and C++. He was the guy who really programmed our first chat room and (almost) got it working. Since we spent most of our fifteen grand on gear, we could only pay Philip $4 an hour, plus lots of pizza and beer.

When we first started setting things up, we used to work so long and hard that we'd occasionally reward ourselves by taking the servers down and dig into long sessions of *Marathon* (the Mac equivalent of *Doom*). There'd be lots of yelling and screaming. Eventually, we'd hear a knock on the door and there'd be some poor professor telling us to be quiet or we'd be kicked out. We'd say, "Oops, sorry," then put the servers back up.

That spring we were almost ready to go. We got the site up and running but hadn't publicized anything so there was no traffic. We had our home page. Then we also decided to be a mirror for software. So we copied over all the software from UMich onto our servers, making our site an eclectic mix of chat room and downloadable software. That was the best we could do. We had no idea what people would like—not a clue. But we pressed on.

Our second employee was Vance Huntley, who became our top programmer. Vance's previous experience was as a falafel cook at Aladdin's, a local health-food joint. He'd sort of dropped out of school for the moment. He'd been studying to be a high-energy-particle-simulation physicist. I mean, we're talking advanced-theoretical-computational-calculation stuff.

Vance came on board. Between us and falafels, he was working ninety-hour weeks. The guy was just deathly pale. Every day we thought he was going to walk in and collapse. Which is exactly what he eventually did. I remember he started bleeding from his nose at one point. "Oh, my God, Vance!" we said as he stumbled out the door, "you've got to recuperate."

Then we found Garth. He was a big, oafish, hippie type who drew comics. We wanted a strip because it seemed like a good way to develop a following. After all, Netscape had this character called Mozilla, a little green lizard, on its home page. Wherever you went, there was this little character, and since you were always getting lost in the early days of the web, it was a great way to identify which site you were looking at—a branding tool.

So Garth developed a comic strip for our site called "The Adventures of Net Surfer and Glitch." Net Surfer was a cool blond dude on a surfboard, and Glitch was a purple gnome with little antennae and a big nose. Then there was the evil Megabyte and a goofy character named Main Frame. These guys temporarily helped define what would soon become theglobe.com.

We launched the site on April 1, 1995—April Fools' Day. Probably not the best timing given that a lot of people thought it was a joke. Nevertheless, somehow people started coming. Right away, the chat room was the main attraction. People just started flocking to it. We'd made it extra cool by using those support icons, which was our big breakthrough. Instead of just having a string of text, you could pick an icon to represent you. The icons, of course, were the characters from our comic strip. You could be Net Surfer, or you could be Glitch. Believe it or not, this was innovative at the time. Our chat really took off. You could literally watch the surfers as the traffic soared. It would climb and climb and climb, and we'd all hold hands and shout, "Yes!"

In the first month, we got 3,000 users. In the second month, it went up to 15,000 users. And the third month, it was 30,000. Then it was 45,000. Month after month, it was climbing all by itself. We weren't advertising at all. This was strictly word-of-mouth.

Now we could demonstrate that our traffic over the first four months had ballooned. The usage time had gone way up. Our chat rooms were constantly filled. There were almost no other chat rooms on the internet you could find that were always filled, but ours would have thirty people in a room chatting away at 4:00 in the morning. At prime time, there would be two hundred people simultaneously chatting. We had continuous chatter.

Obviously, we could see the commercial potential. The time had come to bring in advertisers. But how? Then there was the issue of bringing in new investors—we were running low on funds again. That's where we found ourselves as we approached the summer of 1995.

That May, we officially named the site theglobe.com and incorporated the company as WebGenesis. Working with our parents and a team of lawyers they helped set us up with, we addressed the question of valuation. One lawyer said, "You could argue that this thing is worth a quarter of a million." Todd and I were like, "What? Our project worth a quarter of a million? Holy moly!"

Of course this was a completely arbitrary enterprise value. But at this point, to get anyone beyond family to put money in, we had to have a real value so that people knew they were getting into something official. And we really needed money. We'd been hearing about other companies, like Lycos, that were aggressively raising capital. We could no longer think of ourselves as a little project.

We set up a Subchapter C corporation, incorporated in Delaware, and went with the value of about a quarter of a million dollars. What we didn't know was that in California, where baby web companies were opening left and right, they were going with values of at least $1 to $10 million.

This was also around the time when we first heard whispers that Netscape was going to file to go public and that they were going to be valued in the hundreds of millions. The numbers were astronomical. Todd and I knew that we were onto something big and we'd now be compelled to raise a lot more money if we intended to play in the big leagues. Yahoo! had already secured about $750,000 in financing from Sequoia (a venture capital outfit), even though they were still a project at Stanford. After that, they'd decided to move off campus. Jerry Yang and David Filo were dropping out of their Ph.D. programs, which they were about to complete. (When we first launched theglobe.com, we'd emailed Jerry and David to put us in their search engine. They replied, "Sure, no problem.")

Todd and I started debating. "Should we blow off Cornell? Do we drop out?" Our parents said, "Hold on a second." We were torn. Maybe we should hold on. Ultimately, we decided to try and graduate—even if it killed us. We might finish late, but we were going to continue taking our classes. My junior year was just a horrendous workload. This was where you faced the real meat of computer science, and I was just miserable; I was taking five classes, all high-level computer science, but I stuck with it.

At this point, we'd barely managed to secure another $30,000—again, mainly from friends and family. It wasn't anywhere near enough money, but it was just enough for us to move off campus and look for real office space in Ithaca. Altogether, with temps, we had about ten people working for us now, and we were seeing more than 50,000 users a month. Working with other people's money created a sense of responsibility and reality. In a few months, we'd morphed from an experimental dream into the real thing.

We were twenty-one years old.

We had no idea what lay ahead.

3

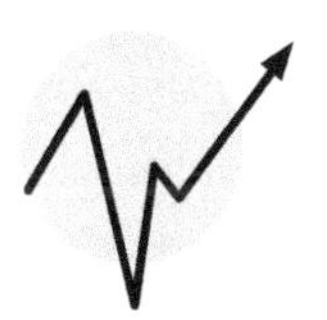

The Early Days

Paying in Pizza and Minimum Wage and the Hunt for VC Dollars: Ten Meetings, Ten Rejections

In the summer of 1995, we moved off campus to Collegetown, into our crappy little corporate office in the Student Agencies building on College Avenue. We wanted it to be perfect, meticulous, beautiful. So we lined up the computers in a straight line. It was a start.

In order to make the rent and cover the employees we hoped to hire, the first thing Todd and I had to do was raise more money.

This was a process we'd soon become experts in.

We started in the early summer, putting informal financials together and talking to my dad. The idea was that with another $30,000 we'd be "there."

Then my dad said, "Well, Steph, why don't you work out what you really need for a longer period of time rather than just the minimum?"

For Todd and me, this was the first time we'd ever heard about raising more money than the minimum we actually needed to get by. *Hmmm,* interesting concept.

So, we started beefing up the financial plan—maybe we should go for $50,000? Or $60,000? Maybe we won't even cap it. Maybe we'll just keep increasing the amount of money we're trying to raise until we've gotten enough.

That summer, Todd and I started traveling back and forth to the West Coast, a frequent journey that would continue into the fall and well beyond. When I look back at the years between 1995 and 1997, it seems like most of our time was spent raising money.

This was not an easy time to raise money for an internet site. No one really understood what the internet was. Every time we met a potential backer, we had to run through our whole "Let's talk about the internet and what it is" spiel and explain why this was indeed a viable medium.

We made our initial moves out of Todd's house in Atherton, California, which is just north of Palo Alto. But we really did most of our setup work in Kinko's, printing up business plans and making corrections; then we'd set up meetings. Todd's dad happened to know a few venture capitalists on the West Coast. We cold-called all the other potential investors. We went to Sutter Hill Ventures. We went to Kleiner Perkins, Greylock, Crosspoint Venture Partners, and many, many more. We had no idea what we were doing.

Todd and I had never pitched before. The whole process was a complete trial by fire—how to pitch and modify your business plan as you go along. From an original fourteen pages, we were revising the plan every two months, bulking it up with more industry background, competitive analysis, detailed financials, management bios, traffic statistics . . . all the new essentials, while also describing all the software tools we'd developed and hyping theglobe.com.

Mainly, we got blank faces. A few people knew that Netscape had raised $5 million after a thirty-minute meeting with Kleiner Perkins. But most people were still on the periphery. This was back in the day when VCs only knew technology companies. Everything was about software and hardware. Venture capitalists weren't into investing in games or entertainment. They'd classically always stayed away from the entertainment sector—film, media, things you can't think about in terms of product upgrades, new versions, and distribution channels. When we arrived out there, the only real response we got, if any, was, "Okay, talk to us about these tools you guys are developing."

By late summer, we were leaning toward describing theglobe.com as a community and thinking about it as a media play. That would be the biggest potential, we thought. We had these chat rooms, which had taken off. We had this massive activity and addiction. On the other side of the business were these technological tools, which we were only interested in selling as a way to make quick cash up front—we really didn't think selling software would be a great business to be in.

Still, for the VCs, tools were the only things they seemed to be able to latch onto. People would say things like, "This chat room you've developed . . . have you guys ever thought about doing it in Java and then licensing that out?" or "What about your registration software? Your survey tools?"

We took dozens and dozens of these meetings. They're not exactly a barrel of laughs. You sit there; you have an hour. They *look* interested. Todd and I would look at each other, wink-wink, nudge-nudge. We'd think things were going pretty well. Then the meeting would end, and we'd get the ol' "We'll get back to you . . . this is all *very* interesting." Then we'd never hear back from them. A big problem was our ages. If Todd and I had been two gray-haired geeks with thick-rimmed spectacles fresh out of Microsoft, it would have been a done deal. But who could blame them? Would you do business with two baby-faced twenty-one-year-olds?

And we could barely pass for twenty-one. I looked maybe twenty, and Todd looked even younger. When we walked into meetings, the VCs always had this expression like, *Oh my God. Can we possibly even consider this?* VCs liked to invest, at a minimum, in quarter-million to half-million increments, but they preferred $5 million lumps. They would look at us as if thinking, *These kids can't even handle a quarter-million-dollar investment.* (At first, they were probably right.)

Our other problem back then was that the VCs were extremely geographically focused. They would only invest in companies that were in San Francisco, particularly in the Bay Area, so that they could be within an hour of their money.

Then here we come—not just from the other coast, but from Ithaca, New York. Upstate, the boonies. This was simply a no-go. Meanwhile, we couldn't find any VCs in New York City. At the time, 99 percent of the industry was based in San Francisco. Not to mention the difference in mentality: East Coast investors were much more involved in high finance and banking; West Coast VC was about constantly digging for nifty new technologies.

Industry analysts were just starting to see the potential of a pure, highly efficient electronic world where everything moved at the speed of light. That season, you could feel the global aspects coming into play. Still, the internet was tiny at the time. When we went online, there were somewhere between five and ten million users worldwide. But that number was doubling month to month. It was growing exponentially, and we were right there from the beginning to watch it. So we stayed with the left coast, where the minds were a bit more open, and things finally happened.

By mid-1996, Yahoo!, Excite, and Lycos had all gone public. Each had raised $30 to $35 million at $150 to $200 million valuations. They'd gone public at somewhere between $15 and $20 a share; within six months they were trading at $2 to $7 a share. Internet mania didn't exist yet. It would be a full twelve to eighteen months before their stocks all started taking off like speed-fueled bulls. Only then did people really start saying, "Oh, maybe I should get some internet stock. Maybe this Net thing is really something."

One day, through a series of lucky breaks, we found ourselves in a meeting with Bob Halperin, the former CEO of Raychem, the multibillion-dollar material sciences company. Bob, a guy who you might—mistakenly—think would be stuck in an old paradigm, seemed to instantly take us under his wing. He was recruited in World War II as one of the five greatest brains working for the Pentagon as a strategist. In other words, a brilliant guy. Todd and I sat down and pitched him. We'd get so excited that we'd finish each other's sentences. Bob asked, "You boys always interrupt each other like this?" He had this warm, gravelly voice that was very contagious. "I love the energy you have," he'd tell us. "You gotta clean it up a bit, but it's fantastic. It feels like you guys are real believers."

Bob looked at our numbers and showed us how we could ramp things up to a million dollars in revenue the next year, and then to $2 million and then $3 million the following year. Bob said, "Boys, to really interest venture capitalists, you need to show five to ten times the revenue growth you do." Todd and I realized it was time for a quick modification of the plan. Bob invested $100,000 and became our first board member.

Now the plan was to project $1 million. Then we would increase it to $10 million. Then $30 million. We just instantly curved it up. What else could we do? With those numbers down on paper, Bob was willing to personally make a few introductions for us.

One was Vinod Khosla of Kleiner Perkins, a quintessential entrepreneur well known on the West Coast. Now, VCs like to outdo each other in the way they manifest their power—it's a White House thing. They want you to feel that you're on hallowed ground, that you're entering the domain of the mighty. When we walked into the Kleiner Perkins offices on Sand Hill Road, we passed through this massive doorway with huge wooden beams.

Inside, there was a cavernous room with an enormous glass wall. We were impressed. The day we walked in, there were other investor meetings under way, and we just knew that those heavies behind glass could raise half a billion in one shot.

Kleiner Perkins was (and still is) considered the Ivy League of venture capitalists. Everyone knew that they were the best. And that was certainly what they thought of themselves. Todd and I were in total awe.

Not that you could tell from how we dressed. We always wore casual clothing. Todd wore khakis and a button-down shirt. I wore jeans and a T-shirt. You have to remember that, despite the setting, we were still two college students with no money, living in an absolute dump. It's not that we chose to skip the suits—we just didn't have any.

I suppose we could have borrowed a suit. But just as Kleiner Perkins was a well-known firm, it was starting to become equally well known that young kids were driving the new internet world. They didn't necessarily trust us with their money, but it was the guys in suits who generated more suspicion when they pitched Net businesses. The VCs were skeptical that anyone in a suit actually used the Net. In our case, there was no doubt we were plugged in.

We were sweating bullets when we met Vinod. This guy was tough. He grilled us about our business. There was a board on his wall with charts and all these comparisons to other Net companies. "Do you boys have a chat?" he asked. "What can your chat do? Okay, it's Java. What features do you have? Is it 3-D? Do you have icons? Do you have this, that, and the other?" He'd start talking about all the other little start-ups he'd heard of on the West Coast. There was one 3-D chat set up with streaming audio that had just received a $23 million investment. These were just insane sums, and here was Vinod comparing us to them.

We'd proceed through endless meetings. Each would basically be two hours of nonstop pitching—our chance to raise the money that could make or break the whole company. The energy we put into the process was mind-boggling. But to little avail. Vinod had a famous line he loved to trot out: "At Kleiner Perkins," he'd intone, "we don't just create companies, we create industries." We were starting to think maybe we had the makings of an industry, even if no one else did. And even though we were a tiny player with 50,000 users, compared to Excite's (one of Vinod's proudest investments) three million.

Adding another worry was the sudden arrival of genuine competition. Other companies that were barely out of the box were proclaiming themselves to be community players, too. They were raising a ton of money and generating the hype and the buzz we thought we deserved. Todd and I were really bitter about that—but also excited. If others were joining the game, we figured there must be real potential. As a result, we put massive pressure on ourselves to hurry up and get to the finish line. And yet every time we'd think we had Vinod's money in hand, our meetings would end with him saying, "Thanks for the update, boys." *Arrgh!*

Ultimately, Vinod passed. But he liked us and wanted to see if he could set up something else. Vinod introduced us to the guys at Excite, which would have been a fantastic relationship. Very quickly, Excite began referring to us as "the boys from theglobe.com." They wouldn't take us seriously. No one would. All our VC discussions kept ending with, "Why don't you guys sell your chat? Why don't you sell your software?" It would always be the same song—and that wasn't what we were looking for. We could have sold our software, but it wouldn't have been valued at much more than, say, $10,000 per system. We had a registration system. We had cool chat software. We had survey software. This could have brought in money. It could have been our bread and butter. But even then we knew the bread and butter would be tiny. And after a while, we'd grow malnourished on just bread and butter.

Besides, we knew that if we went into the software business, we'd be crushed by Microsoft whenever they decided to make something just a little bit better than our stuff. Todd and I debated it for a while, and we decided once and for all that we'd place our bet on the site itself. It seemed so much more exciting. We would proudly call it a media play and go for broke. (Besides, Todd and I wouldn't even know how to manage a software licensing business.)

By the end of our first trip out west, we only managed to raise a paltry $100,000.

But then we met David Horowitz. David had been the founder and former CEO of MTV. He happened to sit on the board of daVinci Time & Space with Bob Halperin, which was developing next-generation CD-ROMs (back when CD-ROMs were all the craze). Besides his business experience, David had another great asset going for him: he was based on the East Coast. Todd and I knew this was a fantastic opportunity.

As soon as we got back to Ithaca, David called. "I've heard of some project you're working on," he said in this comically loud baritone. "How 'bout a meeting?" These guys always have booming voices. You sit there thinking about the powerful industries they've run, and you can feel the hairs tingling on the back of your neck at the prospect of getting together.

When David called, Todd and I were sitting in our tiny office. We could barely squeeze into our desks, which were two feet away from each other (a detail that actually ended up becoming a major problem). After David made it clear that he really did want to meet with us, Todd and I got in my Corolla and drove to New York at ninety-five miles an hour. My Corolla was in bad shape. Every time it took a left turn, the freezer coolant in the air-conditioning would pour onto the passenger's leg. We had to take turns driving because it was complete agony. David had an apartment on the Upper East Side in a Park Avenue doorman building. It was one of those apartments where you could tell the resident had achieved something. It felt *money,* baby—well furnished, nice art, etc. The elevator opened right into his apartment. We said "hi" to his wife and then went into this handsome office packed with books.

At this point, David was one of the few execs actually using the Net. He would log on and everything—it was quite amazing. He had a 28.8-kilobit modem, which was twice the speed of anything Todd and I had. There was this amazing picture of him holding a statuette that said *MTV and VH1*, taken shortly after he'd started the whole thing up. It seemed like a perfect match. David was clearly someone who understood media. We could learn so much from this guy. David realized that theglobe.com's model was in many ways like MTV—they really didn't make any money from subscription fees. It was all advertising based.

After a sweaty and intense meeting in which we pitched like maniacs—we'd started to get pretty good at it—he said, "Guys, I'm in for $50,000." Hallelujah! Now we could say Bob and David were on our board. Back then, when nobody really understood anything, it was all about who invested, who sat on your board. Naturally, we were thrilled, especially since the checks we were writing to our employees were practically bouncing.

As a young businessman, there was a lot to learn on the fly. In the early days, when we were constantly battling for financing, we were extra paranoid about competition. We didn't know how to manage a business, so we behaved like a little clandestine operation.

We never told our employees what our financial situation was. We thought that they'd be scared shitless if they knew we had almost no cash. We never even told them we were raising money. We'd only tell them once we had closed a round. "Hey, guys, we got some more money," and they'd say, "Really, we were raising money?" In fact, during those first few years, our employees had no idea of the stress Todd and I were experiencing, most of which had to do with one simple fact—we were not making money.

Any profit Todd and I had made at this point was through the buying and selling of our software. In late 1995, we landed our first story in *MacWEEK*. *MacWEEK* was mainly writing about the Macintosh world; it was not yet addressing the internet. Still, the magazine wrote about our tools. When that happened, people started coming to our site and buying the software. So when we met with VCs, our financial model was based partly on what it would look like if we could sell advertising on the site and what it would look like if our software tools took off.

Very quickly, we started having formal board meetings and promoted this new strategy. Todd and I established a pattern: we'd race from Ithaca to NYC in my car, meet for an hour, and go over the details of our business. Sometimes we were just feeding updates to David. When Bob came to the meetings, he would fly in on the red-eye from San Francisco. He'd show up in a trench coat, wheeling around his two pieces of luggage, fresh off the subway. "Bob, you're a billionaire," I'd say. "What are you doing on the subway?"

Amazingly, neither Bob nor David ever condescended to us. I think they genuinely respected that we were on the cutting edge, at least in terms of understanding this emerging market. For them—and, to me, this is an amazing American concept—business was a culture bred on making your money and then reinvesting it into the great ideas of others—young or old, or in between.

At our meetings, Todd and I would give all sorts of statistics on traffic; everything was growing fast. Of course, as I said, we weren't really making any money. I don't know how Todd and I got away with it, but for two years we managed to give Bob and David updates that never really showed major revenue growth. Revenues were growing, but in tiny increments. And not from software. In fact, by the end of 1995, Todd and I had entirely abandoned the software thing. As we went into 1996, it was a whole new ball game.

We had reached the critical mass of 100,000 users. This was a major watermark. Major. Once, we'd met with Apple Computers on the West Coast. Apple's abortive eWorld community was still up; they had about 75,000 subscribers. I remember them telling us, "You know, it's going to be tough for you guys to make money on this unless you get to the 50,000-user mark." (Later, we'd have more than a quarter million monthly users, whereas eWorld only got up to about 75,000 subscribers and then just gave up.) Now we had twice that, and we knew users were something we could profit from. Around this time, we met Kevin O'Connor, founder of DoubleClick—the first online advertising network.

Slowly but surely, the web advertising craze started to happen as banner ads standardized and suddenly became the rage. Advertising, we decided, would be theglobe.com's business.

We signed up with DoubleClick, and they put their banners on our site and distributed ads. All of a sudden, Todd and I were making $20,000 a month, $30,000 a month, $40,000 a month, $50,000 a month. In October 1996, we hit $85,000 a month in revenue, and our costs were only $50,000 a month. It was the most amazing feeling. We could actually go to the board and say, "Guys, we had a month of profitability." We could show real growth in revenues. The board was super excited. This was particularly amazing, since we only had about twelve to fifteen employees—and we paid them next to nothing.

Still, Todd and I realized that we had to get bigger to survive. So, reluctantly, in mid-1996, we went back once again on the financing circuit. Since we'd never really received any substantial VC money, the only alternative for us was to continue with individuals and angel investors—but this time we weren't going to rest until we hit the millions.

It was a wild ride. At one point, there was interest from the owner of a winery in upstate New York. Todd and I got in my Corolla, drove an hour and a half up to a winery, and sat down to a wine tasting with the owner, simultaneously pitching her and sniffing bouquets. The owner listened quietly and finally said, "Yes, I'd be interested in investing. I might be able to put in $25,000 to $50,000." That's it? Ugh. Better than nothing.

A couple of weeks later, she wasn't interested. She didn't understand the Net.

Another time, we met with a private investor based in Florida (Todd and I were always skeptical about Florida). This guy ran all sorts of bizarre enterprises (for instance, he was heavily involved with a deep-sea, treasure-hunting operation). He started throwing around crazy numbers. At one point, he said, "I'm prepared to invest $7 million in this puppy."

Oh God, please be for real.

There was just one problem: every time we raised a new round, we'd also raise the stock price. Mr. Florida was willing to put in $7 million, but it would have to be at a massive discount to our prior round. Todd and I hit the brakes. This guy would have eaten up 90 percent of our company—for $7 million.

We met another investor, a sultan of something or other, who said, "You boys have created something that's going to be a chat universe—a chat of every shape and size." "A chat universe? That's not really what we want to limit the business to," we'd say. But the sultan seemed adamant.

He said, "When I give you money, it's going to be a chat universe."

Every time we got a fish on the line, it turned out to be too good to be true. We needed money. We were desperate for money. But at the same time, did we really want investors who would force us into crazy ideas? Once again, we walked away from good money.

Later, we went back to California and met with more angel investors. We met with a guy named Doug DeVivo who had founded the Aldus software company and he was willing to put in $100,000. A miracle! We were finding people, but it took an unsustainable amount of time. Eventually, by the end of 1996, right as our funds were running out, the alumni relations office at Cornell, which had caught wind of our company, suggested we meet with a former alumnus named David Duffield, who ran PeopleSoft, a large California-based tech company.

Todd and I had just come back from California. We were exhausted from our constant scurrying around. All we'd done was fund-raise, and we didn't want to turn right around and fly back to the West Coast. As luck would have it, the Cornell office informed us that Mr. Duffield was actually in town, visiting Ithaca. We still found it hard to get excited about another meeting and were especially suspicious of an entrepreneur who actually enjoyed visiting Ithaca. But we weren't in a position to turn anyone down.

So, for the umpteenth time, we got in the Corolla. It was snowing. It was foggy. You couldn't even see through the window. We kept our coats on inside the car because it was freezing and the heater didn't work.

We finally arrived at a dive bar, our arranged meeting place in Ithaca. There's David with this look on his face, this spark in his eye as he sees us—two kids—walk in. "God, this is fantastic," he said. "It reminds me of my story.

It reminds me of when I had to mortgage my house, and my first few companies failed. But then I created PeopleSoft, guys. Now my net worth is getting close to the billion-dollar mark."

Then he said, "What do you guys intend to raise?"

"We're looking to raise $4 or $5 million," we said, "but we're not getting close to that."

David looked thoughtful for a moment.

"Put me down for $200,000." We were so happy, I don't remember getting home that night. Between David Horowitz, Bob Halperin, Doug DeVivo, David Duffield, family and friends re-upping, and a few other angel investors, we cobbled together about $600,000 and managed to keep our doors open. But this time the momentum continued, and by the spring of 1997, we had closed our third round of financing for nearly $1.2 million (again Duffield was our biggest contributor: this time he put in $500,000 for the round). It was short of our goal of raising a few million, yes, but it was still a new lease on life. And it was just enough for us to step up the pace.

Just as we were raising the stakes in the money sweepstakes, theglobe.com was growing as a company. We'd come a long way. We'd long since discarded our comic strips, and decided to stop mirroring downloadable software from the various sites. That just didn't seem to be a real business model.

It may sound obvious now, but we'd only just learned that it was all about increasing the number of page views—that was what would generate more ad dollars. So, more chat rooms, more sophisticated technology. We'd launched a home-page builder that let you create custom pages and add graphics. We added a personal ad section, where you could post greetings. (By the way, that feature attracted an almost-90-percent-male audience; it was almost embarrassing.)

Our personal ads were actually a turnoff to a lot of VCs. At the time, advertisers were very scared of chat as well. They would go in and see chat room talk about sex and say, "Oh, we don't want to get into that sort of thing." So chat soon became somewhat taboo.

So we focused instead on making the site a more sophisticated and richer community experience. We put more money and effort into beautiful graphics, a nice layout, and navigation assistance. Now you could get around the site much more easily.

Unfortunately for Todd and me, many of the technological advances came while we were away. Although we were intimately familiar with all aspects of the site and continued to serve as the main proponents for innovation, we found ourselves being increasingly limited in terms of the quality time we could focus on enhancements. As we spent more time looking for money, we had to delegate responsibilities for the first time. Actually, we were forced to learn how to delegate—not a talent either of us was born with. Meanwhile, we still had to finish all of our classes. This was just unbearable. We both had a full course load—all day long—right up until the summer of 1996, when we finally graduated by the seat of our pants.

I graduated with roughly a B-plus average, but most of the final months of school are a blur. I do remember the commencement ceremony. That afternoon, in front of five thousand graduating students and ten thousand spectators, Hunter Rawlings, the president of Cornell, interrupted his speech to say, "I'd like to put out a special thanks to Todd Krizelman and Stephan Paternot, who created the largest Macintosh website in the world. Congratulations to the two of them."

We had no idea he even knew about us. It turned out that Bob had put in the word to Rawlings. Either way, we felt totally vindicated.

Suddenly, all our fellow students knew what we'd been up to and why we'd disappeared for two years while they were partying. Our teachers finally knew why we'd been missing classes. One of my professors came running up to me and jumped on my back. "I knew you'd been doing something great," she said. We were heroes that day.

After we graduated, we were still running our entire site on Macintosh computers, which is laughable because Macs are hardly made for servers.

Nevertheless, just as Rawlings said, we'd firmly established ourselves as the biggest Mac-based World Wide Web site in the world, generating fourteen million hits a month, probably somewhere around a quarter-million monthly users, and Apple had begun to officially use us in their marketing material. That was a big coup. Since we had no money for advertising, it was critical to get press and piggyback on other people's marketing campaigns. Now we were on every Apple brochure. It was Target, Valvoline, and theglobe.com—a bizarre mix of companies to showcase Apple, or at least we thought so.

At one point we were even Mac representatives, wearing Apple logoed T-shirts at the Siebold conference in San Francisco, and demonstrating the tools that we'd built to run on Macintosh servers. Any free exposure we could get was worth it. Another conference presented itself in Austin, Texas, and we were offered free booth space for our company. Todd and I jumped at the chance and once again headed back to my old favorite state. Not much of a business plan, but it got us noticed a bit more. On that trip, we were so broke, we rationed every penny and stayed in a Super 8 Motel.

We may have been attracting some notice in the marketplace, but we weren't doing much in the personal-life department during the first few years. Ever since Elayna and I had broken up, I'd decided to focus all my energy on the company. By and large, my social life disappeared. There was no time to travel, no time to bum around, no time to hang out at bars, and do all those classic undergrad things.

Our life in Collegetown revolved around three stops, all of which were right beneath our office. A bar called Rulloff's, a Kinko's, and a Wendy's—the three essential building blocks of any fledgling business. It was the standard combo no. 1 for $3.51, which consisted of a burger and fries. Then we'd go to Rulloff's for a shot of Jack, and then to Kinko's to make a few copies. That was it. That was my life for two years.

And through it all, Todd and I were together twenty-four hours a day. It was getting brutal. That was the real test of our partnership. We had moved in together, worked together, raised money together, and we hung out in the same places. Twenty-four hours a day, sitting at the office, facing each other from two feet apart. We started to get really antsy and aggravated and began fighting about little things. It's almost like a husband-and-wife relationship when stuff between partners goes bad. We'd have vicious arguments.

Eventually, we realized the problem was simple: we were in each other's faces far too often. So, after that year, we got separate places. We decided to live our social lives separately, and voilà, our professional relationship flourished. As of this writing, we still get along, and trust each other with our lives.

Of course, getting our own places didn't ease the burden of working so much in our tiny space. At the office, hygiene essentially went out the window. All I ate was Wendy's. I would speak extra fast. I would walk extra fast. Everything was just hyper speed, hyper everything. That's exactly what it felt like. We could feel the competition of this pioneering new medium; everyone was beginning to notice. We felt this rush. It was like a new religion, a religion being invented.

Next would come the Crusades.

4

New York Groove

How 3,000 Miles in a Toyota Corolla Turned into $20 Million

By 1997, we'd freshly closed our third round of financing with a total of $1.2 million. We thought that would be all the money we'd ever need to reach profitability. And profitability was actually quite close, mainly because our burn rate was super low. Now there were new decisions to make. Todd and I had just graduated. We had fifteen employees. We were still in Ithaca, but I didn't want to spend the rest of my life there.

At the time, Ithaca was desperately trying to retain businesses. The town was hoping to refashion itself as a bustling metropolis, but frankly, it didn't seem so interested in keeping us. We tried to get help from Cornell, but the university bureaucracy didn't allow it. The business-people were just academics, or people who had some vested interest in wanting things to stay the way they were. Some people even seemed threatened by what we were doing. We had really no incentive to stay, so we decided it was time to move. And we'd have to move somewhere that was in the middle of the activity in our space.

That meant Boston, New York City, or San Francisco. Everything was in San Francisco at the time. The problem was that neither of us really wanted to go there. Our perception of San Francisco was that it was a one-track town—all engineers. It would have been *Revenge of the Nerds* for the rest of our lives, and I desperately did not want to end up like that.

Besides, if we went to San Francisco, we'd be a tiny fish in a giant pond; we'd be crushed by the competition. There were issues of employee attrition in San Francisco; people there went from one job, across the street to another job, across the street to yet another job. We'd never be able to hold on to our people. We didn't have the money to retain them. We barely had enough money to advertise and compete.

After ruling out San Francisco, we decided against Boston, too. After Cornell, being in a college town didn't really appeal to either of us.

So, in January 1997, we made the decision to move to Manhattan. Guess who was chosen to explore our future location? I headed down to scout it out. The first time I drove to NYC to find an apartment, I was blasting techno music in my Corolla, going faster and faster and faster. Half an hour away from the city, you start to see the sky-line approaching. By the George Washington Bridge, I'd feel the chill of excitement down my spine as I saw the big city arriving. That's how I felt about New York.

Up until then, my impression of Manhattan was based on what I'd heard and seen in the movies. I pictured something straight out of *Highlander:* people running around dark alleyways, whipping out machine guns, sword fights, the whole nine yards. Drug City.

But that's what drew me to New York as well, the threatening element. I got excited by the notion that there would be danger (and opportunity) around every corner. At Cornell, I'd heard all the stories about how you're guaranteed to get mugged within six months of arrival. One of my friends once had a shotgun held to his head at an ATM.

Of course, Mayor Giuliani had already sanitized a lot of the city by the time I showed up. After a few days strolling through gentrified neighborhoods, my thought was, *What danger?*

It quickly became apparent to me the ease with which a Manhattanite could meet friends, go out, have a phenomenal time, and meet beautiful women. The food was fantastic. All the possibilities made me feel as though I'd picked the perfect moment in my life to arrive; I could sort of power up and energize myself on the blood of the city.

When I arrived, I didn't know anything about Manhattan. I didn't even understand how the grid system worked. I had no sense of geography. Every time you turn left, everything looks the same: straight streets that go on forever. I tried to find an apartment but didn't know where to begin. So I called up a realtor right away. He showed me a bunch of pricey apartments I could barely afford. One after the other was a disaster: basement apartments, closets, dumps. My finances revealed the reality of being an entrepreneur: Todd and I never paid ourselves during the first two and a half years. In fact, when we arrived in New York, we'd just made the radical decision to start paying ourselves $35,000 a year. After taxes, that left me with about $20,000, which after rent . . .

Simply put, it wasn't enough.

So I arrived in New York with about $4,000 in my bank account (the meager remains from the internship in Texas), and I knew it was going to be depleted fast. A few days in, I made the mistake of leaving my car unattended on a sketchy block for half a day. When I came back, my car was pushed up onto the sidewalk, parked against a fire hydrant, with three or four parking tickets. Meanwhile, someone had decided to deflate my right rear tire. After peeling the tickets off the windshield, I drove around at five miles an hour—*kaklunk-kaklunk*—to find another parking place. I was completely lost. I drove the car around, found another parking space on another street (not near a fire hydrant), and parked. The next day, I went to pay off the tickets and plead my case. By the time I came back to the car, all four hubcaps were stolen and my left front mirror was torn off, left dangling by a couple of wires. I was lucky when, a few months later, I negotiated the car's sale for four grand.

I found a little apartment on Sullivan Street, in the West Village, between Bleecker Street and West Third. It was 283 square feet, but you couldn't beat that neighborhood. A beautiful 283-square-foot apartment for only $1,325 a month. My bedroom was the size of the bed. I couldn't even open and shut the door. The bathroom? You could effortlessly sit on the toilet, stick your feet forward into the shower, and turn on the sink and brush your teeth simultaneously. For the first month while I scouted for an office, I worked from my apartment. I had a tiny desk, one of those square one-foot-by-one-foot jobs with little flaps, and a little plastic chair. After a few hours of work, I took any excuse to get out of my apartment.

Every time I stepped out into the street, I would tell myself, *I'm here. I'm thousands of miles away from family and friends. I don't know anyone.* Every time I walked on the pavement, I could feel the city's vibe. Car alarms going off, people yelling, motorcycles roaring, students throwing beer bottles in the street, sirens and laughter every few minutes. The noise was what I liked the most because I could shut my eyes and drown out everything else. Most people like to get rid of the noise.

I wanted it.

I spent the first three months in a mad rush to locate and complete a deal for our office space. Ultimately, I found a loft on Twenty-First Street, a huge raw space, 4,800 square feet, beautiful eighteen-foot ceilings, and wooden floors. It looked like a total hole when I first arrived. After the team came down, we polished the floor, put in the lights, built up some papier-mâché walls, and made room for twenty-five people—a huge risk, since we were really living off the month-to-month money we had. At the time, we had about twelve to fifteen people in Ithaca, and we knew maybe only ten of them were coming. But we weren't in a position to over expand and get a sixty-person office. Making room for twenty-five right out of the gate was a stretch. We debated for quite a while. Then we decided to just hope things worked out. When Todd and the staff arrived, the construction team was still building the walls. Literally, the only thing that had been completed was one conference room. So Todd and I put all ten people in the conference room. We gave ourselves our own little executive office that was maybe 200 square feet.

Because everyone was on top of each other, we all invested in big earphones that were supposed to muffle out noise but instead made us look like helicopter pilots. It didn't help much. After two months, we were ready to kill each other.

Back in Ithaca, our whole site was being run from a few big database machines in one small room. When we moved, a few of the tech guys stayed to run the site. After a couple of months, the time came to bring the server to the big city. So, one weekend morning, we literally took the site off the air while they raced down to the city (we put up a notice that said, "We apologize—the site is temporarily down for maintenance"). Six hours later, we plugged the whole thing back in, wires, everything.

During this period, theglobe.com still had a free service and a subscriber service. This was back in the day when everyone was going free; the concept of subscription as the sole driver of website revenue hadn't yet been proven to be a failure. For $2.95 a month, you could get yourself private chat rooms, and $4.95 a month got you a silver or gold subscription, with more features. For $10 a month, you were platinum, which gave you more home-page storage space.

Then there was the free part of the site. What we realized over the next year or two was that although the subscription service drove decent revenues (something that attracted quite a few investors), it had massively slowed our rate of user growth while everyone else was just rocketing. If we had not done that for those two years, we could have been a Yahoo! or a GeoCities in terms of size. But instead, people had to choose between us or a free service, and a lot of them went somewhere else. In hindsight, subscriptions were a bad early move. But it gave us the experience, and we learned from it. And it's what I think really attracted Michael Egan (our soon-to-be new chairman). Mike came in with these visions of creating tens of thousands of communities, each with ten members, all paying $10 a month, and if we did it, it would work out to billions of dollars in revenue.

By May, after what seemed an eternity, the construction was completed. Everyone got their own cubes: the classic communal office space of the internet start-up age. This was the big time. We were in New York City. Everyone was excited. Some were scared. They didn't know what to do in New York or where to go. As a four-month vet, I was dishing out suggestions to all the employees, showing them all the restaurants and the different things to do.

At the time, New York was trying to attract business. Giuliani had set up an economic development program, trying to attract and retain businesses. From that, we got our first major press: a tiny mention about our arrival in the *New York Times*. The article said something like, "IBM moves 10,000 employees to New York City, and WebGenesis sets up office in New York City." (We'd officially changed our name to theglobe.com, but people still kept calling us WebGenesis.) "Mentioned in the same breath with IBM!" Todd and I groaned. "Everyone is going to think we're a multitrillion-dollar company now."

At the time, there was still no such thing as Silicon Alley. There were a few web shops, but none had the sophistication of the major companies found in San Francisco. The first snippets of what would come to be defined as the new economy were coming out—you heard about people working around the clock, sleeping under their desks, things like that. We had been living it, too. It wasn't unusual to find Todd and me in the office at 2:00 in the morning, watching the servers, rebooting the ones that kept crashing. But we loved it. It was a fever.

Although we'd been briefly profitable the preceding year, we knew the expense of setting up in New York City would put us back in the red. Nevertheless, our traffic kept climbing. Ad sales kept rising. We really didn't have much of an in-house sales force, but we'd made some hires to do marketing and sales. Todd and I were set to return to profitability by that fall. All it would take was $100,000 a month. It became clear that we couldn't get enough customers to pay for the service. Sure, we had some 30,000 paying subscribers, but that would only earn us $100,000 to $200,000 a month in revenue—hardly matching the big advertising dollars out there. We scrapped the subscription business model. And as soon as we did, our traffic rocketed out of control to the point where our servers exploded. I mean, they were melting. We couldn't even keep them up anymore. At the time, it was more important to be a big player with expensive ads than a niche provider. There was much more glamour and power in advertising revenue, and we were all attracted to that.

Sometime in mid-March, I got a call from Hunter Rawlings, and everything changed. Rawlings said, "Hey, boys. I'm down in Florida meeting with an alumnus. Name is Michael Egan. He runs this car company, Alamo Rent A Car. Turns out the guy's looking for his next great hurrah. He wants to get into the media business, and I thought I had the two perfect guys for him to meet."

We looked at each other. "Oh God, the car business? Another flake from Florida? What the hell is this?" Needless to say, we were very skeptical. Rawlings wouldn't hear it. He said, "The guy wants to meet with you. He's flying up to Ithaca."

Todd and I had vowed to *never* return. Now there we were, flying to Ithaca, depressed out of our minds. But when we arrived, we saw Mike disembark from his private jet.

Out rolled the red carpet. Then came the entourage. *My God,* we thought, *this guy has a private jet! This is for real.* That day, Mike's entourage included Ed Cespedes, formerly of J.P. Morgan and Mike's new M&A guru; Rosalie Arthur, Mike's chief accountant; and several others. Todd and I were with Rawlings.

Hunter decided to let us meet at Statler Hall on campus. We had this huge lunch behind private doors; everything was shut down around us.

Why was a guy like Michael Egan interested in a couple of twenty-something kids? At the time, Mike had just sold Alamo Rent A Car for $625 million to Wayne Huizenga's AutoNation, which allowed him to get into the M&A business. Mike's net worth had gone up to about $1 billion (though mostly in stock). Ed had left J.P. Morgan to help start Dancing Bear Investments, Mike's new angel investor group in Fort Lauderdale, Florida. Ed had essentially negotiated the whole Alamo deal while managing Mike's personal finances; he was considered an M&A whiz kid, and he was only in his early thirties.

So we had our meeting. As usual, Todd and I tried to sell the idea of community, still a fairly pioneering concept in those days. We'd become pretty good at our pitch.

We now used the phrase *media play.* We knew about the evolution of the advertising market. We knew the online social dynamics—what worked and what didn't—right down to the kinds of icons that people preferred. We also had the confidence of knowing that we'd progressively raised more and more money each year. Up to this point we'd probably raised close to $2 million. At the time, we were twenty-three years old, and people were still taken aback by how baby-faced we were, which only forced us to improve our pitch. We could literally finish each other's sentences, machine-gun style. We could take on anybody.

At the end of the meeting, Mike said, "Well, I want in."

Mike was a big guy, vaguely reminiscent of Leslie Nielsen (think *The Naked Gun*), only larger, with a friendly face, baby-blue eyes, and white hair. Despite his size, he was always in an impeccably tailored suit. We were struck by Mike's tremendously engaging, enthusiastic personality.

The air seemed to be sucked out of the room after he spoke. There was a pause. Then he added, "I'm ready to put in $5 million." Todd and I looked at each other. A few months earlier, we would have been screaming. Now we felt ambivalent, like *Hold on just a second here.* We'd just raised $1.2 million. We didn't critically need that much money right now. We didn't want an investor with some hugely disparate agenda co-running our show. We felt really unsure about the offer.

But.

This could be the money that would finally open our door into the big leagues. Remember, everyone in San Francisco had been raising $10, $15, even $20 million. This could be our chance to catch up.

We agreed to move forward with Mike, but made it clear that Todd and I would continue to run the company. This was our venture, and we wanted to grow with it. We were doing it because we loved the business.

As we spoke, Mike got this childlike look in his eyes. He seemed like one of those rare people who could really understand what Todd and I were talking about. As soon as we finished, he looked like he wanted to take it to the next level. You could tell that he had this exciting dreamer quality about him. His entrepreneurial vision was obvious.

It was boring holes through the walls, inventing possibility out of anything it wanted to.

Beyond Alamo, Mike was one of the main investors who'd helped start Nantucket Nectars, which had taken a huge market share away from Snapple and Ocean Spray on its way to becoming a $100 million business. He had won the Horatio Alger Award for outstanding Americans who succeeded despite adversity. It was very clear that whatever Mike touched turned to gold.

I should mention that our style of dress still hadn't changed much. In fact, what did quickly change were Mike's clothes. He went from wearing a suit, which he had done his whole life, to wearing nothing but black. It made him look more contemporary, and for a fifty-six-year-old guy venturing into uncharted territory, that was key. Mike jumped into the internet with a great intensity. It was inspiring to witness someone well into middle age changing his lifestyle and his mentality.

Lunch ended five hours later. Not only were we skeptical about Mike's $5 million offer, we were also convinced that either we wouldn't hear back from him or he'd call and change the terms. We'd certainly learned our lesson after all those rounds of financing—things never work out the way you hope.

As we suspected, despite Mike's enthusiasm, the negotiations dragged on through April, May, June, July, and August of 1997—five months. The process involved far more due diligence and painful negotiations than we'd ever endured with any VC firm or investor. This was the biggest drilling ever, and, in the end, it turned out to be fantastic. Todd and I became more intimately familiar with the details of our business than ever before, modeling out all the numbers, the projections, everything. We had to bust our asses to get all this stuff worked out. We'd negotiate, negotiate, negotiate.

Mike had his law firm in Florida; we had ours in California. We were constantly negotiating back and forth. The difficulty was that Mike used a more conservative law firm while ours was high-flying and technology driven. The principles of how things worked—stock options, contracts, non-compete clauses—were all so different. In California, non-competes are taken much more lightly; in New York they're taken very seriously and are actually enforced. Mike wanted to negotiate these stringent non-competes that basically stipulated that if Todd or I ever left theglobe.com we could never even contemplate working in the technology or computer field again. It was just ridiculous! That part of the negotiation took a great deal of time but in the end was resolved to everyone's satisfaction.

Through it all, Todd and I were flying to California constantly. Every time we thought we were almost closing, it kept getting delayed and delayed. This was a time, by the way, when our spending had ramped up in anticipation of the deal closing. It wasn't massive, but we'd gone from spending $100,000 a month up to $150,000. The problem was, at this rate, our $1.2 million was going to run out. Actually, it was imminent. We had $1.2 million at the start of the year. Ten months later, we were down to our last few dollars.

Headaches. Gnawed fingernails. Sleeplessness. One afternoon, as I was walking home, I started trembling with the realization that we were either on the verge of death or on the verge of massive success. It was tearing me apart. I began getting terrible stomachaches.

It turned out that I had become lactose intolerant and allergic to a dozen other things. I discovered that when you undergo astronomical levels of stress, your body can change. You can become allergic to things that never bothered you before. It was terrifying and painful and only resolved slowly over time.

Over the course of our meetings, Mike made it clear to us that he wanted to own at least 50 percent of theglobe.com. And Mike played hardball. He wanted to put in $5 million for that 50 percent stake and own half of a $10 million business post-financing.

Our board was enthusiastic: "Guys, if you can get $5 million on a $10 million valuation, that would be a miracle. Don't push it." But Todd and I still believed we were worth more. I remember a fateful day early on in the negotiations, at a meeting down in Dancing Bear's offices in Florida, sitting down with Mike and saying, "I feel like you're really lowballing us. I really feel like this business is worth (okay, here we go, fingers crossed) $40 million." For an internet company, especially after what I'd seen Yahoo!, Lycos, and other companies go for, this was perfectly reasonable. In fact, I thought we were worth *more.*

Then Mike said, "Look, guys. I don't mean to lowball you. I'll need to talk to Ed and my staff about this." They actually went to another room to do so. Sitting in silence, Todd got a look that said, *If we pull this off, Steph, I'm really going to love you. But if we don't . . . !* It was like poker. The minute we looked nervous was the minute they'd know they had us.

They came back from the board meeting, and we regrouped around the table. Mike was going to put in $20 million instead of the original $5 million.

Oh my God. We had danced with the devil in the pale moonlight. All kinds of crazy things started going through my mind. Of course, we'd find out later that Mike had been wildly hesitant. It was a lot of money. He'd never made an investment that big (*no one* had ever made a personal investment that big in the tech industry).

On top of that, Mike was used to traditional businesses, the old multiples of profit calculation. It is obvious today, but in the context of internet companies, standard methods of valuation simply didn't apply. It was thrilling, new terrain for Mike (and anybody else) who was trying to figure out what an internet site was worth in 1997. It was also practically impossible. Rosalie, a conservative accountant, was dead set against a deal at this price. Fortunately, Ed sat down with Mike to do comparative analysis, after which he said, "Look, Todd and Steph are right. There are valuations out there that set a precedent for this. Despite the risk, this could be the biggest thing you've ever done in your life." He wrote this in a memo that recommended moving forward.

As a reward for his influence with Mike, Ed came to New York City and spent the next five months with us. He'd just relocated his entire life to Florida, including his fiancée. For the first time, it wasn't Todd and me who had to keep the process going. Now Ed was pushing it and challenging us to keep up with him, until we were working twenty-four hours a day, falling asleep at odd hours at our desks and waking up surrounded by stacks of half-empty cartons of Chinese food. Internet mania felt like the Indianapolis 500: fast and furious.

Among the first things that had to be negotiated were our contracts—Todd and I never had one. We had just started making $35,000 a year. We looked at each other practically in a trance—"What an opportunity, what should we ask for? Should we ask for, I don't know, like, $100,000?" That seemed like an outlandish number to us. Of course, CEOs of traditional companies were making far more than that. But could we really dare start there? What if that was too much, and they decided to walk away from the deal? Did we want to take the risk? Maybe it would be better to take the money from the investment and ask for $40,000. We decided to live large.

So we sat down with Ed. "Ed," I said with the deepest voice I could muster, "Todd and I would like to do $100,000 each."

And Ed said, "Guys, let's just call it $125,000 each."

We were taken aback. "What? You just made it more? Done!" This time the poker faces slipped. When you have enough bad experiences, you learn to accept when something seems to have gone well. (Ed, we subsequently discovered, was a stellar negotiator. Not only was he brilliant financially, his power play was that he knew how to befriend the people he was negotiating with. He made himself much more than a go-between. We ended up feeling like he was giving us the inside scoop from the other team, even though he was the negotiator for the acquiring party.)

Naturally, $125,000 each made us feel very comfortable, but the reality was that Todd and I never wanted to sell our business. We never wanted to give up control of anything. But he persuaded us. Ed said, "Mike's only doing this if you guys stay as CEOs, if you guys commit to a ten-year contract." Yikes, that seemed a bit too long of a commitment, with a new partner and all. So we negotiated more. Ultimately, we got it down to a five-year contract, which was two or three years more than anyone else had been signing in California. Again, to make us feel smart, there was a kicker. In addition to the $125,000 each, to soften the five-year commitment and the loss of autonomy, Mike was going to give us $500,000—in cash—each. This, as they well knew, was something we just couldn't refuse. Todd and I were broke, our bank accounts were down to zero, and we had accumulated large debts. (Of course, then we discovered the US tax law, and realized that 50 percent of it was already gone. Nevertheless, the net $250,000 was a new lease on life. All of a sudden, everything we'd worked for wasn't evaporating. Finally, I could hold my head up to my Cornell buddies who were already making $200,000 or $300,000 a year at Goldman Sachs. Mike gave us the first chance to get out of our crappy rentals and actually buy real apartments. How were we supposed to know that it would be the biggest fortune we'd ever accumulate?

When the deal finally seemed to be a sure thing, Todd and I flew yet again to California. We decided we were going to sit at the conference table at our law firm and stay there until the deal was done.

Finally, after thirty-six hours, the final agreement came in, we exchanged documents, and we signed. Todd and I hopped back on the red-eye, flew to New York, arrived first thing in the morning, went to the office, and shut our door. Todd conked out on a futon. I was lying on the floor. We just passed out for an hour.

When we woke up, we checked with our bank and confirmed that the money had been wired in. Twenty million dollars in the bank! It was a done deal. We called a meeting with our staff. They had no clue what was going on. Some of them had speculated that because we'd been gone so much, we were selling the company. When we announced that we'd just closed $20 million, everyone's jaws dropped.

Within a few days, we ended up in the *New York Times.* A front-page story in the Metro section. You couldn't miss it. There was a picture of Todd and me—me still with my stupid ponytail. (My hair, by the way, had grown longer and longer. Later, in the fall of 1997, my sister came to visit and talked me into shaving it all off.) The picture was from the computer conference in Texas. The headline read, "Whiz Kids Land $20 Million for Their Chat Room." It was labeled the biggest investment in internet history by an individual. It began a huge wave of press. Suddenly, the West Coast took notice. Until then, the West Coast had a serious superiority complex—it was still the classic *Revenge of the Nerds.* Any tech company outside was considered inferior. For them, it was as though they were the engineering town, the smart guys, and everyone else was cow dung. (In some cases it was justified. The New York internet world was, for some time, mainly an artsy scene, an opportunity for people to dye their hair, don thick-rimmed glasses, and tote around little portable iBooks.) We were suddenly big fish in an even bigger, more deluxe pond, and certainly the leading player in New York. We had $20 million, and more important, we had secured the mezzanine round of financing needed for an IPO.

The IPO was the final stage, the ultimate rite of passage. It was the stamp of approval that proved this was not just hype and that there was actual money to be made. Being public meant you were legit. It meant that you'd attract more advertisers, and it made it easier to attract even more money and employees. Suddenly, we could envision that TGLO symbol moving across the ticker—just like we'd seen with Yahoo!, whose revenues ballooned after they went public. The dream was to do it in under eighteen months.

Twelve months later, we went public.

5

A Whole New Life Awaits You

Michael Egan and the Road to the IPO

We got the $20 million financing on August 13, 1997, and the events of the next few months happened very quickly. First, we had the getting-to-know-the-new-partner period. Mike was so proud of his new investment that he built his entire office shaped like a globe: he made a circular space with a conference room and super-high-tech monitors connected to computers. All his furniture was circular.

Unbeknownst to us, Mike already had visions for theglobe.com. He'd been simultaneously working on other little investments, things he was interested in folding into our company. Among the first of many companies we heard about from Mike was something called InteleTravel, a network of seventy thousand travel agents. InteleTravel was Mike's multilevel online travel marketing concept. It was run by guys who always seemed to be sporting slicked-back hair and tans. The main guy seemed to ooze money and didn't appear to have nearly enough time to spend his newfound wealth. When Mike introduced him to Todd and me, our initial reaction was, "What in God's name are we doing with these guys?" But Mike had a concept. He'd experienced great success in the travel business. Now he wanted to combine InteleTravel with theglobe.com and sell trips online. "You guys could have this huge revenue stream underneath." At first, Todd and I thought it sounded like it had potential. We'd instantly have thousands more salespeople who weren't even on our payroll.

Then we realized Mike was saying we'd be instantly responsible for the entire travel company—and that was intimidating. But Mike was extremely persuasive: "We could have seventy thousand travel priests preaching about theglobe.com." Priests?

Mike couldn't contain his enthusiasm. "Imagine," he said, "seventy thousand people! All of them able to make a little bit of money if they're able to sell subscriptions to theglobe.com." Mike was presaging AOL selling Time Warner subscriptions by wanting his InteleTravel agents to sell $5-a-month subscriptions to theglobe.com on top of their travel packages. It certainly sounded interesting. At least it did until we actually met the team. These guys were like bottled LA oil. Working together would have been the most lethal combination. They wore such crisp suits you could hear them coming by the swoosh of their pants.

We talked Mike out of merging with InteleTravel, but every month or so, he wanted to have a management meeting in which he'd bring together the heads of all his different investments. After InteleTravel, there was New River

Technologies, a little firm that helped do tech for his travel company. Every time we went down to his office in Fort Lauderdale, Mike would sit at the end of this long table and the rest of us would join him. Though he'd made it clear to his staff that theglobe.com was his crown jewel, it seemed from our perspective that Mike was trying to combine his companies with ours in an effort to gain an advantage—for them, not us. We wanted to get busy preparing theglobe.com to go public and keep growing the thing. We considered these potential deals with a grain of salt.

At one point, Mike basically told us, "Guys, we've got to get this working better. We're losing money." He just started slapping the table. "Show me the money. Guys, *show me the money*!" It was right after the movie *Jerry Maguire* had come out, and this expression was getting overused fast.

Through it all, Mike never really yelled at Todd and me; we were always "the boys." He didn't want to scare us off, and he knew his best chance of having anything to do with the internet was keeping on board the two young guys who really lived and breathed this medium. It was difficult—Mike wanted total accountability for everything. But this was back before statistics were standardized. It was so hard to measure everything.

Even with our traffic—now over the million-user mark—there were always questions about performance. Fluctuations would be hard to explain. You would think your numbers were going up, then you'd reprocess your logs and see they had actually gone down. We spent a lot of time explaining to Mike and others that this business was hard to measure.

By February, Mike backed off a bit and we postponed the meetings. He stopped forcing us to come down to Florida. Somehow, Ed had been able to convince Mike that for theglobe.com to grow, he had to let it really run. Mike responded by sending Ed to New York to supervise us more closely in the lead-up to the IPO. At the time, Ed was thirty-two. I had just turned twenty-four. Having Ed in the city was fantastic. We had a great time. He was a former banker and could speak banker lingo. He knew everybody and had access to bankers that Todd and I couldn't get to. With Ed in place, we started the IPO process in earnest.

Still, it wasn't easy getting the bankers on board. We had a tough time getting a response because there was no IPO or internet mania—yet. Bankers were doing their usual deals. The big guys—the Merrill Lynches, the Goldman Sachses, the Morgan Stanleys—were backlogged with traditional IPOs: Fox, all these major telecommunications companies. They had no real internet analysts, no internet divisions, no internet focus at all. Merrill Lynch, for instance, had zero internet focus (their CEO would get beaten up in the press for not having any internet strategy when this stuff all hit the big time).

In addition to fighting for financial attention, we were working simultaneously on the preparation of a major ad campaign. One of the most notable things Todd and I had discovered the preceding year was that all these new sites that were competing with us for the same audience had launched their first television ad campaigns. Excite had launched the "Are you experienced?" campaign; Yahoo! had goofy fishermen pulling a giant bass out of a pond after having searched for bait. The visibility of our competitors had really picked up. To keep competing in the big leagues, we needed to create greater visibility for our brand.

We'd been preparing for this since the month after Mike's investment closed, meeting with a lot of different ad agencies, trying to figure out who could come up with the right campaign for us. We ended up choosing Kirshenbaum, which ultimately developed an amazing campaign for theglobe.com. The tagline was "A Whole New Life Awaits You" in neon-green text on black. There was a reason we picked those colors. DoubleClick had proven that neon green on black provided a 17 percent higher click-through rate on banner ads. For the first time, you were able to measure the effectiveness of a color. Neon green it was.

We decided to spend $8 million on a massive campaign—$8 million out of the $20 million we had. It seems ludicrous now, but back then, investor mentality had gone through a major evolution. We were just entering the phase when investors had gone from getting excited about mere internet concepts to believing that a site's traffic determined which company was the biggest and the best. At the beginning of 1998, losses were irrelevant. Growth rate was *everything.* Coined by Netscape, the industry's operating expression was GBF, "Get big fast," and it was quickly used by everybody. We were looking ahead to an IPO and the dream of a lot more money. Even Bob Halperin said, "Guys, spend your $20 million as if you had $40 million. Ramp up, that's what matters right now." We agreed. We'd take the $8 million and really advertise the bejesus out of this site.

Kirshenbaum developed an incredible ad campaign for television. We had several different commercials, but they were all very ethereal. In one, there was a black background and our logo would come rotating in this sphere out of nowhere. There were futuristic pulsating lights, and this sexy British female voice that said, "Is this the Age of Aquarius? If so, you could meet your partner online . . . theglobe.com offers chat, home-page building . . ." We played up all our novel concepts.

We launched nationwide—on cable channels, MTV, networks, the whole nine yards. We were the first online community to do any type of advertising and the fourth or fifth site to launch a TV ad campaign. We saturated the New York market. Buses said, "A Whole New Life Awaits You." We had billboards, all strategically placed in front of other ad agencies, so they would know where their clients should advertise online. We tried to hit all the demographics. We wanted the site to appeal to everybody. But the MTV crowd—those responsive twentysomethings—became our best target audience.

People started recognizing our logo. Todd and I would walk down the street in theglobe.com T-shirts. We'd get stopped, "Hey, what is that logo? I recognize it from TV. What is theglobe.com? What's it about?" There's nothing so strangely exciting as having people on the street recognize your logo. At that point, the bankers started getting a lot more responsive. Suddenly, they were thinking that theglobe.com was the next big thing. This community stuff was our hook—and community did make us different from GeoCities and others. Those were really home-page hosting sites. Our philosophy was more about people interacting with other people. Very quickly, everyone started using the term *community.*

The hype was building, the bankers started showing interest, and two of the smaller but more aggressive banks came right after us—Bear Stearns and Volpe Brown Whelan. Now, at this point we had expanded to a staff of maybe sixty people. We had completely saturated our floor; sixty people in a space for twenty-five. It was a rat maze, little *Matrix* cubicles everywhere. Volpe Brown Whelan is a West Coast boutique firm. They came into our little conference room with such thin walls that you could hear the nearby elevator clinking up and down. Todd, Ed, and I walked them through theglobe.com story.

A few days later, the Bear Stearns team, who were always impeccably dressed in suits, came down to pitch us on why *they* would be the right player. Todd and I appeared in dramatic contrast to them, dressed in some completely schlubby outfits. I had just cut my hair, going from my college ponytail to a short messy style. Those bankers must have looked at us and thought, *Oh yes. Young internet kids.* They tried to relax with us, but it was so transparent. There would always be the standard small talk at the beginning of the meeting, all this stilted banter about clothing and clubs. Bankers versus internet guys: a classic divide for the late nineties.

We met with other bankers as well, including Mary Meeker at Morgan Stanley and Michael Parekh at Goldman Sachs. It turned out that Goldman was going to take GeoCities public. GeoCities, a company founded by David Bohnett in LA, was the largest home-page–hosting site in the world and on target to generate twice our revenue. In 1997, our biggest problem was that we'd generated under $1 million in revenues, and we were on track in 1998 to generate $5 million. These bankers typically wouldn't work with a company that only did $5 million in revenue and had massive losses. Our understanding was that the minimum they liked to touch were companies with $10 million in annual revenues and climbing. It was hard for them. We met with a great banker at Merrill Lynch who loved us and wanted to take us public. But we didn't meet all of the required criteria and their analysts refused to budge. We couldn't wait.

Timing was everything; Todd and I could feel the market heating up. We had to be the first in the community space. Second was okay. But no one ever remembers who's third, and the rest would be completely off the map. This became apparent with search engines. It was common knowledge. If GeoCities was going with Goldman, we'd have to race to get ahead, and if we couldn't get ahead of them, we'd have to be second—or else.

Now, we'd heard disturbing things about some of the big investment banks. Imagine two little seals swimming up to a great white shark and kissing the tip of his nose. That's how we felt, giving ourselves to one of these institutions. But we didn't have much of a choice. And Bear Stearns was being the most aggressive—something that others warned could be off-putting. Still, they were willing to fight for us when all the other guys wouldn't.

We signed on with Bear Stearns and Volpe Brown Whelan, and—immediately—the process began. Between April and the end of July, a four-month period, we worked nonstop. Todd and I were barely in the office anymore. We set up a war room down at our law firm at Fried Frank, which was in the financial district, and spent every single day there with all of our bankers, plus all of Bear Stearns's bankers.

We were the ones there because—this was another really tough part—we didn't have a chief financial officer (CFO) or a chief operating officer (COO) yet. The whole company was just a bunch of internet guys, so a part of the deal was that we had to appoint a senior management team immediately in order to go public. We couldn't even file our papers with the SEC unless we had this team in place. So the hunt was on to find a good CFO, right as we were working day and night with the bankers. We hired a head-hunting agency, but couldn't find anyone with the appropriate fit.

Then Frank Joyce walked in. Frank boasted a media background. He had been at the Reed Travel Group, which had $300 million in revenue and 2,500 employees. So we negotiated his deal and injected him right into the filing process, working with the bankers. He had to walk in, accept the financial model that we had developed, refine it with us, and jump right into the pit of fire, which he did from day one.

We'd already been looking to hire a senior director of business development, so we expanded the search to include a COO. We hadn't really thought about a COO before, but we wanted a senior manager with expertise to help us run the daily business. This search was a disaster until the night we met Dean Daniels. Dean had worked in network television at CBS for his entire career. He'd been one of their top guys and was even nominated for four Emmy awards for a piece he'd done on Clinton's infamous "I never inhaled" speech. At first, we weren't sure that he was the right person for us considering his pure television background, but everything he said was music to our ears. "Guys," he said, "I've been working in the television business. When something goes down on the air, you have three seconds to fix it." We knew right away that he was the kind of hands-on business pro that we needed, and right before our final SEC filing, he came on board.

This, by the way, was the first time we'd hired executives who were quite a bit older than us (both in their forties), and we knew that could be awkward. Our ages had been an issue when we were raising money, so we'd made it clear in the search that we were looking for a more experienced CFO and COO who could help us build the company and lend their management expertise to the business. Our experience was limited to the four years of running theglobe.com, and we were obviously missing some of the skills associated with managing a public company. We needed the best help we could get.

And we did need help. As we got closer to the filing process, it felt like we were forming our own ice bridge to skate across. Our entire team always felt on the edge. The reality is that IPOs are a rarity, and few CEOs experience them throughout their entire careers. We were learning everything in real time. Questions kept popping into our heads that would never concern more experienced CEOs. What exactly is a red herring? Why does the SEC have a thirty-day wait period? We were learning on the fly, but also had to project ourselves to the public like executives who had being doing this for a long time. It was like our brains had to be running a billion cycles a second. Todd and I had always focused on the technological and operational details, down to the last megabyte. For example, every home page had to be done just right. Ultimately, that was good for the business because we'd developed good eyes. But at the same time, I'm sure our team wanted to shoot us because we micromanaged the hell out of them.

The bigger picture needs that came with an IPO forced us to finally delegate. We knew that if we went public we would have to think about pursuing acquisitions, managing financing issues, and meeting other CEOs. We'd need to spend a lot more time doing external things. It was time to delegate and trust that our new executive team could do the job.

That was easier said than done. Every week there was some sort of mini crisis. Take our server room. We didn't have the wisdom to think anything through, so the room had been overpacked and installing air-conditioning was an afterthought. We'd put in cheap cooling systems that started spraying water on the computers, which was not only bad for the servers but life-threatening for the staff since there was wiring all over the place. At one point, we consumed so much electricity that the meter melted and everything shut down. The meter, by the way, was located right next to our only emergency exit, and there were phone lines and other wires everywhere. It was absolutely hazardous. Our best solution for fixing the electricity meter was to take a broom and jam it in there, which kept the switch up and prevented the thing from flipping off. The problem was the broom would slip and fall right across the fire exit. Naturally, there were some complaints.

We also had our share of human resources problems. In the race for Silicon Alley talent, not everyone was a star. We employed a few people who had perhaps a little *too much* job experience. One person in particular, an important hire for business development, seemed to have held as many jobs as years she had lived. And it was no surprise: she was a screaming, threatening, empire builder. After a brief honeymoon in which she established her place in the company, she proceeded to terrorize us with intra-office power plays. There would be days when she would walk down to our office screaming obscenities and reacting to what she perceived as attempts to undermine her authority. It rarely gets more overt than that.

Todd and I were reluctant to dismiss her since we depended on her for so much (not to mention how many people she was in charge of and how many she had persuaded into her corner). This, of course, is a standard problem that any CEO would experience, but she was able to bully us like middle school kids simply because we were young founders.

Then we hired Dean, and his first order of business was to help us with the situation. That same day, we convinced her to resign.

While all of this was happening, we were going to the law firm, day in and day out. Every day, there'd be fifteen people in the room with bankers and lawyers on both sides, in the conference room trenches filled with bagels, sandwiches, chips, fruit, cookies, and expensive suits. Our team, our lawyers; their team, their lawyers. We would go in there at 8:00 a.m., start working, have lunch, keep working, go home at 9:00 p.m., shower, and go back in until 3 a.m. the next morning. Around the clock, including Saturdays when our friends and coworkers were out partying. We could have slowed down, but the reality was that we had to catch up to GeoCities.

Then—we found out that a new company called Xoom.com (a company run by Laurent Massa, whom we later became friends with) was going public at the same time we were. Xoom.com was an e-commerce company camouflaged as a community site in order to take advantage of the community hype. And who was taking them public? Bear Stearns, our very same bankers. In our eyes, a total conflict of interest.

Todd and I had always been overly cautious in general, fearful of others finding out what we were doing and fearful of our competitors. Maybe twenty to thirty years of experience makes you more comfortable with competition so that you don't panic as much, but Andy Grove's theory of "Only the Paranoid Survive" clearly applied to us. And paranoia manifests itself in terms of always looking out for the dark horse. Who that you don't know about is going to pop out of nowhere? We were well aware of GeoCities. But Xoom was an unknown, and their reach seemed to be ballooning. Now, to our horror, Bear Stearns was working with them as well, which was our worst nightmare. We could easily end up being third to the market . . . and we knew what people thought about who comes in third. Despite all assurances from our banker that we were a strong player in this sector, we remained nervous about Xoom.

Our investment banker assured Ed—a big, tough guy, the kind of guy who knows how to intimidate bankers—that there was nothing to worry about, that there was no conflict of interest, that there was a Chinese wall that couldn't be broken. Nevertheless, we were skeptical. How could we not be with so much riding on the IPO?

(The truth ended up being that when the market tanked and it looked for a time like neither company would be able to go public, Bear Stearns tried to convince us to merge with Xoom—because of how "similar" our very different businesses were. We also later found out that Xoom's lead banker was secretly dating our lead banker throughout the process. All that talk about "Chinese walls" was just talk—we were left with a very bad taste in our mouths about the entire process.)

Meanwhile, month after month, as Todd and I worked on our financial model, we learned more about valuation. Around this time, GeoCities went public. They were initially valued at $250 million, but their market cap rocketed to $1.5 billion. We thought this was phenomenal. They were trading at a revenue multiple of 13. Everything was based on multiples of revenue for the following year. So we tried to calculate what our next year's revenue would be. We tried to project $15, $16, $17, $18 million—so we could argue our valuation at a multiple of that. Mike wanted it higher. I wanted it higher. Everyone wanted it higher. But the only way to make our market cap higher was to come out and say, "All right then, revenues will be higher." We had to push our revenues. Todd and I were starting to get really nervous. We'd meet with the board and say, "Um, guys, we've pushed our revenue projection to nearly unrealistic heights. Todd and I will have to kill ourselves to make these numbers." (Turns out we nearly did kill ourselves, yet we managed to beat earnings estimates every single quarter for the first two years.)

Bear Stearns decided to price our deal lower than GeoCities—at $11 to $13 a share. For the ten to eleven million outstanding shares of the company, that would value us at about $130 million. Our offering would be about three million shares, which meant we could raise between $33 and $40 million in cash, which would be just perfect. So, numbers in place, we thought we were ready to file . . . until the next debacle.

In a surprise move, Mike came to us with a proposition: "Guys, I'd like to be a CEO, too." This was the first time Todd and I heard of this idea. We spoke with Bob, who was always there to support us. Fortunately, he went to Mike and said, "It's tough enough having two CEOs, but it's not unheard of. Three CEOs is a nonstarter. When someone comes calling, when an investor comes calling with questions, you can't have three different answers."

Mike backed down, and we filed the whole document on July 24. We celebrated like crazy because the minute you file, the press knows instantly, and the story goes out. Suddenly, theglobe.com was a high-visibility player, and our timing looked good. NASDAQ was at its peak. It had reached something like 2,500 points. The press was going crazy, and Todd and I finally let out a deep sigh. We knew the real work was ahead, but, still, we were relieved. Right away, we'd have to start practicing, training for the IPO and the inevitable road show that would commence in September. We'd have one month to six weeks preparation, max. Todd and I wanted desperately to take some time off. I don't think we'd had a single day of vacation since Cornell. Before the road show, we officially had eighty employees, and we'd been in New York for a year and a half. We had five or six million monthly users.

We never got that vacation. Unbeknownst to us then, NASDAQ would begin to fall the following week. In fact, we had the misfortune of beginning our road show on one of the single biggest point drops in NASDAQ history.

But, as they say, the show must go on.

6

New York, New York

A Brave New World

During the first three quarters of 1997, I was living on $35,000 a year. I was netting $2,000 a month; $1,325 of that went to rent. I had less than $665 a month in spending money, about $600 of which went for food. I still had my original $4,000 savings in my bank account, but that had started shrinking by about $1,000 a month.

So when Mike invested and my salary became $125,000, I could start living. And I did, because suddenly I had more money than I knew what to do with. I could actually afford to go out and spend money at the same rate as my friends who'd gone to work at Goldman or Merrill or law firms.

I was a twenty-four-year-old foreigner who'd just moved to Manhattan, and I'd been working like a dog nonstop. I just wanted to get out and pound the pavement. I had a few friends from Cornell who were also in the city, and we started going out regularly. I'd leave the office and head straight out for dinner around 9:30 or 10:00 (a huge change from Cornell, where everyone dined at 6:00). I quickly realized how international Manhattan could feel, a city of countless cultures smashed together and mixing on a tiny island.

My friends and I would sit at the bar for half an hour, knock back a few drinks, and by midnight, we'd finish eating. The classic thing was to head over to 23 Watts Street, to a club called Chaos. Chaos was an incredible club with plush red velvet, dark colors, red lights, and people in black clothing. My new personal style fit in perfectly: short, funky hair and lots of trendy garb. They'd wave us past the velvet ropes. I don't know why, but I just hit it off with the right people and always ended up knowing someone there. We'd show up, and the manager, Theo, would be wearing a cowboy hat and surgery scrubs. He'd take us straight in, up the winding staircase to the VIP section.

Inside, the music was pulsating all the latest European house and techno. Celebrities up the wazoo. You weren't allowed to dance at Chaos because they didn't have a cabaret license, but that's what made it great. They'd let the regulars get away with it, up on one of those velvet cubes, just gyrating away. There were models, actresses, daughters of models and actresses. It was just mind-blowing.

At this point, I hadn't had a steady girlfriend for nearly three years. For me, this was my opportunity to *live,* my belated coming-of-age. But I was far from a perfect Don Juan. In 1997, I was still living in my tiny closet apartment on Sullivan Street. Whenever I brought a girl home, it was hilarious because the size of my bedroom made us feel like hamsters in a shoebox.

The party at Chaos eventually moved to Spy. From there, I discovered Float. Club after club after club. I'd work until midnight or 1:00 a.m., go home, take a shower, meet up with friends, and then head out to the clubs. I'd go out four times a week, usually Wednesday, Thursday, Friday, and Saturday. At 2:30 to 3:00 a.m., I'd leave the first club and go to another one called Twilo. The music was amazing. Everybody was half-naked. Neon glow sticks were waving all around. I'd never seen this before, and it was phenomenal.

During the summer of 1998 before the IPO, life for me turned into club land. The nights were unparalleled, and everything was about the music: house, trance, ambient. Even Mike got into it. He'd already switched over to an all-black, neo-chic wardrobe and bought himself a plush multimillion-dollar apartment in the Trump Tower. But when he started asking me what Oakenfold trance CDs he should buy, I nearly fell over. I don't know if he genuinely liked it or if he just thought it would help him change his image. Either way, when I was in close quarters with Mike and the bankers, I'd put on my earphones, shut my eyes, and relive those crazy moments in the clubs.

I'd never really clicked with the whole fraternity, beer-drinking thing in college. I was studying physics and computer science. For God's sake, I was starting a company. But in Manhattan, it all changed.

Sometimes, around 4:00 in the morning, we'd go to Coffee Shop in Union Square for a burger. Or we'd go to Blue Ribbon for rich foie gras on sweet, perfectly toasted brioche. Around 5:00 or 6:00 in the morning, we'd head to someone else's place, close all the curtains, sit around the table, and watch old reruns of James Bond movies. Our enemy would be the daylight. That was the one thing that killed the vibe.

In my nights out, I never spoke about theglobe.com to anyone. I just didn't talk about it. It wasn't my style. I'd rather ask people about themselves. I was so much more into discovering New York, meeting people, and finding out what other folks were doing. That little geek feeling always seemed to surface when I brought up what I did. Most of my friends had no clue what I was really working on. It was a secret. Everyone else had normal jobs. People would always say, "The internet? So you work with computers?" That was the extent of it. There was nothing cool about the Net at this point.

It quickly became obvious that between the endless work and nonstop partying, there was no time for sleep. I'd come in every morning with huge bags under my eyes. Somehow, I managed. When you're putting this level of energy into your work and getting so much in return, you think you're invincible.

I'm not even sure why we worked so hard. The concept of being an internet zillionaire was still so remote, so that certainly wasn't the goal. My principal experience as a businessman was the unyielding sense of being on the verge of death: always pushing as hard as possible and in constant denial of the inevitable.

After our IPO in 1998, life completely changed. But before the IPO, the idea of future wealth was just a vague notion. I knew about Netscape's Jim Clark and his fortune. But to me, that was still just some VC in San Francisco with thirty years of experience who hit the lucky number. I was just a nobody working on something that I loved. It was nice to have a chance for money, but in my heart of hearts, I never really thought we were about to get rich.

What did I know?

7

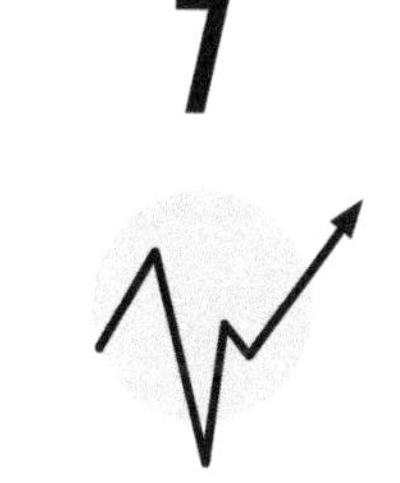

The Road Show

Sixty Meetings, Twenty Cities, Ten Days

They call it a road show. Think of it as two straight weeks of whoring yourself to every single major institutional investor you can, doing whatever you have to do to raise the money to go public.

Again, our timing was regrettable.

At the end of August 1998, just as we were waiting for the paperwork from the SEC that would approve our offering, the market began to collapse. There were 174 companies that had planned to go public but canceled their IPOs. People were canceling in record numbers—even Fox canceled.

Naturally, we freaked out. If we weren't going to go public, we'd run out of money. It would mean the instant death of the company. But the market kept dropping; even the word *recession* started being uttered.

Nevertheless, the SEC finally gave us the green light, and we filed our official documents in September. We weren't exactly brimming with confidence. We wondered if we should even do this. Our bankers were telling us that everything seemed really bad. Bear Stearns felt the market looked like a disaster.

Todd and I decided to roll the dice because we really had no choice. If we put the thing off, we'd run out of money, and we'd already filed the documents. If we suddenly announced that we weren't going public, there'd be a negative wave of press. In our usual sort of brash way, we told them, "Oh, we can do it, we can punch through this storm." And so it was that we prepared to launch the road show in October.

The first thing we did was start practicing for our presentations. When I say that, I mean really practicing. We worked full-time with the bankers developing a full slide show—revenues, projections, competitive analysis, the whole nine yards. We also hired a professional coach for our presentation skills, this guy who came in and helped us with matters of diction and posture. We learned a massive amount. Todd, for instance, used to always stand stock-still and give his presentations like a robot.

My problem? The old genital clutch, in which your hands are clasped together, hanging right in front of your balls. "What are you trying to tell people?" the coach would yell at me. I moved my hands. We practiced for a month with this coach, going down to Bear Stearns, using their conference center. Before we went on the road, we did a mock presentation to the entire Bear Stearns sales force.

They loved it and thought it was fantastic. We could certainly talk the talk: we could show a track history of how our quarters had grown and rocketed, the money we'd raised, the advertisers we had, the management team we had built. We could make everything look compelling.

Too bad it was just practice. The day we got on the road for real, the market dropped another 200 points. But we pressed on, hitting Boston, San Francisco, Los Angeles, and a boatload of other places that I barely knew existed like Minneapolis and Milwaukee—all these places where old, respectable institutions still thrived.

At least we traveled in style. Typically, we'd just get into Mike's private jet, which was one of the coolest things about this entire experience. We'd used his jet before to fly back and forth to Florida. The first time we got in, the hairs were tingling on the backs of our necks—it was that phenomenal. Mike leased his plane from Wayne Huizenga, so this particular jet was a Gulfstream III—nice and spacious with food service. (Wayne also had several Learjets, several Gulfstream jets, and several private helicopters . . . luxury style right out of *Airwolf.*)

Back in the day when it was just Todd and me running the business and trying to raise seed money, we always traveled ultralow budget. To save money, we would share a room and pray for good late-night movies like *The Fifth Element,* which made things a lot more fun. From our separate double beds, we'd talk until 3:00 in the morning. It was like being in camp or something.

But when we told our bankers to just put Todd and me in the same room, they looked at us sidelong—and we slowly realized that this might not look right. So we stayed in separate rooms. We had to get up at 5:00 or 6:00 a.m., go to breakfast (or to a breakfast meeting), and then attend six or seven more meetings a day.

We started in the Connecticut area with these Putnam Trust–type institutions and then headed over to Boston. On a road show, you start off small. The investors you really want are the big ones, and you need the practice.

The plan was to cover twenty to thirty cities in about two weeks. Those are business days, so that really means packing two and a half weeks into ten or eleven business days. It's concert-tour, rock-star dizzying. You start off in one city in the morning, do a few presentations, fly to the next town at noon, do a few presentations there, and either you stop there if you have more meetings the next day, or you get back on the plane, fly to another place, arrive at midnight or 1:00 in the morning, go to sleep, and wake up in another new city. You do a few more meetings, you get back on the plane, you head back out. You don't know where you are anymore. Very quickly, you no longer have patience to listen to new ideas or questions.

You don't have patience for feedback, period. Matter of fact, you don't have patience for anything. The only way to survive this is by isolating yourself, finding moments of perfect clarity and tranquility. As if.

Each of these meetings could be anywhere from an hour to two hours, depending on their interest level. And then we'd zip around in limos because Mike brought his entire entourage (though he'd quickly realize it was wasteful to have everybody there). It was nuts. Institutions normally meet with just the CEO and the CFO. With us, they got two CEOs, the chairman, three bankers, Ed, and others.

Our entourage may have been large and bloated, but our documents were certainly sleek. We insisted that our S-1 form be matte black with hip green graphics, which was very much considered taboo. But we wanted our form to stick out and attract eyeballs and questions: "What the hell is this?" Internet hype was gearing up, and we wanted to show that we were on the edge. A stale black-and-white document would have been just that—stale.

Despite all of this, Mike felt it necessary to always tell us how we could improve our presentation skills—every day, between every meeting. It was frustrating. Mike felt we needed the coaching but at the same time his part of the presentation was much less rehearsed. Every so often, we'd be in a meeting where they wouldn't quite get it or they had a specific question like, "Well, tell us exactly how this functionality would work." Mike would interrupt and say, "Let me take this one." There'd be a long pause, and then he'd start off with something like, "Imagine community like a banana split . . ."

It was comedic, but it left us looking at each other like, "Who needs the coaching?" At this point, we'd been diluted to each owning 10 percent of the company. Mike owned 51 percent. Todd and I ran all the operations, but when it came to issues concerning equity, strategy, the big moves, final decisions on directions to take, we had to work with Mike. In a situation like that, eventually you start to relinquish real control. Right or wrong, we slowly began ceding our territory. Maybe the company would have done better if Todd and I had kept that control and always taken full responsibility for our successes and failures. Maybe we could have forced ourselves to develop these skills instead of moving back a couple of steps and saying, "Well, maybe Mike will make things happen."

So we were out there on the road trying to drum up money, and the market just kept falling. Interest was progressively dropping from meeting to meeting. Their response was less "Great management team, great presentation," than "What the hell are you guys doing out here now?" The feedback wasn't very promising, but we just pressed on, even though no one was signing up for this baby yet. And things got worse. At one point, we were in Texas and had to get to Colorado at some outlandish hour to meet the people from the Janus Fund or one of those institutions. We sat down with two uptight analysts who immediately started grilling us. Halfway through the meeting, another guy walks in, and he seemed to be even more important. So we started repeating everything again. And then, long before the meeting was over, one of the other guys left. Even more distracting were their pagers, which went off every few seconds. It was pure chaos.

I could see that one of the guys was clearly reading from his pager and totally ignoring everything we were saying. Finally, I asked what was so interesting. And the guy just said, "Oh, it's the market. We're down another 200 points." You could literally see a bead of sweat coming down his forehead. You could also see he was thinking, *Why the hell are you guys on this road show? Haven't you noticed 174 companies canceled their IPOs? You guys are a small internet company, you're not some major telecom company. What the hell are you thinking?* Then they cut the meeting short.

Another time we flew out to LA to meet with some generic capital group. These guys looked like they'd rather be on the beach than meeting with us. One guy was sitting on the other side of the table, staring out at the ocean. "Listen," he told us, "can you speed it up a little? I don't have much time here."

And they had asked to meet with us! Then they flipped to the back page of our book and said, "All right, thank you very much." This guy also dropped comments like, "Oh yeah, my son's done some little rinky-dink project like this, too." Even Mike looked over at us at the end of that meeting and said, "Wow, what an ass."

Someone from T. Rowe Price once interrupted us to say, "I just want to let you guys know I think community is a really lousy business model. I really don't believe in it. I don't believe in Lycos, I don't believe in Tripod, I don't believe in GeoCities." And all this was said with a huge smile.

Todd and I were getting more and more frustrated. A road show is something you only want to do once in your lifetime. It's that bad. But we were doing it, and right off the bat, we realized that we might have to do it all over again. And if we did it again, we'd be on the road with the 174 companies that had all canceled; we'd be part of a huge pack. That is if we were even *around* to get that chance.

It was looking like we weren't going to get the deal done. We'd originally been going out on a price range of $11 to $13 a share.

When you file to go public, there's always a range. If it's a good market and everyone wants in, you get the top of the range. If you're really good, they up the range. Not only does the price go up, but you can actually decide to sell more shares. In our case, we were already selling very little in the way of shares—three million total—but we couldn't do it at $13, couldn't do it at $12, couldn't even do it at $11. We tried going all the way down to $8 without any luck. At least we learned one valuable lesson: when the market's dead, there ain't nothin' you can do about it.

Finally, after two and a half weeks with the market precipitously falling, we returned to New York. Todd and I were just so pissed that we'd gone through this whole circus. I don't recall exactly how much money we had left in the company, but out of the original $20 million, $8 million had gone to marketing and a good chunk of the rest had gone into beefing up the infrastructure to handle the six million users that were now coming to theglobe.com.

At best, we probably had enough money to last three or four months if we lowered the burn rate. But that meant all the momentum we'd built up would dissipate. And then there was the GeoCities problem. They'd gone all the way up to a billion-dollar company, but several months after going public, their stock price had dropped to well below their IPO offering. Now people were comparing us to GeoCities. They'd say, "How do we know if we buy you guys, you won't end up below your IPO price, too?" Meanwhile, Yahoo!, Lycos, Excite, all of them had fallen to ungodly low numbers. It was bad, and the consensus was that we couldn't make the IPO. No matter how much power Todd and I thought we had, we couldn't do it.

I wasn't about to do anything drastic, but on a scale of 1 to 10, 10 being joyful optimism, I was at a 2. We'd gone through this four-year sprint, those pioneering days of the internet. And now it would all be for nothing. We would have to fire people. We were going to vanish in one big poof of smoke.

After so much work, we were terribly bitter. Unfortunately, you don't get a grade for effort. When you're unlucky, you're just unlucky, and that was the worst bit of luck we could have ever had.

The plan was to refocus on the business and figure out a way to get our burn rate way back down again so that whatever money we did have left—$5 million in cash—would last us a year. But even that would require so much cutting. No wonder I needed to go out at night.

By the time we reached mid-October, the IPO was officially off, and we convened in Mike's apartment in Trump Tower. I remember standing in his phenomenal apartment with this spectacular view of the city.

Sharing this view with Todd, Mike, Ed, and me was Wayne Huizenga (from Blockbuster and AutoNation), Ace Greenberg (chairman of Bear Stearns), Bob Halperin (of Raychem and an early Intel investor), David Horowitz (of MTV and Warner Communications), and Ric Duques (CEO of First Data Corp., also our latest addition to the board), all standing in a semicircle. In that moment, part of me was thinking, *Never mind all that's gone down. How did I ever get to this point where I'm standing here, a kid surrounded by these legendary, self-made billionaires? I wish I had a camera.*

They all talked about what our options were. But the point was moot—we were really going to have to pull the S-1 and cancel the IPO. But Mike, being as stubborn as always, wouldn't give in. "No," he said, "let's just leave the document out there. Let's just . . ." He kept pleading and pleading, and kudos to Mike because it was his sheer stubbornness that kept the document alive, kept the door open for us to go public.

And what ended up happening? Bear Stearns finally said, "You know what? We'll take you guys. We'll buy all your stock for $6 a share." So we would be, what? A $50 million company. That would make us a drop in the bucket. Even Mike was turned off by the idea. "No, let's not sell our entire company for six bucks a share. That's a steal."

So we passed.

Status report on theglobe.com at this time, late October 1998: basically, we had been growing like crazy. Employee morale was phenomenal, and everyone was so excited and believed in our mission as if it were a religious crusade—too bad they weren't the investors we needed. Traffic was up; sales kept ballooning. Our sales were actually doubling from quarter to quarter—we had awesome growth. We were well on track to doing $5 million-plus in revenues that year, up from $750,000 in 1997. By the spring of 1998, we had fully embraced home-page building and our user count had soared. It was a wildly popular service. But we were still in our crappy little offices with our disastrous little server room, electrical wiring sprouting everywhere, like a crazy weed. We had people staffed 24/7 just to restart the servers at any moment because the site was crashing all the time.

Through all the head-spinning pre-IPO chaos, I was still going out regularly. On November 7, after another long night at work, I went with Julien, a buddy of mine, to a party. I hadn't really wanted to go, but in the city, you never know what you might find or who you might meet.

The party wasn't particularly eventful. People danced, and I watched Julien try to pick up some girls. At one point, I looked over and saw this beautiful woman. She seemed so elegant, with a beautiful, disarming smile. And I did a double take, which is something you learn not to do in New York since just about every other person who walks past you on the sidewalk is worth a double take. I'd been single for four years now: no love, no serious relationship, and given the way my business life was going, I needed something positive to happen in my social life.

That was Jennifer. A girl who grew up on a farm in Kentucky; she was beautiful and warm and intelligent. Even though Jennifer was a model, she wasn't self-absorbed, but in fact rather down-to-earth. We had this long, involved conversation that simply erased what I had been going through at work; I was putty in her hands. Then, in that classic New York way, the party sort of fell apart before I had a chance to get her number.

I thought I'd never be able to contact her, but by sheer luck, I ended up at Spy and there was Jenn with this large group.

This time I went right up to her and asked for her number, and luckily, she gave it to me. I pulled out my cell phone and popped those digits right in, saved. I went to bed that night the happiest guy in the world; a relationship seemed imminent. Little did I know that Jenn would share with me two of the craziest years that anyone could ever expect to live through.

It must have been my lucky week. The following Monday, the market turned up a little bit, just enough that a few offerings that were in limbo suddenly went public. First Fox went public with a modest 15 percent run-up. Next, EarthWeb, an IT outfit I'd never heard of that was trying to compete with CNET, went public and blew up 250 percent. A couple of other companies were lining up to go. There was a murmur bubbling through the market.

On Wednesday, November 11, 1998, I was sitting behind my cheap little Cornell seventies-style metallic desk, when The Call came in. When I started to comprehend what I was hearing, I put the phone on conference, and Todd came over.

Our bankers were on the line with some unbelievable news. "Guys," they said, "you're never going to believe this. Everyone wants in on the deal." I remember Todd and me looking at each other as though we didn't want to believe this. The emotional roller-coaster we'd just been on left us loopy. If it hadn't been for Mike's eternal optimism, we would have pulled all our paperwork. Since it was still in place, there was a small chance we could get everything going for a quick filing.

Bear Stearns wasn't concerned about our emotional state. Every half hour, they kept calling us: "Guys, the demand is going up, going up. We've got to get everything worked out." We called everyone that had originally been part of the deal. Friends, family, everyone that I'd already told it was over, finished. I had to locate people all over the planet; people were on vacation, people were missing. We had twenty-four hours to get everything back together and refile all the necessary paperwork.

We didn't sleep on Wednesday night. By Thursday, we were still cranking through the paperwork. On Thursday afternoon, bankers called to give us an update. "Guys," they said, "there's something like a forty-five-million-share demand for your three-million-share offering." We were incredulous. The next question: What do we do about the price? We were still officially at eight bucks a share, so we'd only be raising half of what we originally needed. We'd only get $24 million instead of $40 million.

We called up Bear Stearns, but they refused to push the number up. "Why?" we demanded. "Goddamn it, look at this demand."

"We can't do it," they said. They'd already told everybody it was $8, and they claimed that was why there was so much interest.

We really pushed and pushed (especially Mike), and finally, they came back to us and said, "Fine, we've got it up to $9 a share."

That meant we'd only raise another $3 million. Still, it was much, much better than nothing. And we really had no choice. On Monday, our S-1 document would officially go stale and there would be no more time. We could have sat there and insisted they let us keep pushing and pushing and pushing the price to $11 or $13, but the risk was too great. If the document went stale, we'd have to refile, and that's a minimum thirty-day period, thirty days in which the market could tank all over again. Todd and I were just the ultimate pessimists and skeptics about everything by then. We had realized the window of opportunity was so small. It reminded me of *Star Trek* when the *Enterprise* had only one chance to get through a wormhole and travel back 70,000 light-years. If we missed our chance, the game was over.

So Todd and I shook hands and said, "Nine bucks it is," and Mike agreed. We locked down that night and confirmed the deal. By Thursday night, everything was filed and ready to fly.

Time for the Theraflu.

You may recall from the prologue what happened next. At midnight, the clock chimed to welcome Friday the thirteenth.

PART 2

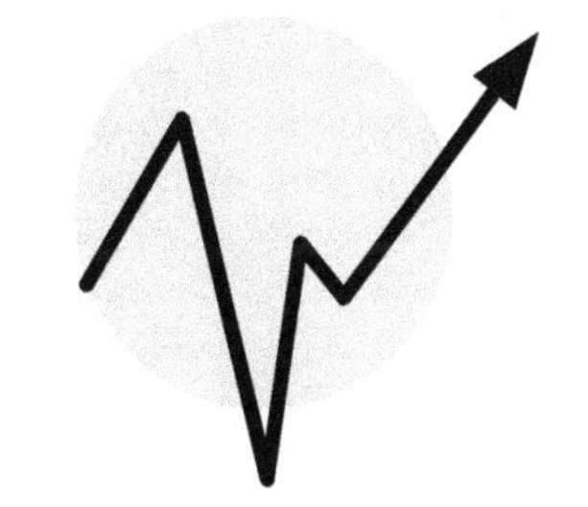

The Reality

8

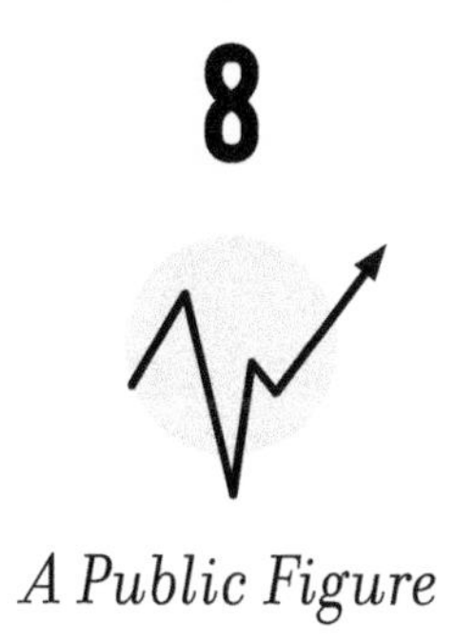

A Public Figure

Life During Internet Mania and a Heavy Dose of Hackers!

The night of the IPO, I kissed Jenn for the first time.

We went out to celebrate at Spy with Julien and Ahmad (my two best friends in NYC), and then about twenty of us came back to my apartment to keep things going after hours. Jenn was sitting in a chair in my living room, and we spoke quietly for a while. She was still just a friend of a friend, and didn't have any sense of the enormity of what had happened to me that morning. As she got up to leave, we kissed, and it was the longest, most passionate kiss I'd had in years.

I went to bed alone that night, my head happily spinning. I remember how excited I was: I'd just kissed the woman of my dreams, and the whole IPO situation was, well, surreal. In a day, I'd been handed an entirely new life.

The next morning, I woke up with what should have been a major hangover but instead felt like this general sense of clarity. My first thought was, *Oh my God, it's done.* The press had already kicked in. The big feature on the cover of the *New York Post* was, "Geeks Make $97 Million." That day, Todd and I began to learn that people react to success in two different ways.

People were either genuinely excited by us and wanted to mirror what we'd done, or they were instantly bitter, wanting everything in the world to ensure that we'd fail, which would make *them* feel much better.

More people than I imagined had heard the news. For instance, I remember leaving my building and catching my doorman smiling at me—everyone knew something big had happened to me in the stock market. Meanwhile, we were already preparing ourselves for the inevitable; our windfall was fine, but the reality was that the stock could just as easily come down.

That Saturday morning, I began my life as a public figure in earnest, running a public company with a trading stock; nothing would ever be the same again. Starting that Monday, we were on everyone's radar, and all of our competitors would be gunning for us.

But enough of that—I know what you're thinking. *What about the money? How did it feel to be worth $97 million?*

Well, hold on. Let's look at the situation realistically. From a personal point of view, I'd have to have been an idiot not to realize the potential for massive fluctuation. Despite our admittedly incredible price, we obviously knew that things were a little unstable at best. After all, we were supposed to go public at $9, and then we hit $87 and went up to $97. That Friday alone, our stock had fluctuated between $97 and $63, from second to second. And something like sixteen million shares had been traded on a three-million-share offering. Day one alone, our stock changed hands at least five times.

As much as I wanted this massive feeling of security and wealth, I knew that it wasn't going to last. If my own net worth could fluctuate up and down by $30 million from one second to another, I knew that over the course of two days, a week, a month, a market shakeup, it could just as easily start rocketing down.

Still, that Saturday morning, I had a big smile on my face. A day before, I was competing with my Ivy League friends who took the safe route, making the usual hundred grand a year, then two hundred grand a year, then three hundred grand. Now, all of a sudden, I'm worth $97 million. It's all over the headlines, all over the world, running on CNN *globally,* every other minute.

But at the same time, I had this eerie feeling. Because I was raised properly, I was taught, "Don't let money change you." So I already had this scary *Twilight Zone* feeling that people were watching me, waiting to see me start spewing money like a walking ATM. The doorman I'd caught smiling conspiratorially at me . . . what was he thinking? Would he expect a bigger tip for Christmas? And if I gave him less than, say, a hundred and fifty bucks, would he call me a cheapskate and give me extra-bad service despite the bonus?

I was frantically thinking, *What do I do?* They don't train you for this kind of thing, especially at age twenty-four. Suddenly, I was scared that people would really start to change, that their perceptions of what my daily life was like would be wildly inaccurate.

The fact was that, given the way things had been going, I'd spent most of my time getting used to the feeling that my whole career would falter imminently. Having sudden financial security really helped. I knew it would fluctuate, but I thought, *You know what? Even if it falls by $50 million, I'll still have $47 million.* I felt like there was plenty of padding and comfort, and even though I wouldn't be able to sell for ages, I'd be fine for a long time.

What did I know?

I spent the weekend at lavish dinners because we all wanted to celebrate. Suddenly, my number of old friends and new ones I'd met mushroomed. We were in a state of total euphoria.

Meanwhile, my actual friends and family—particularly the ones who had purchased stock—were flipping out. People who invested ten grand, acquaintances who I'd coaxed into getting in, all of whom had been fairly reluctant, suddenly made $100,000 that day, a year or two of salary right there. And so we went out again to Spy. Everyone was happy, they brought us to our own table, there was champagne, the booze was flowing, and I was so excited because all these friends had just made a ton of money that they never even slightly expected to make. Of course, *I* ended up with the tab even though I didn't have any more cash than before.

That's the other perception problem that comes with a very public offering. Everyone thought I suddenly had $97 million sitting in a briefcase under my bed. Not true. Not even slightly. The fact is there was *no* cash. There was no real money, thus I couldn't change my lifestyle even if I wanted to. But everyone wanted so badly to believe it was real. It was difficult, especially during that first weekend, not to believe it myself in some abstract way. So, I played the part, which meant spending a lot of money on dinner, picking up tabs for cocktails, champagne, and having dinners at a lot of expensive restaurants that wouldn't have hired Todd and me to wash their dishes just a few years prior. At the same time, I suddenly had people looking at me and whispering about me. Often, there was someone at my ear who I didn't know very well telling me something I wasn't really paying attention to. Forget that it became old very quickly, forget that there was no real cash, it was impossible to deny the sudden and overwhelming sense of power that came with several cocktails and the thought that somewhere out there I had $97 million. Tom Wolfe's "masters of the universe" phrase suddenly became a lot more relevant with that kind of paper wealth attached to me.

By the Monday morning after the IPO, my euphoria had evaporated and turned into pure anxiety. I knew that at 9:30 every morning, the TGLO ticker would start moving, and everything we did would be a matter of public record. I didn't know how to run a public company. Mike had never run a public company. It's amazing how a lot of these billionaires get rich by selling their private companies to other companies; most of them never even think about going public.

Think about it: for the five thousand public companies on NASDAQ, there are ten million that are private. Being public is actually a rare experience. And as much as people like to lecture, they don't necessarily know. Thank God Wayne Huizenga had run a public company as had several other guys on our board. They could give us some real advice. But none of them had done it at age twenty-four.

And it didn't seem like any of them had spent much time thinking about what that might be like.

Perception is everything. That's the scary part. If people think you're a gray-haired guy with a nice stable family, a plush house in the Connecticut suburbs, and your daughters ride ponies on the weekend, they get this feeling: "Ah, yes, my money's with a solid, experienced guy."

Conversely, you wouldn't give your money to Groucho Marx. You wouldn't trust him even if he was the most brilliant accountant in the world. This was the sort of feeling that Todd and I started having. People still were skeptical about our youth, even though we'd just made them a 1,000 percent return in one day.

That became the backstory of our IPO: a wildly fluctuating stock and twenty thousand shareholders wanting to know what we were going to do. "What are you going to *do*? Why are you so *young*? What the *#!@ have I done with my money?" The truth was that there was so much sudden responsibility on Todd, me, and the whole management team. We were all a bit scared. Nevertheless, we all jumped right back into business and got ready for the long road ahead.

For Todd and me, it was a pleasure getting back into the meat of running a company. A day would start with us catching up on the market news: the *Wall Street Journal,* the *New York Times,* CNET, and a dozen other sources. We always felt the need to be scanning the industry, waiting for any new blips to appear on our radar, new competitors, new financing, new killer apps being developed, and so on. We'd often then go visit our competitors' websites to see what new products or services they'd launched, how their services worked, and even to speak with their users to uncover what they liked.

Todd and I shared many responsibilities, especially when it came to the major corporate decisions such as what products to develop, strategies to pursue, new management to recruit, new financing to complete—but we also had our own personal interests. Todd's was to manage the financials, something he'd done since the company's inception. Although he had gradually delegated this to our growing financial staff, Todd still liked to double-check the numbers, making projections of revenues and expenses. Although I liked examining financials, too, I had a greater preference for scanning site statistics: how many users visited, average time spent, most downloaded pages, conversion from visitors to registered users, effectiveness of advertising banners, and so on. I loved playing with stats and equations, which was probably a lingering trait from my engineering days. I'd create massive Excel charts and input pages and pages of data with the most minute details imaginable. I'd then play around with the charting functions to try to analyze the data from every conceivable angle. I did this so often that Excel charts were constantly floating around in my head.

We'd often have weekly and daily meetings with our senior managers to hear status reports on product enhancements, sales reports, and marketing plans. Todd and I loved getting into the details and being hands-on, probably to the frustration of many employees who would have preferred more autonomy. Dean Daniels was very useful at injecting himself in the middle and providing Todd and me with the info we needed while improving our communication capabilities with the various departments. Often, I'd walk around our office and do laps, popping my head into offices to get updates. Sometimes, Todd and I would randomly bump into each other at someone's cube. I probably spent half my time sitting in the ad sales offices getting sales reports and then moving down the hall for an update with our tech guys.

Obviously, things were never the same as when we were a private company. Now, Todd and I had the extra responsibilities as CEOs of a public entity. More time on the road, often with Frank Joyce (the CFO) and Dean Daniels (the COO), meeting with analysts, institutions, and the press.

That Thanksgiving, I took a long-deserved break and flew with Jenn to London. We'd been seeing each other for two weeks; she'd get to meet my mother and taste her turkey. We spent a few days in a hotel, and it was just wonderful. I felt like this was "it"—after four years of searching, I'd found my soul mate.

After going public on Friday the thirteenth of November, our first quarterly report was looming. We knew this quarter was in the bag. We were growing like crazy, doubling the previous quarter's numbers. We felt really good about it.

But there was another concern worrying us. Though our traffic had been ballooning, we never had the type of money necessary to really build the infrastructure at a decent speed. Now our site was perilously overloaded. Our servers were melting. We'd given some thought to finding a new high-tech facility to off-load everything and build from the ground up, and now we dove into this plan on the double.

Thanks to our chief tech guy, Vance Huntley, we found a facility in Staten Island called the Teleport. It was a state-of-the-art maximum-security facility way out in the boondocks with all these massive satellite dishes, a no-fly zone, and infrared barriers around it.

By the time we were prepared to break down our New York office and make the move, our server situation was critical. We were still running in this dangerously overloaded room; at any time the servers could literally melt, which would take us off-line. This scenario, which had happened before, was now a recurring nightmare. We announced to our frantic tech team, "We're a public company. We have twenty thousand shareholders. At no point in time can our site just go off the air!"

In October, before the move could happen, we had our worst technical crisis to date—we lost our home-page service. We had millions of people with home pages on our site and about six million at the time visiting the member pages. All of a sudden, the number of pages was plummeting. The traffic was overloaded. And we're yelling, "What the hell's going on?"

It took us about seventy-two hours to diagnose the problem. The symptoms looked like those of a denial of service, one of those monumental attacks. The same kind of attack that took Yahoo! down. That took CNN down. It took the CIA site down. It's an attack in which computers are commandeered from all over the world, broken into by hackers who install little sleeper programs that when activated act like a military assault. The hackers have a command-and-control center, and someone sends an order out around the world, turning these sleeping Unix servers into secret agents. They receive the attack command and home in on a given location.

The computers create false requests at a million attacks per second. You take a thousand computers, and now you're dealing with a billion attacks per second, then it climbs up to a trillion attacks per second. Each of these attacks are false requests coming from a false address. So it's not like you can lock out addresses because every one of them is false. These attacks come far faster than the servers can possibly handle. They can't handle the load, and they crash, hard.

Now this was happening to us. The good news was that investors and users could still come to the front door of theglobe.com and visit the main site. But if they tried to go to a member page or create a member page, they couldn't do it. And that's where the bulk of our traffic was concentrated at this time, which meant all our advertisers on those pages were going down, too. So not only was the traffic down, but users were getting pissed because they couldn't access their home pages, and advertisers were getting really pissed because their ads weren't being shown. Bottom line: this was going to impact revenues.

And it was happening in real time. Our tech team was spazzing. They worked on weekends; vacation time was a joke. They were ready to implode, their multitasking capacity having been exceeded. The quarter was about to close, and we were ahead of the thing, but now, every day we were down, revenues were shot. We were going to miss our first-quarter estimates, and we were in absolute hysterics.

Vance, our first employee and now chief technology officer, was ready to collapse. The workload was killing him. Then, after an entire month with no sleep, Vance vanished. He didn't leave us an email. He wouldn't pick up his phone or his pager; he simply vanished. Dean was marching around the office like a lunatic. He had only come on board two months before as COO, and he kept saying, "This is tragic." We just hoped that Vance was still alive.

Then another tech guy, a brilliant hacker who could diagnose any problem, vanished as well, after a sleepless week. They were dropping like flies, and we still couldn't fix the problem. Was there a place where these techies went after they snapped?

And the problem was compounded by the fact that our setup was so bad. We had so many critical points of failure that one little attack on a single area would create a chain reaction, and the entire system would go down. It was impossible to find which machines were being attacked, let alone know how to fix them, or more important, identify who was doing this. And why.

Of course, we had to figure out who wanted to destroy us. We tried to eliminate all the variables. "All right, is there any way we can locate who the hacker is?" "No. There's no given address." "Okay. What are the motives for someone wanting to take us down? Could it be some random group out there who is jealous that we're worth billions of dollars?" "No. That's unlikely. There are companies out there that are far bigger." Yahoo! and all those other outfits were way bigger than us.

We considered a few potentially disgruntled employees, but we knew it was a long shot that the attack was personal. The few people who had departed on bad terms had been able to flip their stock, and would you really bother to exact revenge on a company that's just handed you $1 to $3 million?

We called the FBI. We tried to see if they had a special division that could help us out with cybercrimes. They said they would look into it, but they needed more information. We were talking to the head of their cybercrime division, and he was just as frustrated. Meanwhile, we were sitting there and our business was decomposing page by page in real time. What do we do? The FBI guy finally said, "Fellas, I recommend you hire a private detective firm."

We hired a firm called Kroll & Associates, and they proceeded to tail another former tech guy twenty-four hours a day. They tailed him through the evening, through the day, and took pictures. They would deliver fake packages to his new office to see who was inside, what type of receptionist worked in his office, stuff like that.

Meanwhile, I started doing my own online research. I found out who his internet service provider (ISP) was. Through his ISP, I found out what his location was and what type of bandwidth he had. Then I went through our log files, trying to pick out Internet Protocol (IP) addresses. The idea was to see if he had been visiting our site or if he'd left himself any back doors into our database system so he could change things around. All I could tell was that he'd been frequently back to our site.

Kroll & Associates ultimately found nothing. They'd followed him to parties, and they followed him to his house. But they couldn't get any concrete information to give the FBI. There was simply no proof of any wrongdoing. So we called it off, but for approximately three weeks our servers were constantly shutting down.

Then, like a cowboy riding out of the fog, Vance came back. He was sorry—he'd completely lost it. We looked at him, asking, "What the hell?" But we couldn't yell at him. Who could really blame him? He had worked more tirelessly than anyone I had ever met. He was the only authentic technical genius we had and the only person capable of counter-hacking the hackers, but like anybody else, he had his threshold.

Shortly after his return, as suddenly as they started, the attacks stopped. It may have been because we fixed a few key components in our network that managed to dramatically reduce the impact of the attack. In any case, we moved our servers fast as hell to Staten Island.

The new setup was as cool as the old place was crap. We created the most phenomenal state-of-the-art facility. There were raised-floor, automatic air-conditioning, fire-suppression systems; the place looked like the CIA, right down to the rows and rows of black cabinets. Every single wire was perfectly labeled. It was all symmetrical; everything was doubly redundant. If anything went down, we could flip over to the new systems in real time. We spent millions to make sure this baby would be boss.

In the end, we finished the quarter with a 10 percent drop in our total traffic. Still, we made our quarterly projections. That may not sound like much, and if you're a private company, who gives a hoot?

But when everyone's watching, and you miss by a penny, it can crush your stock. Ten percent? My God! That could be the difference between hitting your numbers and missing them by a mile. The first quarter is the one you obviously never miss. You just don't do that. It would destroy your whole business.

We made it, but it was close. That was just November.

By Christmas 1998, we'd done tons of press and we were everywhere—even Europe (a European press tour in the spring of 1998 had helped gild the lily). My family was so excited. My sister, Maddy, who'd been a starving artist her entire adult life had put $200 into the company. That $200 was now worth something like $20,000. My dad's net worth in the company was $10 to $20 million. No one had ever in their wildest dreams expected anything like this.

I was thrilled that all these people—friends and family—had made a bit of money. But they couldn't sell; that was the sad part. Bear Stearns had locked everyone up, even the small investors. Of course, the SEC doesn't require a mandatory lockup. This is something that the banks ask for. The reason? They want to make sure that when institutional investors are brought in, no one in management just flips the stock and gets out, causing it to drop. Instead, they lock *you* up, get the institutions in, and then the institutions are free to sell.

Once our IPO was done, all of the Bear Stearns clients who were in on our deal were the same guys who would get to flip the stock the first day. It was almost a guaranteed moneymaking arrangement, regardless of how much demand there was. As investment banks did, they held the price (even though the stock could have shot up) and offered it to their preferred clients. Ironically, many of the clients who profited most were the same ones who'd told us to get lost during the financing. The whole IPO process is truly fascinating; but for us, in the thick of things, it was becoming disconcerting. Seals kissing sharks.

I knew the cash wasn't real, but I wanted to treat myself to something. I've traveled a lot, and one of my lifelong dreams was to fly first class. Since I was going home to Switzerland for the holidays, I inquired into a first-class ticket on Swissair. Swissair was a total monopoly—their prices were insane. It was $1,000 for a coach ticket. First class would cost me $7,000. "Fuck it," I said, "I'm doing it!" Never mind that I didn't have the actual cash. (I learned a valuable lesson: if you fly with a monopoly, you get the same pathetic service up front, too.)

That was my biggest perk, and my last one.

I spent most of late December in Verbier (in the Swiss Alps) with my family, even though I wanted to be with Jenn (she was with her family). In Switzerland, I was a hero. Any hometown is going to be proud of a favorite son, but I was Switzerland's first internet millionaire. They treated me like royalty.

When I got back to New York, it was a different story. Jenn was staying in my apartment while in between apartments herself, and my love life was heaven. Elsewhere, the honeymoon was definitely over.

That January, Todd and I were still traveling like crazy. We had to keep meeting with institutions. They all needed to know right away—should they buy more stock? Should they sell their stock? We had to quickly digest the lessons of public accounting and prepare for our next report. We'd never done any of this before. We studied quarterly conference calls by other companies. We listened to Yahoo! over and over. How did they do it? Who speaks? Is it scripted or not? We had to understand everything.

Then there was the question of who gets to attend the conference call. One hundred institutions? Several thousand investors? We didn't know. And, of course, the stock had fallen. Like any stock that goes up 1,000 percent, we'd come back down. In those first few weeks, we'd fallen and fallen and fallen. By the end of January, we were somewhere around $22 a share, down from $97.

We knew the whole thing was inflated, but we couldn't help but take any downward momentum personally. We'd seriously think, *Oh God, what are we doing wrong?* It's ironic because, as anyone who's been in this position knows, a stock can take on a life of its own, but you can't expect people to stop drawing conclusions. When we started going south for the first time, just a few weeks after the IPO, some friends of mine told me, "Oh, you guys have fallen to $22. I guess business isn't going well." We hadn't done squat! Nothing had changed. But that's a simple reality no one seemed to get.

Our stock fell, of course, because the people who had stock at $97 thought it was overvalued and sold it. They sold it for $87 because that's what someone was willing to pay for it. And then those who bought it at $87 sold it at $77, or someone who had bought it at $9 and made a killing wanted to sell it at $60, and somebody was willing to pay $60. At that level of volatility, your price constantly changes, and it can keep dropping, dropping, dropping, with no apparent correlation to the daily business. It was like bad voodoo.

As our learning curve evolved, our second philosophy was, "Don't check the stock every day." Fat chance. I'd secretly be checking our price every five minutes, refresh, refresh, refresh, refresh. Todd would say, "You watching the stock, Steph?" "No. Not me," I'd lie. And, of course, I could see Todd clicking away, refresh, refresh, refresh, refresh.

But as I said, it was all new, and despite the fear, it was exciting. At that point, even at $22 a share, it was hard not to be excited when we knew that, theoretically at least, we had a net worth still over $20 million. It wasn't $97 million, but you know what? It was still in the multimillions, and I was twenty-four years old. I felt pretty damn secure.

And so it was, with this newfound security, that we began life post-IPO. We had the money to properly build the business, show massive growth, and watch the revenues climb. The stock stood to be positively impacted. We finally felt we could control the company's market cap. Suddenly,

Todd and I were thrust into the limelight, poster boys for internet success and internet excess.

The reality was, for the first time ever, the stock market had become a giant game. Like some very serious, very compelling PlayStation game with these huge, real-world stakes. For the first time ever, IPOs alone were getting all this press, and everyday folks were suddenly rabidly interested in the market. In a sense, Todd and I might as well have just been innocent bystanders. The thing had its own life, and when it flagged, the press played it up more than ever. The term had not yet been coined, but we were watching the dawn of *internet mania.*

In the spring of 1999, it exploded. What does this all mean? What *are* internet stocks? How are these things valued in the first place? Everyone thought there was a whole new set of rules at work.

It's ironic—a lot of people still have problems with this. I remember listening to Z100 on the radio, and the DJ was talking about the stock market and how something can be worth $50 at one moment, and the next moment it's worth $40, and he's lost $10. The DJ wanted to know where his $10 *went.* As more and more regular folks started trading stocks, everyone tried to wrestle with this notion.

With internet mania came the birth of the day trader. All of a sudden, there were seven to ten million day traders, trading stock online. It no longer was a matter of well-connected stockbrokers or savvy institutions trying to figure out which stocks to buy. Where once-exclusive research held by the wealthiest people helped the rich keep getting richer, it was now a free-for-all. With the internet, the very nature of research changed. Now things were impacted by rumors, stray comments, inside information, and the almighty opinions of a few powerful analysts.

CNBC took off, turning market coverage into the equivalent of sports broadcasting. The finance industry took on the drama of a hot auction. Everyone was watching. There was easy money to be made. The contagious nature of the mania became ridiculous. And Todd and I—even Mike—started getting infected. Running the business was subconsciously becoming secondary. For a good three to six months, it felt like the only thing investors cared about was for us to get the stock up.

Suddenly, Todd, Mike, and I were like drill sergeants. "Let's push it up! Let's push it up! Let's push it up!" Then we had a great first-quarterly result: we blew away earnings estimates by some 20 to 30 percent. The stock picked its way up. We went back from $22, up and up. Then GeoCities was bought by Yahoo!, and that alone thrust us way up. By May, we'd worked our way back to as high as $84 a share. I was worth over $80 million.

But $84 a share wasn't enough. Todd and I had promised ourselves that we were not going to rest until this thing got to $100 a share. And it looked possible; we were on our way.

These were heady times. Now *everyone* was aware of the internet, everyone wanted to get into a dot-com and get rich quick. Companies were going public left and right, and not only were they able to get their stock price at the top of the range, they were able to move their range up twice as much. Instead of selling three million shares, dot-commers could sell four million, five million, six million shares.

The end result of all this insanity was that we didn't look so flush all of a sudden. We'd raised only $27 million with the IPO—the bare minimum. Considering the competition was now raising $80 million, $120 million, $200 million, we felt pathetic. The worst part was that many of these companies were calling themselves communities.

One company was called iTurf. They were going to be a teenage community. This had to be the most bullshit thing I'd ever seen in my life. They had no users, no advertising, no commerce, but they raised $100 million! We were ten times their size, infinitely better known, a better business, and we'd raised a fraction of the money they did.

We'd raised a fraction of the money that *everyone* after us raised. And that marked the beginning of our problems. "Oh, Christ. We have to compete, and they're all going to outspend us in every way. We *have* to raise more money."

To help the situation, another idea came along.

Mike had become heavily caught up in internet mania. While we were still at $65 a share, he came to us beaming. "Guys," he said, "why don't we do a stock split?" Todd and I weren't exactly thrilled. Yahoo! had waited till they were at $250 before they'd split.

But Mike had a plan. "It's very simple, guys," he said. "The theory is that everyone feels richer when they have twice as many shares. And that drives the stock up further." Our initial reaction was, "Well, do we really want to do this? What if we fall again, and then after the split, we're trading at $20 and below? There'd be such a negative perception." Todd and I were hesitant. We ordered a lot of research to be done by Bear Stearns and our lawyers, and they determined that the NASDAQ average for splits was around $50 a share. We were at $65, so we thought, *Okay, it's justified.* We were well above the average.

So right after we finished the first quarter, on March 31 during an interview on CNBC, we announced that we were going to do a stock split followed by a secondary offering to build up our war chest.

We were still stuck in a standard six-month lockup, which was the reason we still didn't have the personal riches everyone assumed we did. That was supposed to last from the November 13 IPO through May 13. Then the lockup was supposed to expire. But when we decided to do the secondary offering, we had to be locked up again, for another three months. (It wasn't until September that any insider could sell. And of course, by then, our stock had fallen to about $13 a share.)

As Mike suspected, the split did drive up our stock, but these drives were illogical to say the least. Why? Because the day traders rush in, going, "*Whee!* Buy more stock!" Just because you've split your stock, it doesn't mean that anything has changed in value—there's just twice as many shares at half the price!

Still, things looked good. Then I looked online.

Internet mania had also given birth to the ascension of message board culture. If you wanted information on a company, you could get everything you ever needed (and lots of stuff you didn't need) simply by checking the Yahoo! message boards.

When I checked our message boards for the first time, I couldn't believe what I was reading about my company. It was a cesspool. "Buy! Sell! The company sucks!" The general tenor of the discourse was astounding.

It was about to get worse.

One afternoon, I got a call from Ed. He wanted to give me a heads-up. It seemed he and Mike were talking about something that had appeared on a message board. He said, "There's some sort of salacious comment on the message board that you might want to take a look at." I said, "What?" "Yeah," he said, "it's about you and some call girls." I felt myself starting to get sick.

Ed continued. "You know, Steph, we're not here to judge or anything, but you have to realize that as a figure in a public company, you've gotta be very careful . . ." "Yes, I'm well aware of that," I said. *But what the fuck?*

I went to the message boards and found it right away. There was a message posted by (of course) an anonymous user. The message was, "Watch out for this company, especially the CEO Stephan Paternot. I hear from the doorman in his building that this Paternot is a real sleazebag. A total sleazebag. He has call girls over all the time." The next message posted my home address, in case anyone wanted to send me some hate mail.

I was furious. To be told about this by my own board . . . and for them to assume that it was true? I was so pissed. I was also humiliated (and paranoid—did my doorman have it out for me now that I was worth millions?).

Needless to say, there had never been any call girls, so I was trying to think what could possibly give anyone this idea. I thought back to all the partying I'd been doing the year before. I'd been going out a ton. I knew all these great party people. I'd invited a lot of girls over. I'd always had beautiful *friends* coming over. Not call girls. These were my friends.

I had to explain lots of other things to people. I remember sitting down with Todd on Fox's *Good Day New York* to talk seriously about the company, and instead we had to answer questions like, "So, how does it feel to be so rich? Can I pinch you?" I actually got pinched on the air.

How do you answer a question like that? "It's, um, *fine*." Then we'd try to explain. "You know, it's all in *stock*. We don't really have the money."

They didn't want to hear that. "Have you bought yachts?" they'd ask. "Have you bought cars?" It was almost like they just wanted us to say yes to satisfy viewers and let people live vicariously. They didn't want to hear that I didn't have any money.

Meanwhile, a similar problem was affecting me in my social life. Very quickly, I started to figure out who was a good friend and who couldn't be trusted. People I'd just met would act like my new best friends. Then they'd force into the conversation, "Oh, yes, I'm working on this new business, and I was wondering . . . I mean, no pressure and everything."

They may have interpreted it as rudeness on my part, but these overtures had to be cut off quickly. The reality is that you have to set rules right away, even though you may look at someone and think, *Wow, I was once that guy.* When the word gets out that you look at stuff, you start receiving a thousand business plans a year. And since we were thinking about expanding, we had to be on the lookout. Of course, if you don't know how to stop and filter and be systematic in your analysis, you're going to make bad investments. Everywhere I turned, people wanted a piece or had something to show me.

Anyway, we survived all that—the crazy questions, the character assassinations, the "friends" coming out of the woodwork with business plans—and we just knuckled down and focused on the process of becoming a big independent company. We started ramping up content, adding news, stock quotes, e-commerce, everything. Yahoo!, Excite, Lycos, and GeoCities had been doing all this, and we felt like we were in a race to keep up with them.

The reality was we started taking on too much.

9

Acquisition Mania

How We Almost Bought Sunglass Hut

After the stock split, we turned our attention to chasing after the latest holy grail—e-commerce.

In the spring of 1999, Amazon had ballooned like crazy, and search engines, which had already been big, were getting way bigger. There was a six-month stretch in which companies just rocketed like I've never seen. E-commerce was the talk of the town. Analysts like Henry Blodget were hailing Amazon as a $400 stock. Everyone lusted after it, and acquisitions abounded. Which may explain why Mike uttered the following famous words: "We gotta buy a commerce company."

By the spring of 1999, theglobe.com had blossomed into a half-billion market cap. We'd entered an interesting phase in which you're able to use your market cap to swallow up other companies and still be open to considerations of being swallowed up yourself.

The logic was that if we wanted to stay big, we had to show investors that we were moving along with the times. Forget that we'd just reached the big time ourselves. No matter that we were still in our diapers; now we had to learn to become astronauts. Now, Todd and I *liked* the idea of acquiring companies. Mike began forwarding us info on a huge variety of companies, and what we quickly became concerned about was the particular companies we seemed to be chasing after. Todd and I would wonder why on earth he was forwarding these things to us. Granted, Mike never forced anything on us; he never told us we *had* to buy something. Which was really great, considering he was the chairman and majority owner. But sometimes he just forwarded too *many* ideas, while we just wanted to focus on a few and do those right.

One of the first companies Mike brought to our attention was called buySAFE.com. It was supposed to be a front door to all sorts of different shops owned by different companies. They were a little network where you could link from one site to another without so much as a common shopping cart. You'd end up going to all these different places; there was no brand identity. Moreover, what type of name was buySAFE? Was that something people were going to get hot for?

We looked at them. They thought they were worth $80 million. They appeared to have growing revenues. They also had *very* low gross margins. They were practically giving away products because they were flush with VC cash. Something was very wrong. We backed away with our hands in the air. Goodbye, buySAFE, and a good dozen other pretenders.

Eventually, we came across a company in Seattle that looked very clean and had a great brand identity. It was an online department store called Azazz.com. They had fourteen different commerce categories. They sold everything from glow-in-the-dark doorbell ringers to Dirt Devil vacuum cleaners to PalmPilots. We flew out, and Azazz proceeded to give us the best presentation ever. They were growing like crazy. They were going to do $7 million in revenues that year. With their growth and our traffic, we'd make beautiful music together.

One of the things Azazz most impressed us with was their self-proclaimed phenomenal personal shopping service. The idea was that you could click on a dialogue window and a personal assistant would pop right up to help you. It seemed nifty. Of course, it had absolutely no scalability. What if 1,000 users wanted to shop at the same time? You'd have to have 1,000 customer support people. Still, at the time, it all looked sexy. Mike liked it. Todd and I liked it. The entire board believed in it. We decided, "Let's do it." So, we negotiated a pretty hard deal. The initial price we'd worked out with them was $15 million in stock—that was 5 percent of our company.

Right as we were closing that transaction, over the wire there was a flash of breaking news. GeoCities had just been acquired for $3.5 billion in stock by Yahoo!. Now, at the time, Yahoo! was rocketing, so essentially that transaction became worth $4.5 billion overnight (and if you look at where the Yahoo! stock price would eventually go, GeoCities became worth something like $20 billion). There was something very wrong with these figures. Their revenues had been about $5 million a quarter. *Our* revenues were about $5 million a quarter, too, but *we* weren't valued at $4.5 billion.

And thus began the era when we started learning about the injustices of how valuations are determined. Everyone thinks this process is mathematical and empirical. The reality is that there's more fuzzy math to this whole thing than you could possibly imagine. There is no logic. Seriously. In many respects, your net worth is nothing but the reflection of the mood swing of some analyst's emotions.

When GeoCities was bought, everyone zoomed in: "Who's the next community that's going to be bought? theglobe.com! Buy! Buy! Buy!" Literally overnight, our stock started to rocket. We exploded all the way back up to $84 in the course of one day. Up from $30! A huge swing. The press was all over us: "Well, do you have any comments?"

Publicly, we said, "Well, we think it's great." But the truth was one of our competitors had just been swallowed up and now enjoyed the backing muscle of a much bigger player.

On some level, we were pleased. The rationalization was, "There'll be no more focus on their brand. There will be no focus on GeoCities as an individual company. They'll lose market share."

But privately, I was scared shitless. First, it meant GeoCities would be there forever; it also meant that if we didn't capitalize on the whole acquisition fever fast, people would think theglobe.com was getting left behind. That could have a vast negative impact.

Still, our market cap rocketed. Suddenly, since we'd worked a fixed ratio to buy Azazz, that $15 million we were buying them for was now worth $45 million. This was totally unjustifiable. We were not going to buy them for $45 million in stock. They had no revenue because they'd been created virtually overnight. They had no market leadership and barely any audience. The pitch had been great, but, damn it, it was not worth $45 million. And this wasn't simple hubris. At the time, we had over eight million users. We were one of the market leaders. We were producing at least $1 million a month in revenue.

So, we renegotiated. We were able to get the price back down to maybe $25 million in stock. We closed the transaction; everything seemed great. Of course, shortly thereafter, when we sent over our transition team to Seattle to meet with them, we started to realize that they were viewing us as big Wall Street corporate titans, like stiff, money-hungry, megalomaniac types. They seemed to have this vision of themselves as the cool little entrepreneurial wing of the company. I said, "Hold on. Have you seen our office?"

Now, when Yahoo! took over a company, there was no question: that company was moved to California and rolled into their organization. Half the company was fired, and either you got on board or you got out. They had a real tough management style. Typically, Todd and I were more of the philosophy, "What does it take to keep them happy?" We said, "Hey, you know what? They're happy out there. Let's not bother them. Plus, it will keep our costs down by not having to relocate them." But it also meant we'd have to run two separate offices.

After we bought Azazz, we shuttled all our shoppers to them. We probably drove 250,000 users a month to these guys just like *that,* but sales weren't really picking up. So we started getting frustrated. "What's going on? What do we need to do? Is it time for a redesign?" They wanted to keep a separate look and feel, and we said, "No, let's create the same look and feel. There's no reason to make our users feel like they've gone to a completely different site. They're not going to necessarily trust a different site."

That meant butting heads more with Azazz. This got very frustrating very fast, and we spent an inordinate amount of time just trying to manage them. Once, we went out there with Mike and listened to one of their guys talk about his sales strategy, which went something like this: we buy a product for $100 and sell it for $80, thus losing $20. He smiled serenely and waited for our response.

I had to make sure I was hearing correctly. "Um, well, how do you *make* money that way?" "Simple . . . we scale up." "You scale up?" With scale, they planned to win. I found myself thinking, *Cool. If you scale up a $20-per-product loss, you will end up with losses of $20 billion. That's just fantastic.*

It was a bad dream. This was not going to work, and we were stuck with it. Remember, when the e-commerce craze hit, every internet company was selling products for less than cost. Literally, they were giving away product to beef up numbers that were as arbitrary as the valuations that went along with them. Like the rest, Azazz was quickly turning into the same disaster. The worst part was that whenever you make an acquisition, the press is all over it and the analysts want your new financial numbers. They want to see new projections showing how big you're going to get. So, we had to give them new projections, and we started worrying. If Azazz told us they could do $7 million in new revenues this year, we'd tell the analysts we'd do $3 million with Azazz to give ourselves some breathing room.

This was when things started getting ugly. By the third quarter of 1999, Azazz was supposed to be producing at least $1 million in quarterly revenues. Halfway through the quarter, they had maybe produced $50,000. We were in total hysterics. We were pushing *our* guys harder than we could possibly push them, but we still weren't getting there. Azazz also had millions of bugs in their software—the thing would never work properly. From their perspective, everything was great for them in Seattle on their own internal network. From anywhere else, it sucked.

Moreover, in Q3, we had a weak ad sales month for July. That set us off on a really bad pace. We'd produced great previous quarters, but our sales team had simply dropped the ball. Combined with the fact that Azazz had *completely* missed their numbers, it turned into an ugly third quarter. Now, we'd still beaten our earnings numbers because we kept our costs down. We beat earnings per share (EPS), and that's the number the analysts cared about most. In truth, it wasn't that bad. By Q3 1999, we were doing about $5 million a quarter. When we went public, we had only been doing about $800,000 a quarter. In short order, we'd ramped up like absolute mad. We were on track for $20 million in annual revenues, up from $5 million the year before.

But some people see things differently.

Despite our massive ramp rate, despite having beaten our own projected numbers, Bear Stearns gave us a scathing review and downgraded us. They were the only one of our four covering analysts to downgrade us. They'd been our lead banker and the first to drop a bomb on us. (Of course, shortly after we went public—a record-setting IPO, out of the gates crushing all their revenue estimates—Bear Stearns pushed us like crazy, telling all their institutions we were the greatest thing since sliced bread.) Now, instead of a buy rating, they came out and put us at neutral.

It was the most insulting, infuriating situation. A downgrade is the ultimate slap in the face. When it came down to it, it meant a no-confidence vote, and when your lead banker does something like that, it really doesn't matter what any other analysts say. The press starts picking up on it, and most likely, you're dead meat.

Meanwhile, there we were, drowning with Azazz. To help alleviate stress, I developed a technique of drawing things on our big white board. One of the things I drew was this huge dam filled with water. The water represented our user base and the massive revenue potential; the dam was Azazz, the name of which had now been changed to Shop.theglobe.com. On the other side of the dam was this little picture of Azazz's president. He had a mini tap switched on, with this little trickle coming in, and he had a glass. He was singing, "Ooh-hoo, guys, things are going great. The glass is almost a quarter full, it's a great trickle."

For Q4, we needed Shop.theglobe.com to produce $2 million in revenues. So we came up with all sorts of coupon strategies, discounted products, anything to make that number. Remember, in 1999, revenue was still king and losses were still . . . acceptable. If you lost money but grew faster still, all was forgiven. Take About.com. They were one of those classic Net companies. Just after they went public, they raised $80-plus million and spent $20 million in one quarter on advertising. They were losing a ridiculous amount of money, but the analysts just kept giving them top reviews.

So, based on that theory, we did an abrupt about-face and said fine. Instead of spending less and less, like we'd done during the ramp up, we'd launch a massive ad campaign. Thus, in late 1999 we announced our new $27 million ad campaign, to show our aggressive new commitment to growth. Like lemmings—and during the Net bubble of the late 1990s it was difficult to truly differentiate lemmings from trendsetters, copycats from change agents—the analysts loved it. And as usual, our timing sucked. The mentality of the industry was changing so fast. By the time we started implementing the new campaign at the end of Q4, internet mania had reached its crescendo. By January

2000, people were officially sick of losses and things started really turning around.

We'd also poured a huge amount of money into Shop.theglobe.com. We shoveled so much in that by the end of the fourth quarter, we'd generated that precious $2 million in revenue. But at a cost of nearly $6 million. The losses were just *ridiculous.*

In January 2000, our CFO, Frank Joyce, suggested we wind it down and take a write-off. At first, Todd and I were dead set against it. But the truth of the matter was that our stock price was shrinking so fast we could never get ahead of the investor hype curve. We got rid of Azazz's senior management and brought in a heavy hitter from Eddie Bauer. The impact was felt immediately and sales really picked up, but it was too late. Despite rocketing revenues, the margins were just too small and caused us to lose money at a faster pace. In the end, we made the tough decision to shut it down.

But Azazz was only one of several acquisitions. We made another major purchase in March. The Attitude Network, a gaming network comprised of Happy Puppy (a leading US site), Games Domain (a leading game player in the United Kingdom), and Kids Domain (a leading kids' site in the States). Attitude Network seemed like a reasonable acquisition. The business plan was there because they'd been around for several years growing their site. They had some revenues, and they were already talking to Lycos. Then Lycos walked away, and we pounced.

It was a no-brainer. They had an advertising-based model very similar to theglobe.com: users show up; they spend time; you sell targeted advertising in the games category. Moreover, we thought games were awesome. The site had an audience of hard-core internet users, and that was great for community. There's nothing like gamers sitting in chat rooms, talking up our other games and citing them in their own websites. They added a perfect audience . . . that we knew how to sell to. "Let's do it," we said.

So we negotiated a deal just as our stock moved to the point where we were a $600 million company. We ended up buying Attitude for $43 million in stock—just under 10 percent of our business. That was a great purchase. They became Games.theglobe.com. Unfortunately, it turned out to be one of the only positive acquisitions we made.

But it wasn't all roses. Their UK subdivision, Games Domain, turned out to be the sort of thing that made Azazz look like fun. It was run by a couple of blue-collar blokes from Birmingham who seemed to think that everything America produced was *shite* and that everything that came out of England was *fecking fantastic.* Granted, they ran a tight outfit with twenty-five employees, but the average person was probably making $15,000 a year. Todd and I really believed that in the internet space *people* were the asset, so we tried to accommodate a situation that quickly became a clash of transatlantic internet cultures. In hindsight, Todd and I should have moved them to the States right away and demanded total control like Yahoo! would have done. But we didn't.

Then there were the acquisitions we didn't make. It just so happened that one of Todd's friends was the CEO of Sunglass Hut. Now, at the time, they were a private billion-dollar company. Mike got wind of the acquaintance and wanted to turn it into an acquisition. "You know what?" he said. "The great thing about Sunglass Hut is that they're the leader in their vertical. You automatically know that brand and what they represent. Let's do it."

If we did make a move like that, people would accuse us of a lack of focus. They would think we were completely nuts. Todd and I would become laughingstocks. As I said, Mike wouldn't *force* anything on us, but the thing about him was . . . he was relentless. He just kept talking and talking and talking until the point where we just had to give up. He didn't force us technically, but it was exhausting to keep resisting him.

At this point in 1999, Todd and I were still at our old office, the barracks. The place was just falling apart. Even the elevator with its slow-clinking chain gave way a few times as we fell several flights. Mike would always sweep in with his full entourage, close the door, and sit with us on our rotting futon. "How's it going, boys?" he'd say with this big smile, flashing his baby blues. He'd rock forward, start talking, and Todd and I would glance at each other knowing that it was time to clear our schedules. Those conversations could go on for five hours.

We really couldn't blame Mike's gut feeling for Sunglass Hut. It was a great company. If we could own them the way GE owns hundreds of different companies, we could do really well. The reality, of course, was that we didn't have the power. Yes, we were a billion-dollar company on paper, but we were just doing $20 million in revenue. We simply weren't in a position to start buying up new industries. That argument finally convinced Mike to give up on Sunglass Hut, but there was an infinite supply of other companies for him to obsess over.

One afternoon in the fall, Mike called to say, "Guys, I've got conversations going with Vitamins.com. They have stores all over the country, they're setting up online, and they've got $20 million in revenue. What if we buy them? I've spoken with their guy, and he's really interested."

We stopped that adventure, but the process continued. It was always like this. Mike would read some article at 5:00 a.m. in the *Wall Street Journal.* By 7:00 a.m., phone calls were in, voice mails, faxes. "Guys, what do you think? Please look into this. Let's have a full report." *Ugh.* Todd and I would put our heads down. I have much less patience and tolerance than Todd. Sometimes, I'd just start screaming.

In all fairness, we'd been at this with Mike for a while. Back in 1997, even before we went public, Mike told us about some connections in the adult publishing business, which didn't surprise us at all—it seemed Mike had connections in every industry. They produced some sort of porno magazine. In short order, Mike set up meetings. Actually, Todd and I didn't think this was a completely outlandish idea. We could charge subscription fees, for instance, but we knew it would be difficult to manage. How do you maintain a separate little subdivision of your company for the scanning of porn photos? My stance was that either you're a porn company or you're not.

We met this one guy who was draped in gold chains; you could almost make out the porn stars dancing naked in the next room. The rational part of me thought, *Wait a second here. Do we really want to get into this industry?* In the end, we passed. Professionally speaking, it would have been a bad move even though the porn business was, and still is, the most profitable venture online. But it would have prevented us from going public. I also knew I would have had a hard time explaining it to my grandparents.

In the fall, as our stock kept dropping, Mike said, "What do you think about theglobe.com buying AutoNation?" AutoNation, which was run by Wayne Huizenga, was the big car company that had bought Alamo. At first, it had gone way up in stock price, but then everything collapsed, taking with it a lot of Mike's hard-earned fortune. The car business has low margins, they weren't driving new business, and their price had plummeted. They'd sort of settled into their role as a $4 billion slow-growth company.

Mike thought we could buy AutoNation for a good premium. We tried to dissuade him. "God, Mike," we'd say, "we're having enough trouble as it is. We need to get down to the nitty-gritty of running our business. We need to start really figuring out how to get theglobe.com working better and not letting ourselves get distracted by grandiose ideas."

But he pushed and pushed, and Todd and I eventually said, "Okay, let's look into it further." We had such little experience, and that makes anyone start second-guessing themselves. We'd gotten to a point where we'd say, "If Mike's so into this thing, maybe it is worth checking out." Mike wanted us not only to check it out but to save it. "You guys are the internet wizards," he said, "figure out AutoNation's strategy."

So we'd sit down and try to figure out what to do to bring AutoNation into the web-driven future. We came up with a bunch of ideas, and then Mike called up Wayne Huizenga and said, "Todd and Steph, tell Wayne your internet ideas." God, we felt so awkward. Wayne was this massive businessman. He didn't need two kids with an online community telling him how to run a car company. But we tried. Then Wayne, of course, answered, "Well, guys, we already spent a good year with my people strategizing over these things, and we think that's a bad move for the following reasons . . ."

Ouch.

But remember—there was a reason why a zillionaire like Wayne Huizenga would consider listening to people like Todd and me. There was a moment in the late nineties when the collective financial world basically said, "Bet *everything* on the Net business. And get yourself some Net kid to run it." If you were in health care, finance, whatever, everyone said, "If you're an internet kid, you know how things work."

Hell, it happened with my dad, a successful (albeit old paradigm) businessman in his own right. Very quickly, he was asking me questions like, "Steph, what do you think about WebMD?" I responded, "Dad, I don't know *anything* about the health care industry." "But they're an internet company." "So what? Okay, fine. Make sure that the banners are black and green so that people click on them." I mean, why not? For some reason, it didn't matter that we didn't know anything about the vitamin business or e-commerce. Actually, we really didn't know much about *regular* commerce. But it just didn't matter.

Now I'm not trying to cast blame on other people. Todd and I were the CEOs; the buck stopped with us. To Mike's credit, he was a brilliant entrepreneur with a proven track record. He built multiple billion-dollar companies, and he had great ideas. Many things he told us were brilliant. He was fully on board with the four acquisitions we did make and had many more great ideas to share with us. It was our fault for not putting a stake in the ground and saying, "No, this is how it's going to be. We're going to stick with what we know."

After backing away from AutoNation, we'd managed to convince Mike that we needed to only buy companies that were similar to us. So, with that in mind, we looked at other home-page-building companies. Eventually, after a few near disasters, we found a company in California called WebJump.com. They were a professional web-hosting service, and they'd grown a ton. We scooped them up for about $17 million in stock. After having dealt with several acquisitions already, we were getting really good at this. We had an entire mergers and acquisitions team in place, headed by Ed. They would do all the research on the market segment of our target, do due diligence, meet with their management, go through a matrix of checklists, and then propose a deal to the management team and the board. Upon making the deal, Dean would then lead what we called the transition team into the acquired company and start integrating the new assets. We would bring in our top managers to meet with their top managers and rapidly start mixing and matching our protocols so that we could get to work. Acquisitions were great. Although cultural differences could often make new entities difficult to integrate, the benefit was that we could move at light speed and grow the company more aggressively.

Everything with WebJump was great . . . at first. We appeared to be getting a tremendous amount of reach, along with the assets that come with new servers and traffic, all of which we transferred to our system. Of course, in short order we realized that the management out there was complete schlock. The good news was that this time we had detected this during due diligence and Ed, Dean, Todd, and I had decided just to buy their assets and not give contracts to their management. It was brilliant. We got all their valuable parts without burdening ourselves with sketchy people. Shortly thereafter, we found out that their leaders had filed for personal bankruptcy protection, and we also discovered that they were running another site called Web1000—a massive porn-hosting service. We had to laugh. People are always complaining about accidentally landing on porn sites while online; we had managed to accidentally do *business* with porn site owners.

So at this point, we were juggling three outside companies. Instead of just being theglobe.com, we were four companies with challenges that needed our attention every day of the week, twenty-four hours a day. We were absolutely exhausted, and the burden continued to build. The situation was becoming untenable.

Still, through January and February 2000, we tried to hunt down more acquisitions that would grow the company and goose the stock. Our price kept dropping, even as our competitors—companies that were way smaller than us—were going public for ten times the price we were worth. eToys, one of the newest kids on the block, was now a multibillion-dollar company!

Come spring, we decided to beef up our gaming network. We found a company called Strategy Plus, which was a games magazine that had a subdivision called Chips and Bits, an e-commerce outfit. They were producing $12 to $14 million in revenue, and they were just becoming profitable; it looked fantastic. We scooped them up for about $17 million in stock.

Strategy Plus was based in Vermont, a seven-hour drive from New York. The first time we drove up to meet with them, there was a hailstorm and we nearly ran over a moose that had run across the road. As always, things were fine at first. But very shortly thereafter, we realized that the founders had staffed the place with family members. It turned out that many of the financials were misleading.

By this point, our management team knew how to deal with this and we felt confident we could eliminate the problems at the top with minimal collateral damage. The biggest surprise was the reaction. Sensing that we were about to eliminate them, they literally took their money and ran, hopping on a plane to Monte Carlo. We were dumbfounded . . . *Monte Carlo?* Overnight, we sent up a team to manage this thing, just as the guys at Games Domain were getting in another tizzy. Todd and I were always pleased when we would hear from some of our friends at Yahoo! that life was the same over there. Difficult at best, chaotic at worst. You just had to deal with it. Amazingly, there was still a light at the end of the tunnel. The assets of all our companies were good. Despite all our troubles, we'd ended up with the number one gaming network in the world. And it was *profitable.*

As a result, we decided to officially scrap the whole e-commerce thing. We had just eliminated Azazz and taken a massive write-off. At least we stemmed the losses, which was the right move.

Even though we were the number one gaming network with tons of traffic, the problem was that everything we did was buried beneath theglobe.com stock price. No matter what we did, we couldn't seem to convince anyone in the media that we were anything but a sad stock story. People simply knew us as a stock—they barely even glanced at what theglobe.com was doing or how fast we were growing, let alone bother to consider our games. It was so frustrating. Little did I know it was going to get worse.

Let me give some sense of how we looked at the time. We'd gone from 80 employees at the IPO to about 120. By the time we completed our last acquisition in the spring of 2000 (Chips and Bits and Strategy Plus in Vermont), we were 260 people.

We made these acquisitions, we were becoming a solid company, and we'd gone from $5 million in revenues in 1998 to $18 million in revenues in 1999. We were projected to do nearly $30 million in revenues the next year.

We were twenty times bigger than at the IPO date. But instead of being twenty times more valuable, we were worth one-hundredth of what we were at the IPO date. It was totally unjustifiable. And there's nothing we could say or do. Todd and I made plenty of mistakes, but most of the variables that affect market cap and perception are beyond anyone's control. We began to get our first taste of the soon-to-be-familiar sensation that things were spinning very much out of control.

This was something that Todd and I could have never imagined. Just a few years earlier, we didn't know what going public meant. Now we had 260 people dependent on us for paychecks and thousands more affected by our stock price. And yet despite all our troubles, I still felt like I was on top of the world. When I walked down the hallways, I'd walk with pride. I felt good about what we'd achieved, and about myself. That would soon change.

10

The Double-Edged Sword

The Media Attacks My Black Plastic Pants and
My "Disgusting and Frivolous Lifestyle"

Exactly why was the internet such a hype machine? What allowed a string of web companies to raise such huge amounts of money? I like to think of it as a kind of mass hypnosis: an unshakable idea that something phenomenal was happening.

Which brings us to the press.

From 1995 onward, there was tangible evidence in the business press that the world was changing. We were on the cusp of something revolutionary, on a scale that hadn't been seen maybe ever. As the word *internet* entered the public's vocabulary, people became convinced that we were witnessing the greatest technological leap since movable type.

It was a great time to be a reporter. So many crazy stories to write. Reporters on the web-business beat seemed to have an insatiable appetite for those crazy internet entrepreneurs and their amazing stories. Here were young Americans working so hard they didn't go home anymore. Here were people sleeping under their desks, bringing their pets to work. This new breed didn't wear suits, and they didn't hold regular hours. People were turning their jobs into all-night cram sessions for a crucial final exam.com.

We started reading about this, and we didn't stop. The public developed an obsession with this amazing new universe. Especially when it came to all the new fortunes being made, and the head-spinning magic of inexplicable internet stock valuations.

The reigning headline of the era was "Company with Massive Losses Is Worth $300 Million," and the formula for determining the value of a company was no longer about profit or even revenue. The more you lose, the bigger you are.

In that setting, we became the quintessential web story, the global poster boys for internet excess. Generally, the press reacted to theglobe.com—and by extension, to the whole web—in two ways. The first was benign optimism: "How can this be? Two young kids running this huge company? Simply amazing!" The other reaction was complete pessimism: "This shouldn't be. This is all *bull.* Just keep waiting, and the bubble will eventually pop." One side wanted to build us up and tell our amazing story, and the other side wanted to tear us down. During the early days, we'd certainly had some coverage, but the real explosion took place starting on the day of the IPO. From there, it built and built, eventually ending up as a tidal wave that left us treading in its wake.

But long before we knew how to handle the press, we strolled blithely into its sights. My relationship with the media started out fairly pleasant.

We did our first European press tour in the fall of 1997, right on the heels of Mike's investment. We had scheduled interviews in the United Kingdom, France, Germany, and Sweden. The basic idea was to hit four countries in one week.

Though we'd go back to Europe in the spring of 1999, our first overseas romp was pre-IPO. We were hot at the time, and the Euro press had just been converted by the coattails of internet fervor and its attendant IPO mania. We thought the timing was perfect, to help us build our brand in Europe before the big IPO rush to come. We began in England, where we spent most of our time explaining how it was possible for young Americans to start these new businesses and why it worked more easily in the US than it did in Europe. Naturally, some people looked down their noses at us. I remember these staid British interviewers saying, "Righto. So, how do you *boys* do this?"

Still, we took on as many media outlets as we could stand. We would do press from 5:00 a.m. all the way to about 6:00 or 7:00 p.m. We'd do two different BBC radio interviews, Sky News, BBC News on television, a few magazines, a few tabloids, whatever. Our public relations head, Esther Loewy, packed in the meetings. There must have been twenty-five or thirty interviews in five days. Since England is a relatively small market, somebody would invariably recognize us from earlier in the day. And it actually affected traffic on the site. We saw our UK audience grow from 200,000 users per month to 500,000 in the course of only a few weeks.

After the United Kingdom, we hopped on a plane and headed to France. There, instead of stuffy Brit journalists, we found ourselves being interviewed in cafes through a haze of smoke. "Let's have some steak," the reporter would say. There'd be questions, but they were definitely more interested in eating and pointing out that the ketchup I was having with my fries was sacrilege. Meanwhile, the reporter got sauce all over his shirt, a cigarette dangling from his mouth (and we were sitting in the nonsmoking area). In France, the main question was, "Okay, so how much money did you make? Twenty million, right? That's nice, that's good." We left Paris, hopped on a Lufthansa flight, and headed off to Hamburg, Germany—a city without a center.

Surprisingly, the Germans seemed more relaxed, so we gave in and started drinking with the reporters, and the interviews became sillier and sillier. Maybe that was why we got such good press. We did *Stern* magazine, *Der Spiegel,* and several other German publications, and they all had a wry sense of humor that really suited two internet guys like us.

From Germany, we headed off to Sweden, and that was the most unique part of our Euro travels. I remember arriving in Stockholm at 2:00 a.m. We got off the plane, and it was absolutely freezing. We drove along in a Volvo to the Grand Hôtel, and there were icebergs outside. I remember thinking, *What the hell am I doing here?*

It turned out that the Swedes loved us. They'd already been writing all this positive stuff about theglobe.com, and they were just infatuated. Sweden was well known for being very wired, and somehow, we'd surfaced there in advance of our arrival.

Still, by the end of the tour, the back-to-back interviews had taken their toll. The endless repetition, repetition, repetition, started to become a blur. I couldn't even remember anymore what I'd said a half hour earlier, and the interviewers were starting to look at me funny. It couldn't have been that bad, though, since our numbers went up in Sweden, too.

The press was almost entirely positive. Seemingly victorious, we went home. One thing had become crystal clear to us: the more press we did, the more people heard about us, and the more our traffic grew. More traffic would lead to more advertisers, generating higher revenues. And, of course, higher revenues would make our shareholders happier. The best part about the press was that it was all free.

After the IPO, the first thing Todd and I noticed was the power of CNN. Of all channels, of all media sources, when CNN put you on the worldwide circuit, it was a mind-blowing adventure in global communications. The whole world had CNN.

We were on CNN the week after the IPO, and they re-ran it for the next few weeks. They'd put together this minutes-long story, with Todd and me clinking champagne glasses in front of the NASDAQ screens. Everyone saw it. Everyone knew. I got a call from people all over the planet.

The punch line of the clip was, "And it's run by two twenty-four-year-old kids." This had the effect of turning theglobe.com from a news item into more of a lifestyle story, a pop culture bit. This in turn attracted all the consumer press. Esther was brilliant at public relations. She and her team got us into everything. We were receiving endless phone calls and requests for interviews, and the entire team was inundated. During the peak, we were averaging 1,200 mentions per quarter in the US print press alone. That's an average of thirteen mentions per *day* without counting international exposure. Esther and her team truly brought the art of public relations to a whole new level none of us had ever seen before. Often, the first question we would get from our peers in the industry was, "Who does your PR? We want the same!"

We were on Fox News, *The Montel Williams Show*, MTV, *Charlie Rose*. We did the morning show *Wake Up New York*. The female interviewer said silly stuff like, "How does it feel to be worth, you know, a trillion dollars?" "Well, we're not," we'd try to say. "So," she'd continue, ignoring what we'd said, "have you gotten lots of marriage proposals . . . ?"

The Montel Williams experience was great PR, but a little bizarre. It was an episode about entrepreneurs. One guy had started a muffin business and built it up to $4 million in annual sales. There was a woman who had developed a line of handbags called "trash bags." Then there was Todd and me—the internet guys. People could relate to muffins, but this Net thing was still a bit vague, so they'd made a little video clip about the site. Everyone in the audience was just like, *Huh?* And then Montel Williams said, "So, how much is this company worth again?" And Todd and I would try to explain it wasn't that simple, but the guy just wanted to hear us say it. So we did. "Well, it's about three-quarters of a billion." "I love the ring of that," he said. "*Billion.* You boys are billionaires."

It was surreal and often achingly awkward, but it was also effective. These things would air a few times, and our audience would rocket upward. We saw shopping activity go up, traffic go up. Between the IPO and our secondary offering in May 1999, the press was overwhelmingly positive. The pieces varied, but they usually made us look intelligent, and the stories were often flattering.

Talk about brief honeymoons. There were two groups that began the negative tide. The first one was called *Silicon Alley Reporter,* a small local rag run by a guy named Jason McCabe Calacanis. Jason had gotten along with us super well before our IPO. We did several pleasant interviews. When we had company parties, he was invited.

The day we went public, the first story that came from him was practically, "Oh, these guys are a scam." This was a major lesson for our team. It was suddenly clear that some people were going to turn on us.

The other guy who started relentlessly bashing us was Jim Cramer of TheStreet.com. Cramer never had anything positive to say. His mantra was that theglobe.com was wildly overvalued.

Cramer had never met us, and he'd never interviewed us, but he still felt free to portray me and Todd as two little jerks who had absolutely no experience. How do you fight something like that? He was all over TV. The negative press began to take on a life of its own. People had a short attention span, and when they were once fed something nasty, it was hard to convince them later they might actually like it. By loudly singling us out, Cramer created a snowball effect. Any writer considering a positive story had to worry that it would look too soft. It was amazing to us that of all the many good reporters out there, just a few bad ones could steal the limelight.

Once the story crossed over from the financial press to pop culture, things got more and more ridiculous.

We did a photo shoot for *SmartMoney* magazine. They shot Todd and me in our theglobe.com T-shirts, running down a hallway and jumping in the air. They said they wanted a shot of us in flight. Seemed cool enough.

But they took the shot with some sort of fish-eye lens, which made our heads look distorted. The story became: "Todd and Steph jumping for cash!" We looked like smiling idiots just begging for a punch in the face. I wanted to punch myself in the face, too—it was that cartoonish.

But sometimes there were surprises in the other direction. We went to Los Angeles to meet with a *Los Angeles Times* writer named Jonathan Weber. Weber was working in this huge office with tiny cubicles everywhere, and had this old Mac, a relic in a place that otherwise looked pretty modern.

He gave us nothing through the whole interview, blank expression, no reactions. For the few moments when he actually seemed engaged, he was fairly critical of our business, asking probing questions, tougher questions than most interviews.

On the way back, Todd and I yelled at Esther. "We've really got to get better at screening these stories. This guy's probably going to write a horrible piece on us." We were so pissed. A month goes by, and all of a sudden, this huge *Los Angeles Times* story comes out, super positive, hitting on all of the key elements of our business. The piece got picked up by the *Washington Post* and then ran in the *Boston Globe.* Thank you, Jonathan Weber.

Shortly after that, Weber mentioned to us that he was starting up a new magazine about the industry (just a magazine, not an internet business), which ultimately became the *Industry Standard.* He said he wanted to do a story on theglobe.com.

"Come on," he said, "we'll do an interview with you guys. We'll set the whole thing up." Since we had this relationship, we agreed to let him put one of his reporters on us. And so, for three months, we did interviews with this one writer, who practically followed us around. She came to New York to meet with us. We met up with her in San Francisco when we were there on business. We did phone interviews, everything. We thought it would never end.

Then, one day, after months had passed and we wondered if the story had been killed—there we are, on the cover of the magazine, smiling like hucksters behind a cover line that says, "The Selling of theglobe.com." The piece was about how Todd and I were more teen idols than businessmen.

When I saw the cover, I knew. My first reaction was, "That can't be good." My heart was pounding. Whenever a story came out, I was always nervous that some quote would get twisted around. Todd was always critical of how I spoke my mind so openly to the press. Therefore, I'd learned that the best interview format is doing it live. As much as live television seemed scary, at least they can't re-edit your comments out of context. Now, as I flipped through the pages of the magazine, I saw comments attributed to us that were totally distorted, vapid, wrong.

It belittled everything we'd been building. And it started a snowball effect.

From then on, getting ambushed in the press was a regular occurrence. We'd always be getting calls from Mike or a friend: "Did you see the story?" I would drop everything I was doing and try to control my breathing.

Through all of this, we were laying the groundwork for our secondary offering. One of the last days before closing our offering, Alan Greenspan issued his now-infamous proclamation about internet mania and investors' "irrational exuberance" overheating the stock market. This was followed by the Fed rapidly raising interest rates.

Just like that, our stock plummeted. It had dropped before, but this time things were a bit more complicated. When you gear up for a secondary offering, you're trying to raise new money. If your stock keeps dropping, it screws up your whole plan. It means you must sell twice as many shares to raise the same amount of money. Once again, we ended up raising half as much cash as we'd intended. Instead of selling 8 million shares at $40, we only managed 6.9 million at $20. That was still $140 million, but it was far less than we anticipated.

The press didn't miss a beat. And to make matters worse, there was a huge story in the *New York Observer.* The gist was, "Globe management plunders Globe financial assets." It said Mike had cashed out and left everyone hanging. Which was a gross exaggeration. Mike had decided he was going to sell 20 percent of his holdings during the secondary offering. Todd and I had decided to sell 5 percent. We'd been locked in for so long, we jumped—carefully—at our first chance to taste even a little of our own profits. The article was the most scathing story about us I'd ever seen. It essentially said, "How *dare* they make money in the secondary offering? Shame on them for raising money and putting some in their pockets."

Of course, that was picked up by Steve Frank, a *Wall Street Journal* reporter on CNBC. And then, once again, by Jim Cramer.

At the time, one thing that made the negative press tolerable was that CNN was in the process of doing a huge documentary on us. Lou Dobbs had already done a general overview documentary about the craze of theglobe.com ("And how old are the founders? Twenty-four years old!"). But now, Jan Hopkins was preparing something for CNN *Movers. Movers* was all about people, old and young, and their great ideas that were moving and shaking.

Given the context, it was hard to imagine we were getting into anything but a positive story. So we cooperated. They wanted to film Todd and me everywhere. They really wanted to follow us around, get into our personal lives. I remember one of the producers saying, "Guys, let's make this well-rounded. Let's see who you are as *people*."

In the course of running the company, Todd and I had essentially been living double lives: each of us was simultaneously the wise CEO and the twenty-five-year-old guy. I told them, "Screw it. If you're going to follow my life, that means out to dinner and on to the clubs. You want to do that?" And they were like, "Yes!" So that, ultimately to my detriment, was what we did.

For Todd's story, they followed him out to the Hamptons, where he was playing badminton and hanging around at a barbecue. From there, the story cut straight to me, the European boy, all dressed up in black for full-on clubbing. I had on some of these cheap plastic pants. Todd, in what looked like a hippie commune, and me in my black plastic pants. It was a funny contrast and *way* overdone.

They were filming me at home—I'd let them into my apartment—and a couple of things happened. They were filming some B-roll, off-camera stuff, and one interviewer asked me, "So, what's it like being rich? Are you living it up?" Remembering the countless prior interviews and the reporters' never-ending fascination with our wealth, the supposed yachts, cars, and marriage proposals, with more than a little sarcasm, I replied, "Oh yeah. I'm ready to live a disgusting and frivolous lifestyle."

Now this was off camera. The cameraman was literally setting up. And I, of course, was just joking. I even said, "No, no, I'm just kidding." And then I proceeded to tell them, not for the first time, that it wasn't at all like that, and my lifestyle hadn't changed a bit. If only I wasn't so boring.

Of course, what ended up happening was that they lifted that specific quote, "I'm ready to live a disgusting and frivolous lifestyle," and then superimposed it onto a scene where you see me, on camera.

Todd was horrified when the tape aired. "Steph, why would you say that?" I tried to explain, but it was no use—I was done. I had to stop talking to the press. I'd always been so open, and I liked speaking my mind. (This was one of the bigger personality differences that Todd and I had discovered between us over the years. I was direct, to a fault, while Todd would watch his words very carefully, perhaps also to a fault.) Nevertheless, that was the lesson I learned. As CEO of a public company, I had to be more careful with what I said.

CNN *Movers: The Story of theglobe.com* came out in July 1999. It was a half hour documentary, and it aired worldwide, again and again. A lot of people saw it. The fact is that it was a great story, one of the first big documentaries they had done on the internet. And it was positive, overall—but those plastic pants and the "disgusting, frivolous" line overpowered almost all of it.

The story quickly became fodder for the Yahoo! message boards, a running joke.

Suddenly, my pants were the reason Greenspan came out with his comments and why internet stocks were plummeting. The comments on the message boards were awful, and, of course, all our employees read those same boards.

It got worse. We'd read things on the message boards like, "Those guys have got no clue what they're doing." "They're probably off gallivanting in their private jet." Steve Frank on CNBC ended up doing another hatchet job on us. He got a quote from an analyst at Jupiter Communications, saying, "Well, I don't know about you, but if you've gone on the Yahoo! message boards, investors don't seem to have many positive things to say about those guys from theglobe.com." To me, using a message board as validation was no different from the FBI sourcing the *National Enquirer* for hard evidence.

Despite these negative experiences, and how it all felt at the time, an outside firm that tracks press mentions reported that 75 percent of ours were still neutral to positive. And, truth is, there were some great experiences, especially when it came to speaking opportunities and PR that wasn't quite so focused on readership numbers or viewer eyeballs.

Todd and I were invited as guest speakers to Harvard, MIT, and the University of Lausanne (which made my dad proud), as well as to conferences like the *Industry Standard*'s Internet Summit 99 and the Connecticut Forum. People loved hearing our story as much as Todd and I enjoyed sharing it. Still, even as other internet companies were rising, our stock kept dropping. When we asked investors why they sold, their reasons were often centered around the bad press. "Well, you know, there's this general negative feeling about you guys and how overvalued you are." What else could we say? Our revenues were climbing, we were beating earnings, we were doing all the things everybody does to beat the competition.

But negative press spooked people—and made them sell. And, for us, it happened to be the case that the bad press had a disproportionate impact on our stock as compared with other companies. Normally, most stock is held by institutional investors, who do look at the fundamentals of the business, and don't tend to be spooked by the media. But our institutional investors had largely taken advantage of the insane 1,000 percent run-up on the day of the IPO, harvested their profits, and sold. Instead, our stockholders were largely the day traders, the smaller shareholders, the individual gamblers with a fear of missing out—they drove the price high, and then panicked with every message board rumor. That was why the stock was so volatile in comparison with others, and that was why the bad press was so particularly dangerous to us.

Ultimately, we scaled down the amount of press we did that fall. When people shove you in the trash, there's not much you can do to dig your way out. It would take a miracle, and we'd already had one in getting the IPO in the first place.

That was one more miracle than most people get.

11

The Downward Spiral Part I

The Slow Tumble

One thing no one ever prepares you for in the running of a public company is shareholder resentment.

I'm not talking about the big institutional investors who made a killing in Net stocks (only to eventually lose money in the crash). The big buyers have resources; they work with other people's money. For them, what happened to our stock was all part of the game of fund management. You lose some, you win some.

I'm talking about the little investors, the individuals who have to settle their accounts at the end of the day. These people are often playing Russian roulette with their life savings. That's hard-earned money they've decided to gamble away. But individuals never see it as gambling.

As our stock began to fall, a Greek chorus of accusation and outrage began to rise, particularly on the Yahoo! message boards.

"It's the company's fault!"

"Todd and Steph, they should be fired!"

"They should be killed!"

"They should be lynched!" Nice.

Some of the comments would be about our age, as in, "I'm sure Todd and Steph had their shareholder meeting and handed out milk and cookies to everyone. Milk and Chips Ahoy!, saying, 'Everybody, let's celebrate!'"

It was hard to believe this was a discussion among real people. Talk about the effect of anonymity on the internet. Any potential investors who were looking for a useful tip would suddenly be subjected to a barrage of, "You want to invest in those faggot CEOs? Don't do it! They're just going to jack you off and pump and dump," and all sorts of sage advice like that.

But that was the power of these message boards. One renegade with an agenda had the power to influence hundreds of day traders. And when hundreds of day traders sell your stock, it drops 10 percent in a day. When it drops 10 percent in one day, someone writes about it. When someone writes about it, another hundred shareholders sell. Before the internet, people didn't have the power to get the word out to thousands of potential shareholders so quickly and directly—it even took the SEC a while to catch up to the potential that message boards had to affect stock prices.

We noticed that there was one particular shareholder lurking on the message boards, with the user name Larry_Hey. Ever since the secondary offering, he had been bad-mouthing us and he just wouldn't stop. He almost buried us, single-handedly. Whenever he went on one of his rampages, we would notice a drop in the stock that day.

It became clear that Mr. Hey must have been shorting our stock—in essence, betting on it to drop. Up until then, as sad as it sounds, Todd and I were not all that well informed about shorting—it just seemed like such an unethical thing to do. Who knew you could actually bet against a stock and then go out and ensure your profit by broadcasting what a lump of shit it was?

Larry_Hey kept bad-mouthing us, and getting personal. Things like, "Yes, I just saw Todd and Steph and Mike in their limo in New York. Looks like they are heading to one of the banks to go liquidate." Complete BS, but you never know what someone will believe.

We had no choice but to try to investigate and find out who this guy was. We called the FBI, but they wouldn't do anything. Technically, the securities laws hadn't caught up—there was nothing illegal about it.

Our own internal lawyer advised us to let it go. But I said, "No, we are not going to let it go." So we started tracking him ourselves like wily fox hunters. One of the first steps we took was to file an affidavit with Yahoo! to get hostile member information. They found out what the guy's other user names were and what ISP he used. They gave us the information, and with that in hand, we were able to backtrack. What we quickly discovered was that this user had an account on our own site, not just on the Yahoo! boards.

Here's how we were able to track him down. Some user had set up a club on our site that was the TGLO Discussion Club, a successful group that often had hundreds of traders in it. Larry_Hey, of course, joined the club on our site. That was a mistake.

Through that, we were able to get into his account, find his user name and his password, his real name, confirm it was the same guy as on Yahoo!, and *gotcha.*

So we tracked him down and found out that he was a broker from a small firm in New Jersey. It's amazing the stuff you can find out about a person. I found out which tennis club he belonged to and that he was subscribing to hair growth products on Drugstore.com. I must confess, for a moment, I thought about revenge, posting about him the same way he was posting about us.

What we ended up doing (with advice from counsel) was to send him a FedEx package. We bundled together all these examples of his bad-mouthing and threw in everything else we had found out about him. We put it in a legal envelope with a letter that read, "This is a cease and desist order . . ." We sent this package not to Larry_Hey himself, but to his superiors at work. We added a note that said, "Are you aware that your employee is doing the following . . . ?"

Within maybe forty-eight hours of sending that package, Larry_Hey never wrote another word, at least not under *that* user name, and the level of negativity on the boards went way down. Still, the damage had been done. In terms of market cap, he almost probably cost us tens of millions of dollars.

He wasn't the only one.

Shortly after our stock began its swan dive, a woman started regularly calling our offices to tell us how evil we were. Here's a sample: "I lost my money on theglobe.com. Fuck you, I want you to die!"

She would leave voice mails for Todd and me, separately. She was relentless. Every morning, we'd walk in, ready to face the day, and the first thing we'd hear was, "I hate you! I hate you! I hate you! I will kill you! I will kill you! I will kill you! I invested my money in you. I will sue you! Class action lawsuit! I read this in the message boards, everybody hates the founders. They want you to die!"

Then, the same woman would call the head of our investor relations department and start sobbing. "I lost all my money! Please, please, please pay me back all my money, and I will be fine! Pay it back, pay it back, fuck you! Fuck you!" It was heartbreaking. It was also pure lunacy.

We thought about personal security. I was seriously concerned that some deranged lunatic would find my apartment and murder me. We'd just heard about a day trader who'd gone berserk in Atlanta and shot his colleagues, so it didn't seem that impossible.

In truth, it was scary as hell. And it went on for *six* months. Over and over, dozens of voice mails.

We never did hire protection, but the thought constantly crossed my mind. The whole thing was even giving me nightmares. I'd wake up in a cold sweat, gasping for air. It was a stressful few months. And it would only get worse.

12

The Downward Spiral Part II

My Dad

By the fall of 1999, Todd and I had been running the company for over five years, and the only vacation time we'd ever taken was one week during Christmas.

In September 1999, shortly after the completion of our secondary offering, Jenn and I decided to take a trip. This was particularly meaningful to me because it was the first time I would be returning to the South of France to my grandparents' house, the place where I'd summered as a teenager.

I hadn't been back in part because the last time hadn't ended so well. When I was thirteen, after spending a wonderfully isolated two weeks in France, my family and I packed up my dad's car, planning to drive the six hundred kilometers up through most of France on our way back to Switzerland.

What ended up happening was the front tire caught fire on the road, the brakes failed, and my dad ended up trying to steer the car across four lanes of traffic while dodging the other cars and looking for a soft shoulder.

We all ran from the car as a wall of flame surged from underneath the door.

We backed away and watched as the car burned like a huge torch. In the end, there was nothing left but a wire frame and the remains of our luggage. That event all but kept me from returning for many years.

Fast-forward back to 1999 and I was returning to France with Jenn, the first time that she would actually spend time with my dad's side of the family, including my grandparents.

With the sound of the ocean, the breeze, the crickets . . . it was as far from Manhattan and our fibrillating stock price as I could possibly be. We went swimming and sailing every day, to the local market for cheese and fresh produce. It wasn't perfection, but it was close. Except for my dad and a sudden back pain he was experiencing, growing more and more severe throughout that week. A few weeks after the trip, again knee-deep in the drama of our stock price, I got a call revealing my dad had advanced pancreatic cancer, and needed major surgery, from which he barely survived.

"Steph," my mom said, "your dad may only have a few months left to live." Even though they'd divorced years earlier, they remained close, and she had always loved him.

I got up and shut the door to the office, which was soundproof because Todd and I used to scream at each other all too often. I got back on the phone, and I could barely get the words out. "What are you saying?"

The shock wasn't so much the illness, but the cruel surprise of it. I always imagined I'd have my whole life to get to know my dad, to rely on him as I began my own family and continued my own business ventures.

That evening I booked a ticket to Switzerland. I arrived not having slept for two nights. I looked like a day hiker who'd been lost in the Alps. I went straight from the airport to the hospital. My stepmother, Monica, and my half brother and half sister were already there, waiting for me.

Before the nurse on duty let us in, she mentioned that my father was still on heavy painkillers post-surgery and that he'd be in and out of consciousness. As I listened, my stomach twisted in knots.

He didn't look like my father. He was lying on his back with tubes going into his stomach, his arm, and up his nose. They'd cut so much out of him. It turned out that they had to open his leg and take out nerves and veins to reconstruct the canal system in his stomach. My dad had always been such a larger-than-life character, a powerful figure. He was a lion of business and politics. Now he looked so thin and weak, the skin sagged from his neck. He'd been asking to see me. He sort of looked over, but his eyes weren't really focusing, they were wobbling from side to side. He said to me (in French), "You know, Steph, I think I've been dealt a really poor hand." Then he was crying. "I wanted . . . I have no time now to say anything to anyone." I told him everything was going to be fine, and tears welled up in my eyes.

My family was sitting at the end of the bed, completely quiet. Dad said, "There are so many things we need to work out. I have so many business issues that are unresolved, that we need to wind down. I need your help, Steph. There are these businesses in the States."

He started going through all of them. My father had always been a businessman, and once again, everything was coming out business, business, business. All the while, he was crying, and he couldn't stop.

Then, just as quickly, he calmed down and immediately dozed off. We stepped out, and the nurses went in to look after him.

As I waited outside, I thought about my dad's role in theglobe.com. After initial skepticism (but never negativity), he had become a big believer. He'd invested in an online medical company in Atlanta, and that company had merged with WebMD, and then WebMD merged with Healtheon. Suddenly, my dad was an investor in one of the biggest health care companies online. Even so, he always told me it was all a massive bubble that was going to burst; it was just a question of time. He was the first person who told me, long before anyone else, that people should absolutely not believe the hype.

As my business grew, my dad would always give me advice about how we weren't being handled correctly, whether I liked it or not. I'd say, "Yes, Dad, thank you. I have already heard this a trillion times," but he was always right. Still, the Net became the one place where he'd ultimately defer to *my* opinion—a rare triumph.

On Sunday, I boarded the plane and headed back to New York, to the office.

First thing Monday morning, I told Todd what was going on. As strange as it sounds, my father's illness had a cathartic effect on us; our pent-up hostilities released.

Suddenly, nothing about work mattered to me in the same way. I didn't want to tell anyone at the office about my dad; it was just too tiring to get into. But I still had to put on a good face. I had to get in front of the camera to meet press. I had to keep Mike apprised of how the quarter was shaping up.

Thank God there were two of us. Behind closed doors, Todd was the crutch I had to lean on. This was the time when we were being buried by the message boards and watching the stock sink. I dreamed that we could rewind, un-buy Azazz, un-buy whatever other junk we'd gotten stuck with. It was all a mess. We had weak ad sales. E-commerce had not panned out. The guys in Seattle were just lumps of coal. I started to ask myself, *Why are we doing this?* Todd and I made a pact the day we started the business that we would do it only as long as we were having fun. We looked each other in the eye and said, "Let's not turn this into some silly little saying that just vanishes. We will only do this if we love it every day." Now we were falling out of love.

We knew we were going to be short revenues in the third quarter, for the first time in the company's history—and you can never miss a quarter; it's a death sentence. Todd and I were having our first serious talk about whether there was any way we would be able to survive.

It turned out that the company could survive—but Todd and I couldn't.

13

The Downward Spiral Part III

Mutiny and the Decision

We held our secondary offering during the two weeks that came to an end on May 19, 1999. Those days will stand for me as the beginning of the end.

Obviously, there were hundreds of factors that led us to our finish—including the libelous message boards and vitriolic bad press, and my emotional state regarding my father's health—but the key ingredient was a negativity in the world at large about our company that became endemic and incurable, and how that negative perception became a reality in the form of a plunging stock price.

That, for me, remained the most frustrating part of this whole ordeal because revenues were climbing and we had beaten every quarter right out of the gate. Our dropping stock price had nothing to do with how the company was performing.

For a while, Todd and I had the fighting spirit. "Oh, well, *fine,* we'll prove everybody wrong." But what starts to happen is that you find yourself pushing a bigger and bigger boulder uphill. It eventually gets so big that it actually starts to push you backward.

We did everything to ignore the daily stock price and just focus on the business. But even when you don't seek out the information, someone comes in and tells you your stock price or there's yet another article about its drop. All day long, your employees (and you) are measuring the company's success based on the price. The more the stock price dropped, the more depressed everyone in the company became.

We'd have employees leave for what they thought was their dream job. A month later, we'd hear they were fired or quit, or the company they'd thought so highly of had gone under. Very frequently, they came back. One of our top database programmers left to do high-tech video. Within a month, he quit and asked for his old job back. We gave it to him.

Still, desperate negativity starts to crush you. Inevitably, your clients start to hear it. Clients read. All of a sudden, advertisers start to pull their accounts; new clients are a lot less interested. Now their first question isn't, "Hey, what's your demographic?" It's, "Hey, so how long are you guys going to be in business?" We'd have to tell people, "We have enough cash to last at least another two years. We are in the top 20 percent of publicly traded internet companies.

There is nothing to worry about." Nevertheless, the fact that you have to have these conversations is a bad sign.

By the secondary offering, theglobe.com had gone through some major restructuring, much of it based on how the competition had shaken out. GeoCities had been bought by Yahoo!; Tripod was snapped up by Lycos. In effect, our toughest competitors were removed as brands.

We'd grown from five or six million users at the IPO to fifteen million users worldwide after the secondary offering. Media Metrix ranked us the thirty-fourth biggest site in the world, and that included measurements from every major country. We were very proud of what we had accomplished.

But by then, users had more choices. They could go to Yahoo! where they could get absolutely everything, or they could come to theglobe.com where they could get much less.

We changed from being a pure community to an attempt at a portal. We'd dabbled with being an e-commerce company. We'd suffered greatly from our unfocused search to become whatever was going to be seen as the next big thing.

In June 1999, we decided we would need to make changes. On the heels of the secondary offering, in which we had raised another $140 million, we brought in all of our key managers from around the world, from the United Kingdom, from Seattle, from everywhere. It was amazing to see the great talent we had managed to attract over the years. Between the IPO and the continuous press, our brand had become very well known, and our company seemed hip, truly alive. In turn, this had attracted many pioneering, creative, hardworking employees. We decided to restructure the company to revolve more clearly around the products. We would be product-focused (clubs, home pages, games), and everything we did would be built upon that.

One of the products that had just emerged was email clubs, a product that I personally loved. I truly believed email clubs were the sequel to community. So we implemented the changes, launched the clubs, a new home-page builder, and a whole new site design. Employees became very positive. For the first time in a long while, we felt like we were on the cutting edge with our products. But on the flip side, we were being crushed by a slowdown in sales. It was our weakest link. We didn't quite realize it at first. We had gone from just $0.75 million in sales in 1997 to $18.6 million in revenues in 1999. We had this huge ramp-up and much of that we attributed to our energetic sales force, which numbered in the low thirties by this time.

Our internal goal for 1999 was to hit $25 million in sales. The analysts knew we were supposed to do about $18 million, and when we came in at $18.6, we'd technically beat the analysts' numbers, which was fantastic.

But the reality was that after we went public, we kept missing every *internal* goal we had set. Despite padding our numbers with each additional acquisition, sales just couldn't stay ahead of the curve.

As we headed into the third quarter of 1999, suddenly, revenues were coming in way short. Todd and I were horrified. Then, in July, ad sales fell through completely. We'd been doing about $1.25 million a month from ad sales alone. By the end of July, revenue had dropped to half a million.

We'd dropped $750,000 in revenues! Sales would say, "We had a bad month. We'll make up for it." And so they tried. August jumped to a million. In September, we got up to $1.75 million in sales.

But July's loss of half a million was a fatal blow. After factoring in another million we'd lost in e-commerce, we came in short of Bear Stearns's revenue estimate. We'd actually missed other analysts' estimates by about $300,000, but they'd all said, "That's fine, no problem." Our losses were low enough that we had beaten their earnings-per-share figures.

Bear Stearns, on the other hand, came down with severity. Naturally, the press had a field day. Jim Cramer kept running a story on us, and we were getting crushed.

One of the problems was the sales team seeing themselves as distinct from the rest of the company. They saw us as obstacles instead of leaders. To them, we were these two kids isolated in our ivory tower, running the company without knowing anything. With the endless bashing in the press, our public reputations as CEOs were getting seriously tarnished, and the missed quarter had only made things worse.

From the perspective of our sales team, since they were the ones actually charged with generating revenue, the pressure was on them exclusively—and they resented it.

There was also pressure coming the other way, from sales back to us, for more stock options. Our people were getting stock options priced at $30 a share. Then, after the secondary offering, our stock price dropped and dropped. Around the time it was $15 a share, we began hearing from executives in sales: "Well, thanks for the seventy thousand shares, but now they're not worth anything." These demands became hard for everyone in senior management to ignore.

At the time, we thought it was more important to hit our quarter than to cause disharmony with our sales team. So we caved. Our attitude for a while became, "Okay, fine, have some new stock options." Obviously, the economy was exploding and all around us in New York people were comparing their options packages over drinks, packages that very soon, for many of them, would become worthless. But everyone wanted a piece of the pie, and we had a few people who continually came back to us, trying to renegotiate their options package as the price continued to drop. Todd and I were stunned by their expectations. We felt backed into a corner. They knew how much we were relying on them. But at a certain point, we simply had to say, "No more. You're playing with this stock like its Monopoly money."

Suddenly, as soon as we pushed back, there was a perception that Todd and I weren't willing to reward good performance. Then the stock dropped even farther. And Todd and I had to wonder what kind of performance people expected should be rewarded. It was a mistake to have ever started renegotiating in the first place, but we felt we had no choice. It would take three to six months to find replacements for anyone who left. And if people started leaving, then we would have certainly missed our projections.

If we lost our top salespeople, all of a sudden we'd have to explain to TheStreet why we missed our revenue—not by 5 percent or by one cent a share—but by twenty cents a share or a massive 50 percent. When things fall apart like that, you don't have time to work it out. And the analysts were looking for us to trip up.

It was unbearable, and it would get uglier. I was also dealing at the time with my dad's ordeal. What we'd soon realize was that our top sales managers were privately talking to Ed. They must have known that Ed had Mike's ear.

Fortunately, Ed was loyal to me and Todd. Although he was also loyal to Mike, Ed was phenomenal at being an adviser to us and a buffer to keep the relationship with Mike working. There were a number of times when Todd and I were ready to blow up at Mike, and Ed would be the one saying, "Don't do that. Here is how I suggest you make things right."

Part of this was our fault, for sure. It was our fault that our senior management team didn't act in a stronger and more authoritative way with our own managers. Todd and I didn't have thirty years of experience managing such situations to know that you either attack it the first time it happens or it gets out of hand down the road. But Todd and I didn't handle it well.

It was now December 1999. Everyone was excited about the new millennium, NASDAQ was hitting record highs, Silicon Valley was celebrating. To outsiders, even we were flying high. Todd and I received the 1999 Ernst & Young Entrepreneur of the Year Award. In accepting the award, I said, "You should never give up. You never know how far you can go." But inside, I knew it was about to fall apart. My dad was dying. Our stock was dying. The haters were hating. I could feel that the internet bubble was about to burst and we'd inevitably be one of the first casualties.

At the end of December, I went to Switzerland to see my dad.

I came back, and then Todd left on his vacation. I walked into the office on January 6 to find it half-empty and our stock down to around $10 a share and fluctuating. The energy had left the building. Sitting at my desk and listening to the silence, I had a rushing sense of foreboding. Then Dean Daniels came in to the office and explained that our top sales guys, Will and Bryan, were down in Florida, working on a business deal with CBS SportsLine.

We'd been talking to SportsLine, one of the largest sports sites, for month after month after month. This was going to be a big, big anchor deal, the first huge company wanting to make a deal to use our community. Bryan started talking to them in the fall of 1999. The deal was finalized around late March of 2000, and turned out to be the worst deal we made in company history. We paid out a whopping $8 million in stock with the expectation of making millions in revenue. It probably made less than $100,000 for us. It was a massive loss.

I got a call from Ed at Mike's Florida office.

"What's up, Ed?"

Ed said, "Hey, I just want you to know that Will and Bryan have been here all morning with Mike. They're scheduled to be here all day."

"What?"

"Yeah, I didn't know if you knew or not. I just wanted to fill you in." Ed had broken out of the meeting to tell me this. He said, "I'll tell you more later."

This wasn't good. Up until this point, my relationship with Will and Bryan had been cordial—tense, but cordial, all things considered. Which made this much more shocking. Todd was totally out of the loop. He was skiing and blissfully free; I was on my own and going out of my mind. My heart stopped, and the pit of my stomach was erupting.

I called Todd and left him a voice mail (he never had his cell phone on, which frustrated the hell out of me).

Finally, I got Mike on the phone and let him talk.

"Will and Bryan are down here," he said, "and they're giving us some valuable feedback. They think you guys are not communicating with everybody properly, and they have a list of things they think should change. Oh, and that you should step aside." Mike said that he didn't necessarily think we should step aside, but that we needed to work on the communication problems.

I was flabbergasted that the meeting had even occurred. For a moment, I couldn't answer. I was just trembling on the phone. Trembling with rage. Finally, I said something like, "Okay, okay, *okay.* I gotta call you back."

Half an hour later, Todd called. We had a crazy David Mamet conversation:

"Guess what?" "What?"

"No!"

"No?"

"Yes?"

"Yes!"

I told Todd the whole goddamn thing. Now, between Todd and me, I had always been the guy who was more passionate and aggressive. But Todd had changed, and so had I—and only Todd knew what was happening with my father. Seeing the cancer eat away his vitality, it became truly obvious to me that there was more to life than theglobe.com, but I was acting on instinct and said to Todd, "I'm thinking we should fly right down to Florida and storm in there . . ."

Todd interrupted. "Tell Mike we're out." "What?"

Todd was oddly calm. He was like a Zen master. "That's it," he said. "That's it. Let's go tell him we are out. We are out, we are out!"

"What do you mean, out?" I said. "Do you mean we're quitting?" "Steph," he said, and I could hear the smile forming on his face, "we are fucking out! That's it!"

The minute I heard Todd say it, I knew in my heart of hearts that I was ready to step aside, that this had been too much. Todd and I had always tried to be together on all the big decisions. Over the years, we'd fought about a lot, but on this, we were in total agreement.

And so I hung up and called Mike back.

"Mike," I said, "I just want you to know Todd and I are really disappointed. We are really disappointed, and this is absolutely unacceptable." It was very quiet on the other end. I explained to Mike how upset I was that Will and Bryan had set this meeting without our knowledge. I took a deep breath. "Mike, I want you to know that we're out, Todd and I are resigning."

Mike started in immediately. "Now, hold on. I wouldn't be so brash. We can work this out. There is nothing to be so crazy about." "No," I said. What I wanted to tell Mike was that I was just as pissed at him for having taken the meeting. I said, "It seems like you've really lost faith in us."

Mike said, "No, I have never lost faith in you guys." He was backtracking, but in the end he couldn't stop us from leaving.

After I got off the phone, Ed called. He wanted to know if it was true. I told him we were dead serious. He didn't want us to do anything brash, either. "You have a lot of shares in this company," he reminded me. "The last thing we want is some big scandal to appear in the newspapers."

"Believe me," I said, "Todd and I are not stupid. I believe in this company, and I love the company. It's heart-wrenching for me to have to let go. Don't worry," I told him, "nothing stupid is going to happen. We are going to take our time."

This all went down on Thursday, January 6, 2000. That night, Todd got on a plane and came back. He arrived Friday afternoon and came over to my place. We pulled out the vodka, and Jenn was our personal bartender. We all had tears in our eyes, but we were also wildly excited at the same time. We held up the shot glasses and grinned. We had drink after drink after drink, giddy with laughter and freedom.

That whole weekend was a blur and, all the while, I floated with excitement. I was also delusional and scared. I had no idea what was going to happen. But we had to be adamant about our decision. "We are going through with this," we told each other, "we are definitely going through with this, but we have to ensure a very orderly transition." On a wintry gray morning in early January 2000, we agreed that we'd note our departure at the quarterly announcement, and that we'd put out a press release. The release would make it clear that although Todd and I were indeed stepping aside, we were going to continue as board members. We would continue, just like Bill Gates, as chief strategists. We'd also help the company transition, find a new CEO, even guarantee a new CEO before the end of the second quarter.

There were a lot of factors that fed into our decision. Will and Bryan were merely the last straw. The reality was that Todd and I were ready to go. The attempted force-out, unpleasant at first, became a good reason to exit, and there was little Mike could do to argue with us. This had been building ever since we went public, since that day we realized that this was all falling out of our control. We had designed the car and started the engine, but we were very quickly becoming passengers in our own vehicle. (We'd also learned how few CEOs are actually in absolute control of their companies. It was better to be the founder and then maintain control of your equity by relinquishing the reins to better trained, more experienced people.)

Todd and I used to draw these massive spirals on our whiteboard—these perfectly symmetrical spirals. I called them the spirals of despair. There's nothing worse than the feeling that things can actually get worse. In fact, around the time of the secondary offering, Todd and I suggested that the board seriously consider hiring a new CEO, a leader who could just take over and really push through.

The board's general reaction was, "If it ain't broke . . ." They never believed that the company was broken. After all, we were still a half-billion-dollar enterprise, and we'd also managed to consistently beat earnings every quarter. They didn't believe there was anything wrong with me and Todd. It was just about giving us good advice and making things work. Despite this, Todd and I mentioned that we weren't against the idea of bringing in a new CEO, but they wanted us to stay.

Now we'd made our decision. Life was too important. I wanted to spend some time with my dad.

We'd been in the process of courting a buyout. We'd been talking with David Wetherell at CMGI, but he backed away—partly because we had to keep renegotiating the price as their stock ran up, but largely because Wetherell seemed like an emotional basket case who couldn't make up his mind (the *New York Times* ended up writing an article about him that agreed).

All I dreamed of doing was selling the company, getting back to Switzerland, and spending time with my dad. But the buyout wasn't happening, so eventually we had to actually make the decision on our own.

We'd never started theglobe.com to be slaves to a stock price or to an investor community. We'd never expected to have our lives judged day in and day out by people who formed their opinions based on how much money they'd made or lost in a single afternoon. We had a vision, and we'd gone for it. That's all that Todd and I had originally done. Obviously, when something goes too far, you can't turn back and cry for your days of innocence. Todd and I realized that the only thing we could do was change the future and take control of our personal lives.

Which is exactly what we did.

14

Stepping Away

It's Done!

After Todd and I made our big decision, we had to keep our mouths closed. After all, we had a vested interest in cooperating with Mike and making sure that the cathartic thrill of our departure didn't come at the deadly expense of our stock price. Still, that didn't stop Ed from saying, "I assume you guys won't go and do something stupid like talking to the press." We had no intention of talking to the press. The plan was that Todd and I would keep our lips zipped until January 27, when we were to announce our next quarterly results. It's not easy to keep that kind of secret. We couldn't discuss it with our employees, and I had to swear my girlfriend to secrecy. The only people who knew were our COO, Dean Daniels, and our head of communications, Esther Loewy.

January 27 was a bittersweet day. We'd just happened to be wrapping up our best quarter ever, $7 million in revenue, and Todd and I were proud of those numbers. At least we were stepping aside on a good note.

Once the big news went out over the wire, we immediately held an internal meeting. Despite our silence, rumors had been flying about what was going on. Still, some people were genuinely in shock when we told them.

It wasn't easy. Of course, we couldn't tell them all the things that had gone down behind the scenes. We just let people know that stepping down was the best thing for the company. We explained that Todd and I would be relinquishing day-to-day operations and that Dean would be stepping up as president. We'd continue to deal with the things that he didn't have time for. Over the next six months, we'd announce a new CEO.

After the meeting, we did the conference call with the analysts and spent five minutes placating them about our sudden departure. Then we handed over the phone. It was Dean's turn to talk. Dean gave a whole debriefing about the quarter. He did a great job. We just sat there, not saying a word.

Then we went back to our office and closed the door behind us. We gave each other a hug and wrote on the board, *It's done!* I had a little disposable camera, and we took goofy thumbs-up pictures.

I'll never forget that initial thrilling sensation of freedom, sitting in our office, the weight finally lifted. We'd been on a roller-coaster that had nearly careened out of control to the point that sparks were flying, and we'd actually jumped the tracks. Now it was done. Over the next six months, we'd work out the legal details, gradually give up the reins, look for that new CEO, and try to learn how to enjoy life again. For the first time, we could breathe. It was like taking a huge swan dive off a cliff and landing on a silk bed. It felt so good knowing that we'd finally made this decision, an honest decision. We'd been raising this baby for six years. Now we finally let it go; someone else would be doing the diapering.

On the day of our announcement, the stock was around $9 a share (post-split). In some vengeful reporters' eyes, the price was just another sign of our incompetence. Of course, what we couldn't have known was that two and a half months later, the massive internet bubble would burst, and 90 percent of all internet companies would drop 90 percent in value.

Who knows what would have happened if we'd all fallen together, as opposed to theglobe.com falling just a few months ahead of the curve. Maybe Todd and I would've stayed longer, maybe we would have been willing to put up with everything, and nobody would have been haranguing us constantly about our stock price.

What no one else knew at the time was that we'd entered into intense discussions with another company that wanted to buy theglobe.com. The negotiations had been going on for a couple of months.

We were talking to the publishing company Emap Petersen. They'd been looking to implement a big internet strategy, and they liked that we offered niche services that could work with their niche publications. But Emap had concerns. They could never understand why our stock had dropped so much, and this was always in the back of their minds.

Of course, had we been part of the entire market crapping out, they might have said, "Oh, well, good, theglobe.com is actually no different from the rest of them." But it didn't work out like that in the end, and it didn't help that Mike was pushing hard—perhaps too hard—on Todd and me for the deal. In the end, Emap backed away completely.

Prior to Emap, a number of other suitors had also expressed interest in acquiring us, including Tom Rogers at Primedia, Mel Karmazin at CBS, and Bob Wright at NBC. But those deals also fizzled out, usually because our potential acquirers were unsure of what their own internet strategies should have been.

As a result of the failed Emap deal, we lost a couple of months in our search for a new CEO. In March 2000, Todd and I finally started looking in earnest.

We interviewed several candidates, all from traditional companies. We were looking for someone with the requisite amount of energy to take on something huge like this, and for someone who *wasn't* an internet exec. We talked to one major media player who was among the top people at Random House, and several candidates of a similar caliber.

Ultimately, the man we hired was Chuck Peck, a self-described "challenge junkie" from the AICPA and Simon & Schuster who'd been a lifelong turnaround artist. Chuck had helped build New York Air with Frank Lorenzo. He'd secured $150 million in sales and overseen some three thousand employees. He was a former marine, which added a little discipline to his persona. He was a bulldog, a guy with a gift for raw pushing, and his strength was especially pronounced in sales and marketing.

Just the year before, we had moved into new cutting-edge offices down on Wall Street, and we knew that as soon as Chuck arrived he could revolutionize the organization and really take our sales to the next level. We knew he'd be able to gun it. He wasn't one of those toothless CEOs who overanalyzed everything and never made ends meet. And so, on August 1, 2000, Chuck came on board while Todd and I began our gradual unwinding.

We became the backseat guys, and we tried extra hard to not be backseat drivers. One of the biggest failures many companies suffer is when their new CEOs come in only to find themselves smothered by the predecessors. We couldn't risk that kind of counterproductivity.

In January, February, and March, the market was still up. NASDAQ was holding at 5,000. Meanwhile, Todd and I had all our stock in theglobe.com, which was still—slowly but surely—going down. So you can imagine how frustrating it was when everyone else celebrated. "Whoo-hoo, I've got my money in eToys, in this $10 billion company!" and "Webvan is a $20 billion company. It's just fantastic!"

Todd and I knew all these companies pre-IPO. We knew the people from UrbanFetch and Kozmo.com, two hot start-ups in our backyard, which were on fire. We knew them like no one else knew them. In fact, we knew them so well that Todd and I decided to borrow money against our stock, because at the time our portfolio was still worth about $20 million. We decided to go low-risk and borrow $1 million against it, and put it into UrbanFetch. I figured we wouldn't do as well as a lot of other people were making out, but damn it, we were going to make a dime on the side.

At the time, UrbanFetch had just closed another round of $60 million financing. Our timing looked good. Then, a couple weeks after we closed the investment, the market tanked. The market started tanking like no one had ever seen before; all internet stocks went down 90 percent. All the pre-IPO companies canceled their IPOs, and they all ran out of money. Kozmo.com burned through $250 million in under a year. And my own personal investment tragedy? Over eight months, I watched as the only cash I had left, the money I put into UrbanFetch, evaporated. I had absolutely nothing to show for it but a Rubik's Cube with their logo on it.

Individual trading is rarely anything more than gambling, which is why I probably shouldn't have invested in the first place. I don't blame UrbanFetch for my million-dollar loss. I blame myself.

The month Todd and I stepped aside, Jenn and I took off on my first non-family vacation in a long while. We went to Venice via Florence and then ended up driving through Tuscan farmlands. Something about Italy, along with the fact that Chuck had just come on board, allowed me to ease off completely. There I was sitting in the Italian countryside with my girlfriend, listening to roosters, eating real northern Italian food, watching the sunset, then later, chilling on the beach on Elba. Paradise.

Then we came back to New York, and it hit me like a ton of massive scaffolding: my whole career had evaporated. My income was gone, and my worth, which had rocketed from absolute zero to $97 million, had now dropped down to . . . well, our stock was now mired at $2 a share. I'd seen my net worth drop and drop and drop, and though I was technically still worth a few million bucks, it was all tied up in stock. I didn't have access to it, and I couldn't sell.

Why couldn't I sell? First, I would have inside information. Second, if a CEO or a board member sells and someone notices, it can cause a panic. There are so many restrictions, restrictions, restrictions—many of which were the reason why I could never liquidate anything before. It suddenly dawned on me that I might get nothing out of this, not a penny. For all intents and purposes, I was broke. I'd never really had cash in the bank. Now, I no longer had an income. (But, of course, everyone still perceived me as a billionaire.)

Todd and I had a severance package that gave us enough cash for maybe a year. But the reality was that I had to figure out something new. Fast. On top of that, my dad was still fighting to stay alive.

I needed to figure out what I was going to do with myself and how to make money again. At twenty-six, I was having a midlife crisis.

That's when it happened with me and Jenn. Confronted with the abyss, I stepped away from her, and our relationship ended.

That August, the only thing that sustained me was this vague sense that there was something new I could go after, a new dream, and that the next time around, I would do it better. From then on, I went into the office only on a part-time basis. I started reading fiction again for the first time in a long while.

I picked up the entire volume of *Dune.* I would go over to a jazz coffee bar on Seventeenth and Broadway and sit on a sofa in the back. As I delved into books, I was exploring space all over again and the prospect excited me.

It made me think of when Todd and I were initially excavating the internet and of the time when I didn't spend my days and nights thinking about a damn stock price. It helped me jump-start my mind again, reviving my long-starved imagination.

It dawned on me that what I'd always liked the most about theglobe.com was the creative aspect, the making of something out of thin air, something that hadn't heretofore existed. I wanted to know how I could recapture that inspiration and what type of role would bring some of those elements back to me. One of the things I started doing after we stepped aside was taking notes. I started jotting down the feelings that came with the initial Net euphoria, and before I knew it, I was writing down my memories.

Little did I know they would wind up in a book.

EPILOGUE

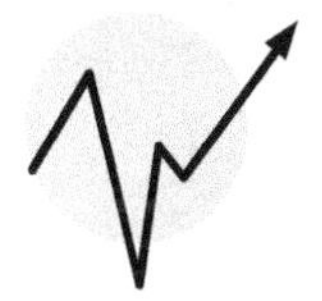

Lessons Learned . . . And a New Adventure!

Only about four months after I wrote those words, this book was released by John Wiley & Sons and I did a whirlwind of press, where I found myself giving glib advice to young entrepreneurs—"Don't go public!" and "Beware of the media!"—and announcing aspirations to leave the tech world entirely and become a Hollywood actor.

Gosh, I was young. And I was tired—exhausted, really, after putting nearly seven years, a quarter of my life, into theglobe.com, missing out on much of the fun of college and young adulthood, friendships, healthy relationships, jobs where every move you made wasn't chronicled in newspapers, industry magazines, and on the nightly news. And of course I'm a little embarrassed by how naïve I was about Hollywood and the film industry, particularly since now I've spent almost fifteen years immersed in that world—first as a producer and now as the cofounder and CEO of Slated, a film financing and packaging marketplace that I'll talk about more in a bit—and I know how crazy those initial acting dreams really were.

But the truth is that I was in shock for a long time after my life at theglobe.com fell apart, and then the internet fell apart, and then, on September 11, it seemed like the whole world was falling apart. It took me a couple of years to start over again, to stop torturing myself with the what-ifs, my envy of others whose companies reemerged from the ashes after the dot-com crash, the frustration that things could have been different if we'd started just a few years later, and that perhaps "community" as a function of the internet (indeed, maybe one of the chief functions) was just a little bit too far ahead of its time.

I'm writing this epilogue with the backdrop of a new television series that may or may not have aired by the time you read this, *Valley of the Boom*, revisiting the birth of the internet, and telling the tale of theglobe.com, along with the origin stories of Netscape and a streaming video company named Pixelon. Todd and I had zero involvement in the development of this series and I was shocked when I found out that our story was going to be included—flattered and humbled, and, honestly, more than a little amused that the adventures of a company I started in college could still, so many years after its failure, make for a story worth watching. (I didn't even know that there would be a scripted portion of the show until friends in the entertainment industry told me there was a casting call out there for someone named "Stephan Paternot"—and it's been a surreal experience to see someone else embodying my life on screen.)

I've only seen the first couple of episodes at this point—so I don't know how the producers ultimately decided to portray our journey—but merely seeing the start of our adventure brought to life up on the screen took me right back to that time, revived all of the emotions I was feeling back then, the ups, the downs. And when I look at it with fresh eyes, the thing I'm most struck by is how easy it is to imagine now, knowing what we know today, that social networking was a given, something that was fated to succeed. We look at Facebook, at Twitter, at Instagram, and it seems obvious that the internet can bring people together and connect people to communities, whether made of people they know in real life or people they don't—but back when we were starting, this wasn't obvious at all, not in the least.

When we began theglobe.com, it was incredibly hard to get people to even understand what the internet was and what it could do for them from a social perspective. Computer users were seen as loners, kids sitting in dark basements staring into machines. Social? No way. A computer was an *anti*social tool, if anything—yes, you could use it to create a spreadsheet, or, if you signed up for America Online, maybe read the news or check sports scores—but a computer was certainly not imagined by anyone as something that could create or deepen relationships. (And the people using computers were hardly seen as people anyone would even want to have any sort of a relationship with.)

We would talk to people about connecting online, and they just wouldn't get it. "What's wrong with the telephone?" they would ask us, laughing.

Even email wasn't understood as the powerful tool it so quickly became. People worried about losing the personality of handwritten letters—who would want to read a message that someone typed on a screen, where you couldn't even see their handwriting? People were so suspicious of the impersonal nature of it all. And when we talked about the instantaneous back-and-forth, they would tell us they have a fax machine . . . so what do they need email for? Let alone discussion boards, virtual communities, online chat. They looked at us like we were crazy.

It all seems utterly inevitable now, but educating potential users as to what the internet could become was absolutely our biggest hurdle at the start. Investors could not wrap their heads around it, couldn't see how this would ever work, or how it would appeal to even the nerdiest among us—let alone the broader general public.

All of which is why it's unbelievable to me that we've moved so completely in the other direction now. Everyone's addicted, posting selfies to Facebook and Instagram, presenting to the world this curated picture of their life, 24/7, unable to unplug long enough to have time with their own brains, with their own (offline) friends and family. It's bizarre, as someone who spent so much time twenty years ago trying to evangelize about the power of these tools, to see how far the pendulum has swung in the other direction: experts pleading with people to put their devices away, keep them from kids, understand their addictive potential, go back to the "good old days" of in-person contact and communication.

Ah, the good old days. Except we've forgotten that the good old days weren't really all that good! There's a reason why social networking has become so addictive to so many people, a reason why we started theglobe.com in the first place, a reason why Facebook and the others have grown so huge. Twenty years ago, the world was a pretty awful place for anyone who didn't feel like they fit in. People were lonely, huge swaths of society felt like outcasts, desperate. They craved community, interaction, and the sharing of knowledge. The offline world was working for some people, but not for everyone.

I wrote "they" in that last paragraph, but I could have just as easily written "we." Because I was one of them, without a doubt. It's only in retrospect that I see it—it wasn't a conscious thought at the time, and certainly I would never have admitted I felt like a lonely outcast—but I started theglobe.com not just because I saw it as a business opportunity, an opening waiting to be filled. I started it because it was exactly what I needed out there in the world, for me personally.

I felt so incredibly disconnected prior to getting online. I lived in a bunch of different countries, the language changed every few years, my school kept changing, my parents were together and then they weren't, I didn't know the cultural details I needed to bond with anyone else my age. I went to college feeling like a total outsider, no family to depend on, few friends. I needed the internet to grow into what I saw it could become in order to create my own virtual family, since there was no way my real one was ever going to fill that role.

And, amazingly, I just happened to grow up at a time when a college student didn't have to sit around and wait for someone to invent the internet that he needed in order to thrive—the technology was so new that Todd and I were in a position to do it ourselves. I know we didn't appreciate that at the time, just how crazy it was to try to do what we were doing—but I see it so clearly now, with two decades of perspective. We were delusional as to what we could accomplish—except, as I know now, you have to be delusional or you'll never accomplish anything.

When people ask my advice about starting an internet company (and they still do, though reading back through this book, it's hard for me to know quite why they would want to emulate our journey, given how it ultimately turned out—do you want to be worth $97 million dollars for an instant . . . and then, pretty soon afterward, be worth almost nothing?), I have to say, it just seems so much easier now. I don't mean the success part—it's obviously hugely challenging to build a truly successful, long-term, sustainable business—but the launch, the day-to-day, the mechanics of running that company. Tech entrepreneurs today don't understand just how hard it was, from a practical point of view.

The infrastructure is there now, in a way it wasn't at all when we started. Yes, the pipeline had been laid by DARPA and the US Department of Defense, and Marc Andreessen had introduced a graphical interface to search the web, with Mosaic and then Netscape, but there were no communication tools, there were no avatars, emoticons, any way to express personality. Connection was unreliable, expensive, slow as molasses. We were using a 14.4 kilobit modem, with storage costs more than a thousand times what they are today. We were just kids, but, looking back at it, we were literally a part of the invention of the internet, we were creating all of these things from scratch. Can you imagine waiting as long now even just for things to load as we did back then?

It's been an incredible journey since way back then, for the internet and social networking, and for me as an entrepreneur and a person—but those two journeys have been very separate from one another in so many ways. It's amazing for me to watch, largely as an outsider (except for the narrow domain of film financing where I now play, with Slated), how social networking has integrated itself into every aspect of our lives, and continues to evolve in technological sophistication. I can finally imagine, in the very near future, our world looking far too much like what science fiction author Neal Stephenson called the Metaverse back in 1992, in his novel *Snow Crash* (a book that continues to inspire me to this day)—an immersive, three-dimensional, virtual reality–based internet, people literally living their lives entirely as avatars online. Unfortunately, as Stephenson predicted, from the early dream of a decentralized internet empowering citizens all around the globe, instead there has been the emergence of a very few concentrated players controlling the tech world, which has led to the loss of transparency, the harvesting of data, and the weaponizing of our highly personal information against our own interests (things we couldn't even imagine back when we were begging users to read our Net Surfer and Glitch comic strips).

Clearly, now that so many of us are online 24/7, being manipulated by the algorithms powering Facebook, Google, and others, the internet—and specifically the social side of the internet—is horribly broken. I find myself personally using social media less and less, more as a business tool than as the vehicle for personal connection and fulfillment that I felt initially, the purity and authenticity having faded far into the background.

I fear a bit that putting this on paper will doom this epilogue—much like the thoughts that initially ended my book back in 2001 when it was first released—into feeling dated all too quickly, but as deformed as the original utopian dreams of social networking have become, as far away as that initial magic of person-to-person connection that drove me to build theglobe.com can sometimes feel, all is not lost. I firmly believe that the future of the internet will give control back to users instead of keeping it in the hands of a few key centralized players with their own goals and motivations.

New technological course corrections are already underway, led by a new generation of young idealists with incredible internet savvy and nothing to lose, ushering in the next great driver of transformation in the internet landscape—Web 3.0, a revolution of open-source, community-driven collaboration intended to serve humanity instead of harm it. I'm a huge believer (and investor) in blockchain technology and its ability in the short term to enable more efficient transactions, more secure digital identities, transparency, and reliability. And in the long term, even more critically, to decentralize concentration of technological, financial, and government power, and to mobilize citizens toward greater social democracy all around the world.

But at the same time as the internet has, in some respects, lost its way, I have spent the past two decades finding mine. For a long time, I was burned out and could never imagine running a company again, being a CEO, dealing with the daily stress, the ups and downs, the accountability to investors and customers, the ever-lurking threat of bad press emerging to hurt me (and it did, more than I should have allowed it to—again, curse those plastic pants!). At the same time, I wanted to prove that it wasn't just luck that led to the initial success of theglobe.com and that I had a genuinely good business sense for what would be successful in the tech space.

Even after we failed, friends and our early investors began asking me for hot tips on new internet companies, to tell them what was next. And I had ideas—as the internet renaissance began post-bubble, I started to hear about new ventures, new companies. Some were fresh developments and others were things that had taken hold already in Europe—around ringtones, downloadable wallpaper images, texting, technologies that were much more prevalent internationally at that point than they were in the US, but clearly headed this way.

I ended up starting a tech fund—Actarus Funds, named after one of my favorite Japanese cartoon heroes from my childhood, a little guy who ends up controlling a far bigger robot, in order to defend the earth from forces of destruction—in large part out of necessity and survival. I had no income, no net worth, just a network of entrepreneurs I knew. My first few bets were successful, 8x, 10x returns, and that just led to more. I built a portfolio of ten, fifteen, twenty internet companies (at this point I've invested in a total of fifty to sixty, though I've dialed it back in recent years), and found that it turned out I was winning more than I was losing. It proved to me that I still had a good sense of product-market fit, a good intuition about teams that would be successful, and a good attitude about being a useful partner for younger entrepreneurs.

I'd cashed out my final remaining shares in theglobe.com after our initial investors, Mike Egan and Ed Cespedes, had gained some traction reinventing the company as an internet phone provider (voice over IP) along the same lines as Skype. (Ironically, after we spent years trying to replace telephones as the primary tool for socializing, the company ended up attempting to make internet phone calls its core business.)

The stock price had lifted for a bit and I capitalized, dumping everything I had and using that money to launch my fund. It was a bittersweet moment. Sweet, as it gave me a financial cushion to survive with, but bitter, as I knew I was saying farewell and severing the last link I had to my first great professional love, theglobe.com. (Soon after, the stock dipped back to zero, ultimately making me grateful I had pulled the trigger when I did.)

I used the lessons from my own experience to inform my behavior as an investor—namely, let the founders do their job, and don't muddy the waters with your own agenda (no matter how smart you think you are). I'd seen all too closely what happened when a company started to raise big money and suddenly had to listen to new, powerful voices in the room that didn't necessarily have the same vision for the company or understand the product or industry enough to add positive value.

I was there for my companies with advice, absolutely—but my hope is they'd say I only offered when they asked for it, and only when I thought I actually had useful things to say. Otherwise, I wanted them to have the freedom to figure it out on their own, to stay true to their business without the "money guy" stepping in to force a direction change. I wanted to be everything I wished my investors would have been for me—and no suggestions that any of my companies buy Sunglass Hut.

Being an angel investor was a huge eye-opener for me—it made me realize, with more confidence than I anticipated, that success is all about the team. The wrong team will fumble the perfect idea at the perfect time, but a great team can correct its course, and pivot to find success.

But the odds are never helped by an investor breathing down a founder's neck, dialing up the pressure, and trying to run the company himself, pushing for reports, pushing for data, pushing for an exit. All the data in the world doesn't make a difference, incidentally. I've seen professional investors ask for report after report, looking for answers in the metrics, thinking if they demand enough information, somehow the path forward will become clear. It's all useless, frankly. You're just a backseat driver trying to micromanage the ones at the wheel. All you need to do is ask, "Is this a good team, and do they know where they are going?" If so, then put your earbuds in, fall asleep, and enjoy the ride.

If a team is lost, no amount of data will make you more useful as an investor. If a team is lost, they're done. But if they're not—if they see a way out, if they understand their business—then it doesn't matter if *you* see it, just get out of the way. Be supportive—offer options, not directives—but let them run their company. The number one job of an investor, having experienced the dynamic on both sides, is simply this: give the team room to perform, room to find its own answers, even room to fail, because if they're going to ultimately fail, you as an investor really can't prevent it from happening.

Of course, not every investor agrees, which is why when young entrepreneurs come to me for advice, I tell them that it's so critical to be just as careful about who is giving you money as the investor is going to be about who he or she invests in. If raising money is necessary for you to keep innovating—and if it isn't, then do yourself a favor and don't saddle yourself with money guys, because they're only going to make your life more difficult—you need to make sure your investors are not going to have louder voices than your own, and that they are going to trust you to continue to invent and iterate, to direct the vision of your company.

Our first angels at theglobe.com didn't pretend to have insights about our product. They were valuable sounding boards for questions about legal issues, business development, hiring and retention, but they let me and Todd continue to figure out our business and make the decisions we needed to make. Once our investors got bigger, so did their personal aspirations, and so did their voices—and it was course-altering. They weren't dispassionate about getting a return on their investment, and, for better or worse, they weren't willing to just sit back and trust.

All of this gets magnified so much further when a company goes public, which is why the biggest piece of concrete advice I gave to entrepreneurs then and still give to entrepreneurs now is to only go public as a last resort. I was scarred by our experience, no question. The public markets prioritize short-term results over long-term vision, to such an extent that it inevitably creates tension between your desire to serve your customers and your need to satisfy your investors. Investors, as a general rule, don't care whether you succeed in the long run, don't care about your personal growth and development, and don't really care about your product. They care about return—instant return. Short-term quarterly reports are hugely damaging to the idea of creating long-term value. As CEO of a public company, you quickly lose the ability to make truly bold long-term bets, like the ones that brought you success to begin with, and you end up gradually trading a culture of innovation for one of incremental gain and managing short-term risk, to satisfy the shortest of short-term investors (hello, day traders).

Simply put, public market reporting requirements are deeply broken. Although the SEC is well intentioned in looking to protect small, unsophisticated investors from fraud and from gambling away their life savings, it has massively rewarded short-term gains over long-term growth and prosperity. A rebalancing is desperately needed.

Just as damaging as the investor demands, incidentally, are the motivations of the bankers themselves. Bear Stearns ended up in hot water for all the shenanigans they pulled during our road show, and in the 1,000 percent run-up in the price of our stock followed by the dumping of it by all of Bear Stearns's "long-term holder" institutions. The *Wall Street Journal* spent weeks investigating, and ultimately ran a huge front-page spread about our IPO and how Bear Stearns had sandbagged our stock. Despite knowing there was 15x the expected demand, they deliberately priced us low so that the stock would pop so high that their institutional clients could make a huge return, making Bear Stearns their hero—at our company's expense. Everyone with an opinion estimated that we'd left at least $100 million in cash on the table by so severely underpricing—money we could have desperately used to match our competitors, who were flush with capital when "IPO mania" kicked in.

At first I was naïve and defensive about our IPO, especially when my own dad told me that we'd gotten "screwed" by Bear Stearns. Admitting it would have made me feel like I'd been played for a fool. But all these years later, it was clear that he was right. Their profiteering and unethical behavior—and probably even more that I will never know about—remained one of my most bitter regrets in the whole adventure. Though I did finally find closure in the market collapse of 2008, when Bear Stearns was the first bank to collapse and get sold for scraps to JPMorgan Chase. Poetic justice, perhaps.

As I write these pages, the public versus private dilemma has been playing out in real life with Elon Musk, who has been speaking and writing about needing room to breathe, and even made a failed attempt at taking his company, Tesla, private again. Contrast this with the perspective of venture capitalists like Fred Wilson, who recently published an article arguing that a solid company should be able to satisfy investors as well as act with long-term focus. Wilson, an early-stage private equity investor, makes his returns just as I do as an angel investor, by betting on a team that's trying to do something big, years before an exit event might occur. Of course he wants companies to go public (as do I), as it's the only way to cash out on a massive scale, after years of waiting. But if you look at his portfolio, you'll undoubtedly find that he doesn't hold on to those stocks once they go public for any longer than he has to, so that he can roll those profits back into a new set of innovative companies still at the early stage. The big gains, the big bets, the big breakthroughs happen at the start—great for early investors, but not so great for the person who has to keep running that public company for the long haul, as his stock price drops from his earliest speculators pulling out their investments as soon as they can.

There are a handful of other lessons I share with young founders, built on my experiences—a big one is that the media is never your friend. You can't let what the media has to say about you and your company penetrate your heart and soul. You need the media—and they can do wonders to publicize your company and help you build an initial audience—but you have to work to stay as dispassionate as you can about what they say, and especially to ignore the ego-stroking of positive press. It may sound counterintuitive, but if you pay too much attention, especially to positive press, you can start to believe the hype, and start to depend on what they're saying to determine your self-worth. Once they turn on your company—and, given enough time, they always will—it then becomes impossible to tune it out, to avoid obsessing about what went wrong and how you can fix it, when, truly, it's out of your control. I learned the hard way that it can end up eating away at your soul and at your team. For a long time, we were the "internet whiz kids." And then, suddenly, we were the "internet cautionary tale." It was a hard transition to accept, and I know that if I hadn't bought into the narrative when it was positive, it would have been far easier to ignore it when it turned.

At theglobe.com, we absolutely benefited from a ton of free press when we went public and needed to grow the business as fast as we could—but I think I gave the media too much credit at times. In an ideal world, you don't need the media. Your product should be so good that it speaks for itself and grows through word of mouth. Ultimately, 95 percent of your growth will (and should!) come from your existing customers spreading the word. You shouldn't be dependent on the media and what they say about you. And you definitely shouldn't try to make a "hard sell" to the press about what might end up being an underwhelming product—you're only setting yourself up for personal criticism in that case. In any event, you need to divorce your own self-image from that of your company. You are more than your business. Ignore what they say, don't believe the good or the bad, and focus entirely on building a better product or service.

This is advice I wish I had back when I was begging the press to cover us. I was too willing to be open with the media, too eager—and from a personal standpoint, this took a huge toll. Todd and I became public figures and were judged on everything we did or didn't do. I was candid, reflective, accessible, and honest. I was also twenty-four years old. Quotes were taken out of context, jokes were misinterpreted, and, day to day, I spent far, far, far too much energy concerned about whatever the latest article online or in print was saying about me. I took it all personally, and it became a huge distraction. (I'm reminded of all of this as I watch Elon Musk flailing in the media right now.)

The media is broken. Just like going public favors short-term results over long-term vision, the economics of being a media company in today's world favor short-term noise and clickbait over real insights and balanced articles. You can't win. Even Facebook, which benefited from positive press for years, is now seeing that it can very quickly turn in the other direction. (And if it can happen to Facebook, rest assured, it will happen to you.)

Another big set of lessons I've learned is about leadership and the management of your team. Todd and I were obviously new to management at theglobe.com—we were so young, and knew so little about how to motivate people, how to treat them, how to get them to do their best. In the years—and ventures—since, I've tried to remedy this, not just through experience but through reading the accounts of others. (Key tip: reading is underrated and not enough leaders do it. There is so much wisdom out there that is virtually free for the taking, and to spend some time scouring management books and incorporating relevant lessons into your own life can pay huge dividends.)

The biggest management principle I've adopted as my own in the work I do now is the idea of "radical candor" (a concept coined by Kim Scott, who was an executive at Google and Apple before launching a career as an author and management expert). You have to be honest, you have to be transparent, you have to be okay with upsetting people. I was so in my own head when Todd and I were running theglobe.com—insecure, anxious, reactive—that I didn't have a lot of mental energy left to truly consider how to manage the three hundred employees we had working under us, let alone be candid and transparent with them about all of our fears and worries. We were positive that if they saw how hard things were, they would have all bailed—immediately.

An unintended consequence of our guardedness was that Todd and I were often accused of locking ourselves away in an ivory tower—and it was true. We always shared a corner office; we felt safer being together so we could debate things out loud and emerge with one unified, consistent voice—which we did, and it's something I'm proud of, but the truth is that if you've hired smart, mature talent, they can handle being brought further into the loop. And, if you give them enough context, you never know what they might come up with—especially if you don't try to micromanage them. As Phil Knight, the founder of Nike, writes, "Don't tell people how to do things. Tell them what to do and let them surprise you with the results."

We did so many things wrong along these lines, not trusting our employees as much as we should have, not respecting their ability to handle the truth, overvaluing our own skills as managers of people. I was so judgmental back then—I would think to myself, when someone made a mistake, *What an idiot.* I wouldn't say it—I'd be "ruinously empathetic" (also from Kim Scott's work) to compensate for those ungenerous thoughts running through my head—but it would be there in the background, when the truth was almost surely that they just hadn't been given the right information to do their job correctly, or Todd and I had simply put them in the wrong role. There are awful performers, sure—people who cannot be saved, toxic people, people who will ruin your business if given the chance—but for the most part, people can deliver if they're in the right role, and if someone used to be a rock star and is now flailing, it's far more likely that it's your fault as a manager and not that they've suddenly become incompetent.

I know now how critical it is to be comfortable in my own skin in order to be a good leader, to be able to connect emotionally and build relationships, to be able to give tough but honest and compassionate feedback, to listen, to trust, and to give credit freely and generously. I used to want credit for everything—I used to want everyone to know every good thing I did. (Especially those positive media mentions—I really was so hooked on those.) Maybe it's because I didn't get enough praise from my dad growing up. But now I realize you serve your business—and your life—a heck of a lot better if you give credit far more than you seek to receive it. If someone helped you make a good decision, if something someone said or did inspired you along the way, made your path easier, contributed even in a tiny way—tell them, recognize them, praise them. It yields so much in the way of loyalty, positive energy, and, ultimately, results.

Next: in building your team, you need to understand your own strengths and weaknesses. One of my biggest mentors (and one of my dad's best friends), Stephen Pond, my go-to for all financial matters in my life (and an investor in everything I've pursued), has taught me about the magical combination of instincts and structure. "Steph, you have great instincts," he has told me. "Good instincts are vital. But they will only get you 80 percent of the way there. And in a competitive market, 80 percent isn't enough. However—if you combine your instincts with structure, you'll get a multiplier effect, which can take you all the way."

What he meant by structure is putting some organization behind how you think, how you approach a challenge, and how you execute. I have always been all instinct—and at theglobe.com, Todd was the structure for me, he brought the discipline, the perspective, the systematic thinking. For me, structure has always been more of a struggle.

When I became CEO at Slated, I wrote a leadership document codifying these management principles I'm explaining here—because I didn't want them to just be in my head, I wanted them to be on paper; I wanted to force myself to create some structure around my thinking. Heck, writing this book initially wasn't just about the cathartic release and letting everyone know about this adventure in my life—it was also about locking down the experience, trying to find a way to turn what happened into a product that I could use to build from—to help me become, in the future, something closer to the CEO I was trying to be. Because I knew I wasn't doing it right back then—I knew I had so much to learn, but in the heat of the moment, I just didn't have the time to learn it.

Now I know better. You have to acknowledge frustration. Help people work past their struggles. Find fault in the output, not in the person. "Your work sucks" is far better than "You suck," but of course far better than either option is "Your work is usually extraordinary, but this time it isn't—so let's figure out what went wrong, and whether I may have set you on the wrong path." Now I try to end tough feedback sessions by explicitly stating that, regardless of what just happened, "I'm proud to be working with you." It seems like a small thing, but it helps. As the one with power, everything you say can feel like a sledgehammer—you have to understand that, and you have to remind people that you don't hate them, even if you're disappointed in their work.

During crises, I now understand that you have to stay centered, stay in control emotionally. Which, of course, is a lot easier to do when you have a solid team around you that trusts you and that you know you can depend on. You have to tell someone when his fly is down, when there's something in between her teeth. You tell these small truths and you establish credibility for the big ones.

It shocks me now when I look back and realize how much I didn't know—but, even so, fortunately, we never had an employee churn problem at theglobe.com. We did lots of things wrong, but I'm proud that I was able to keep our employees inspired about the company's mission, to keep my negative energy largely in my own head, and to keep people excited about working for us. I don't know how I quite managed to retain their loyalty back then, but now, I'm very deliberate about it. If I'm hard on an employee, I know it, and I come back a day later and say I'm sorry—not necessarily for the content of the criticism, but certainly for the tone. Increasingly with age, I've become self-deprecating to a fault, honest, and more and more quick to apologize. A boss admitting mistakes helps humanize him or her—and build trust, credibility, and mutual respect. Rarely admitting mistakes underscores an insecurity and fear of being wrong—it will only erode people's trust in your self-awareness and leadership. Low employee churn is a sign you're doing something right.

Finally, I tell people that continuous innovation is critical. theglobe.com eventually had to die for the same reason Myspace had to die, and Friendster, and AOL, and, if they rest for even a moment and think they've won the game, I'm confident Facebook will go down that same path as well. Once you are no longer able to see one step—two steps, three steps, ten steps—into the future and know what you have to build next, you inevitably will end up having to pass the baton to the next generation of inventors. (And this mental fog—this inability to envision the right next moves—becomes far more likely once you go public and have so many short-term concerns crowding your plate.)

No technology, no product, no paradigm will dominate the market forever. Back in 1999, people couldn't imagine a search engine more powerful than Yahoo! Or a mobile phone company more cutting-edge than Nokia. Even now, it's hard to imagine the next iteration of technologies and companies that are so enmeshed in our lives. What does a post-Google world even look like? And what about industries that have not yet been fully transformed by technology? Medicine, education, the business of financing television and movies?

I mention that last one not by accident, not at all, since it's the business I'm now doing my best to reinvent at Slated. I've always been in awe of stories in film and on television. I often saw the world through a cinematic lens growing up. Movie plots, scenes, characters, and quotes all wormed their way into my life. Watching good movies was always gripping for me, especially imagining myself as a character in each adventure. For a kid growing up without a solid foundation—divorce, moves back and forth around the globe—the movies represented common ground for me and my peers, a language that even strangers could understand. And yet from a creation perspective, film always seemed to me like a parallel universe that regular people could never cross into. I was always a technology nerd, and, sure, some people can see glamour in computers and gadgets, but it's nothing like the incredible stories, fictional or real, that less than 1 percent of the population gets to create and shape for the rest of us to just go and watch. We're consumers, but we never get to actually be a part of the invention, part of the story.

At theglobe.com, for all the mixed feelings I had about our media coverage, every time I was interviewed, I got a taste of what it was like to be on television. I discovered that I knew how to tell stories, and that I liked telling them. It's the same skill set that got me to convince investors to write a check or push employees to come work for us. The need to tell our story, to develop it, to refine it, to perform it for an audience—it was one of the things I missed most after leaving theglobe.com, and it's something I didn't expect to miss. (One thing I didn't miss was the constant refreshing of our stock price.)

After I left, I got this itch I needed to scratch, to become an actor. I was naïve, but I had this romantic fantasy—I imagined being an actor to be the polar opposite of running a company with hundreds of employees. As an actor, you're a one-man show, or at least that's how I pictured it—with responsibility just for you and your own performance, the power to turn yourself into an asset that investors couldn't destroy, no matter how much they tried.

I tried to learn the craft, took lots of classes and fumbled in the dark for a while, trying to understand how it all worked. (As a side note, I would highly recommend everyone try an acting class at least once. You will learn so much about yourself, from a different perspective than you're used to in your normal life, that it can blow your mind. I went to the Baron Brown Studio in Santa Monica, initially dipping my toe in with a six-week program, and got hooked, committing to two years of Meisner training. The insights I gained were life-altering, particularly when it came to matters of leadership.)

Alas, even though I loved acting, living the life of an actor—going from audition to audition with a complete lack of control over the opportunities you are given, let alone the stories you get to tell—required a patience, and indifference, that I did not possess. You can romanticize being an actor from the outside, but once you're on the inside, you very clearly see the downside.

So I took my interest and passion in a slightly different direction, and started to produce some short films. I learned a heck of a lot about the filmmaking process, but also discovered there's no real commercial market for scripted shorts, no chance to get them out to a wide audience, no matter how amazing the story, and certainly no financial model that could prove sustainable. Luckily, the last short I was involved in was coproduced by Kevin Frakes, a highly ambitious recent MBA graduate from Yale. Just as I was looking for a better direction to take my nascent filmmaking career, Kevin just so happened to have a compelling business plan he had put together, picking apart film industry economics and laying out an approach to building a better production company. Together, we cofounded a production company we called PalmStar. Kevin was ready to go straight to Los Angeles to be in the middle of the industry. I was not . . . so we set up a back office in New York with a small development team, and made Kevin's condo in Los Angeles our headquarters.

Kevin and I were both drawn to true stories—the deep dives into lives almost too complex and exciting to believe. We decided to predominantly focus on optioning biographies and other nonfiction material we thought could thrive on the big screen. We quickly figured out that talent (and money) chases after the highest-profile material, so we optioned the best content we could afford, including *Down and Dirty Pictures,* written by Peter Biskind, the story of the rise of Miramax and the independent film movement (and the notorious Harvey Weinstein!), *Lunar Park*, a mock memoir by writer Bret Easton Ellis (the author of *American Psycho*), *Ian Fleming*, the definitive biography of the man who created James Bond, and a dozen others, as we tried to navigate the independent film world from scratch.

PalmStar became my own personal film school, as I split my time and attention between the movie world and my tech company investments through Actarus. I had office space with a glass divider splitting the two sides—on one side were the tech ventures I'd backed, and on the other side we'd be casting a movie, fifty hipsters coming in for a part one day, fifty grandmas the next. The tech companies thought it was neat—and for me, I loved it, watching movies get made from the inside, giving script notes, learning the ropes of the indie film business. Over the years we amassed over twenty properties in various stages of development, but time and time again we found ourselves hitting walls, always lacking that critical bankable actor or director—or we'd have all the talent committed only to see production financing fall through at the last minute. There was always one piece that would fall out and cause everything to stall or collapse. Momentum would build slowly, then fizzle fast, on each project, over and over again. In any given year we had no idea which horse was going to win the race.

We soon learned that our experience was typical of the industry. Even with material that talent and financing was chasing after, unless you were one of the six major studios, it was incredibly slow, inefficient, opaque. Gatekeepers blocked every turn. Overly complex financial engineering was needed to close deals, using complex legal structures and investor terms, always favoring the big distributors at the expense of early equity investors who took the biggest risks. "Hollywood accounting" resulted in litigation with almost every film. Some of the smartest, most well-connected people in the industry often reminded me that getting any movie made was always "a miracle," let alone making a profit on that movie.

A "miracle"? That was not a term I had often heard fellow tech entrepreneurs use with successful start-ups, and it always struck me as odd. Film and television is a $300-plus billion-dollar market, growing year after year, with huge demand for more and more content, all around the world, and yet the process of finding material, organizing teams around it, financing, and getting distribution hadn't evolved in a century. It wasn't long before I realized that the film industry as a whole was a massive, and completely inefficient, fragmented mess.

At PalmStar, we did eventually get a handful of small budget features made, including one documentary I felt particularly proud of: *Life 2.0*, featuring stories of real people living through their avatars in a three-dimensional virtual community called Second Life. The movie premiered in competition at Sundance in 2010, and was bought and distributed by Oprah Winfrey's cable network, OWN. We even made a small but respectable profit.

And yet, despite some small victories, it became clearer and clearer after six years that we hadn't cracked the code. There had to be a better approach to filmmaking—something that could accelerate the process of sourcing good material, packaging it with talent, financing it, getting distribution, allowing filmmakers to make a living and investors to make a return, with profits reinvested into the industry, adding up to a growing, profitable, and sustainable asset class. More and more, I found myself thinking about inventing a new business structure more than finding the next great film project. It was the internet entrepreneur in me coming back to life.

While still working on PalmStar, I kept an eye out for every new internet business model that was coming along, and thought about whether there might be an application to the film industry. Through Actarus, I had begun focusing my investments into a group of start-ups that were successfully reinventing online financing. I had the good fortune of being a founding or early investor in companies like LendingClub, a peer-to-peer lending platform, then Indiegogo, one of the first crowdfunding sites, then SecondMarket, the online secondary market allowing insiders from pre-IPO companies (like Facebook and Twitter at the time) to sell stock before going public, and, finally, AngelList, which made early-stage equity investing in tech start-ups open to just about everyone. Each of these companies helped crystallize how I imagined an online marketplace for the film industry might work.

The next challenge was finding a team that shared my vision. Still feeling burned by my experience at theglobe.com, my biggest fear was that I wouldn't find the right team—and then have to grapple with the temptation to build it myself. (I still could not get my head around the idea of being in the driver's seat again, and fought the urge for a long time. It was so comfortable to write checks for others, to stay safely on the side of being an investor, to just worry about returns . . .) Fortunately, at the end of 2009, I was serendipitously introduced to a bright and ambitious entrepreneur named Duncan Cork, who had a vision for the film industry that overlapped incredibly closely with mine.

With PalmStar's future in Kevin's capable hands, I felt ready to move on, and cofounded Slated with Duncan, along with two other partners. This time, as opposed to when I started with PalmStar, I was finally ready to move to Los Angeles and leverage the industry network I'd built up over the years. Duncan, ironically, was freshly excited to be in New York City and wanted to build the company there. As he was the CEO, and I was only a cofounding investor, taking on a chairman/mentor role, I deferred to him.

(As far as PalmStar, over the past eight years, Kevin has grown the company significantly, successfully producing several dozen more movies, including *Hereditary*, *John Wick*, *Split*, *Collateral Beauty*, and *Sing Street*. I'm so proud to have cofounded PalmStar with him, and witness what he's built—and I look forward to watching his success, and seeing my stake continue to grow in value, for many more years.)

At Slated we set out to reinvent how films could be financed—and it wasn't an immediate success. It took a number of years of different iterations, figuring out what the platform should be, how it should work, where the biggest pain points were for producers, directors, writers, and actors—and coming up with ways to address and solve them. Effectively, we wanted to take a traditional, offline, bespoke, gatekeeper-centric, word-of-mouth business and optimize it using whatever online tools we could.

Duncan successfully started our journey and launched the brand. Eventually, it became increasingly clear that we needed more experience to take it to the next level. At the beginning of 2014, he handed me the reins. After thirteen years of staying safely on the sidelines as an investor, much to my surprise, the posttraumatic stress I had experienced being CEO of theglobe.com had vanished. I was surprised how much my old wounds had healed, and I found myself ready, and hungry, to lead again. Personally and professionally, it has been a far different experience from the first time.

From a product point of view, we realized over time that it wasn't just about creating a Kickstarter for movies and matching investors to projects. It was also about helping filmmakers make their projects better—identifying strengths and weaknesses, improving the script, and ultimately increasing not just the odds of finding investors and talent but of actually getting the movie made and finding true success.

To that end, we developed and introduced analytics and machine learning to the front end of our marketplace, allowing filmmakers and investors to get objective, unbiased, relevant insights into their projects. Our projections, made before release and tested on seventy movies that came out over a two-year period, correctly predicted 8 of 9 hits and 41 of 46 misses. Slated's analytics aren't a crystal ball, but we have provided a massive wake-up call regarding the predictive power of data as applied to what many see as an idiosyncratic, statistics-immune industry.

From there, we provide a roadmap for how to move forward, attempting to match projects with their needs as far as talent, financing, and distribution—more rapidly and effectively than under the traditional model. We've had successes, but we're still figuring it out. The biggest challenge by far up to this point has been that the film industry incumbents—the (relatively few) people succeeding in the current model—are comfortable with how things have always worked, and resistant to this type of disruptive change. Working to our benefit is that there are far more people struggling in the current model than succeeding—even top talent, award-winning writers and directors, and producers working to package absolutely extraordinary pieces of material that deserve to find their way to the big screen.

From a personal point of view, Slated has been such a rewarding experience for me because it has combined my passions—it's the principles of social networking, but applied to a transactional marketplace for the film industry, a platform that can truly transform a business, positively impact the lives of actors, writers, directors, producers . . . the whole industry, and leave a lasting legacy.

But unlike before, two decades later, I now have greater perspective. theglobe.com was such a single-minded pursuit. My attitude, my mood, my self-worth rose and fell with the stock price. I had literally nothing else in my life, no other dreams, no other thoughts, nothing else mattered. I did not have the strength to pick myself up when things were bad, to find a way to get re-centered.

Beyond perspective, I also know now that it isn't just about instinct, and I've implemented the kind of structure Stephen Pond encouraged so many years ago. My road to Slated has been a slow, step-by-step approach, starting with small educational experiences structured around the making of short films, evolving to bigger, more commercial film manufacturing structures like PalmStar, and, finally, the ambitious industry-altering structure I'm developing with Slated. I'm driven by a set of management principles, and I've also learned that I need to surround myself with the right people, who can bring structure to my life. With theglobe.com, it was Todd. And now, with Slated, there's my new team, but in even larger part, it's my family.

In 2013, I met my wife, Anna, and in February of 2017, our daughter, Nova Yves Paternot, was born—her first name like the PBS science show about the future and space travel (we're nerdy parents, what can I say), and her middle name after my father, who after a long struggle with pancreatic cancer, giving us far more years than we anticipated when he was first diagnosed, passed away in early 2016. Anna is a fellow entrepreneur, with a cinema therapy start-up also at the nexus of film and technology. Much like the partnership I had with Todd Krizelman, Anna is my rock. When I'm down, she props me back up. When either of us needs advice, we brainstorm together on a whiteboard. That type of partnership, at a family level, is game-changing for me, and brings a sense of security I've never felt before.

Having a family has brought so much more richness and fulfillment to my life, as well as greater stability and mental clarity, resulting in more focus and structure to help make Slated a greater success. I am so much more than my company, and while I absolutely want to achieve success once again on the same level as theglobe.com, I am at peace with the journey. This inner peace has made me more balanced, focused, and centered—and makes me a better leader at Slated. None of this was part of a "grand plan," but, without a doubt, looking back twenty years, I can see that my family has become my greatest multiplier effect yet.

I used to be defined completely by my work, but now I know, if Slated fails, I'll still have my family, and that's so much more important. I can bounce back from the inevitable valleys, because I know that I'll be okay—I know I have people in my life who I care about, and who care about me. I am hungry for the billion-dollar business that can transform the entertainment industry, but not at the price of my sanity, and not if it has to have the same volatility as theglobe.com. Slated hasn't been a rocket ship, and doesn't need to be. It has a far stronger foundation—and so do I.

The whole journey has made me realize what I love most—reinventing things from behind my keyboard, and then going out into the world and evangelizing for them. With Slated, I get to scratch the storytelling itch, the actor itch, I get to do something with a potentially massive scale, connect with customers, impact an industry. Over half of all nominated Academy Award films, and over half of what appeared at the Sundance Film Festival over the last few years, have been either produced, directed, or written by Slated members, and I'm incredibly proud of that, incredibly—and I'm confident that the best is yet to come.

I'll put it on paper—Slated is the last company I plan to build from the ground up. If I've learned anything from theglobe.com and now this, it's that we only have a small number of legacy projects in our lives, a couple of times we can truly find a venture that makes the sacrifices worthwhile. I'm prepared to run Slated for the next twenty years—but I can confidently say that the only other big project I plan to take on is helping my growing family achieve their dreams.

Now that I am a father, I feel a need to be a better leader, to actively codify into my company culture the very same value system I want to share with my growing family—the same values I want my daughter to live by and to experience in her own journey as a future leader.

Each time I reread this book, I'm struck once again by what a crazy journey I've had, and what an unexpected set of circumstances led me to be, for a short time, worth such an astonishing amount of money, at least on paper. It has taken me a long time to be at peace with what ultimately happened, and to look exclusively forward instead of sometimes, with more than a tinge of regret, looking back.

Todd has been on his own journey since we left theglobe.com. He went to Harvard Business School in 2001 for an MBA, where, ironically, they were teaching case studies about how our company broke, and how to fix it. Todd happened to be there at the very same time that Mark Zuckerberg started at Harvard as a freshman in the fall of 2002. I'm not sure how much (if at all) our story influenced Mark, but right as Todd was finishing up his MBA in the spring of 2003, Zuckerberg was getting ready to launch Facebook in February 2004, before dropping out of Harvard that spring. To us, it felt like the passing of the baton from one generation of tech entrepreneurs to the next. And, a few years later, it felt like a complete vindication of our initial ideas—virtual community was here to stay.

After getting his MBA, Todd went to work for Bertelsmann, the multibillion-dollar publishing powerhouse, where he learned everything there was to know about the magazine publishing and ad sales business—and how they had virtually no analytics to help them make better business decisions. Todd left at the end of 2006 to found MediaRadar, a cutting-edge analytics platform for the media world, now the leading player in that market. MediaRadar, incidentally, was also one of the first ventures I invested in through Actarus Funds, earning me one of my bigger returns to date.

As for me, after fourteen years in New York City, witnessing the boom and bust and rise again of the internet, and making safe bets from the sidelines, I was ready to embark on a new mission, in a new city, in a new industry, with a massive new opportunity. A new vision, powered by two decades of perspective, making me ready to lead again.

At this very moment, Slated reminds me in so many ways of the early days of theglobe.com, at the dawn of a new era, nearing an inflection point and sudden explosion of awareness, growth, and change. As always, who knows how this will all play out. Only time will tell. Until I write again . . .

Our first employees . . . pizza anyone?

Our first office, with plenty of leg room.

Our death trap server room in NYC.

Traveling in style! From left to right: Frank Joyce (CFO), me, Mike Egan, and Todd during the IPO road show. Fall 1998.

Morning of the IPO . . . Ace Greenberg does his trademark card tricks in a futile attempt to relax us.

"$97!?" The pit at Bear Stearns where it all happened.

Todd, me, Mike, Ace, and Ed Cespedes.

At the NASDAQ headquarters, Friday the 13th of November 1998.

The Metro Section

FRIDAY, SEPTEMBER 19, 1997

The New York Times

'Wow': Infusion of Money for 2 Internet 'Kids' With Chat Room

Computer Chat Room Began as Idea For 2 Students in Their Cornell Days

By DAVID W. CHEN

Stephan Paternot, left, and Todd Krizelman, shown at a conference in Texas in 1995, joined forces to start an Internet business known as Web Genesis. They were Cornell students when they came up with the idea.

On the front page of the *New York Times* Metro section after Mike Egan's $20 million investment in 1997.

Industry Standard cover . . . three months of interviews for a teen heartthrob story.

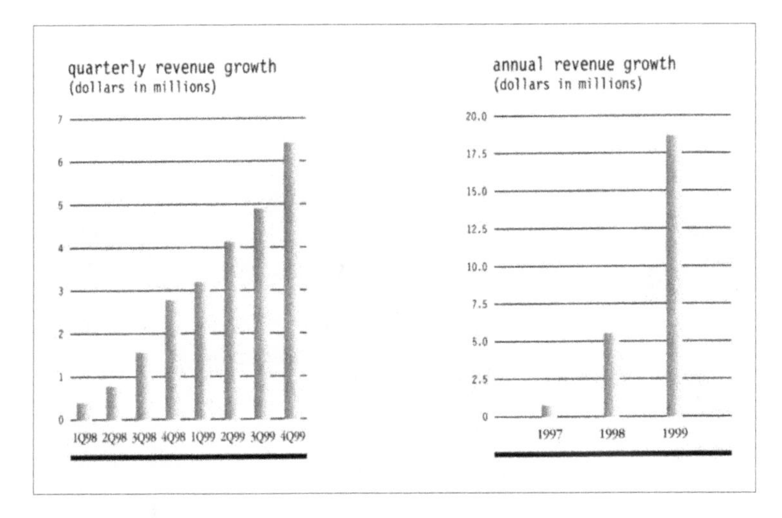

Our revenue performance as a public company: rapid and steady growth, despite stock price volatility and decline. We were proud to step down on the heels of our best quarter ever.

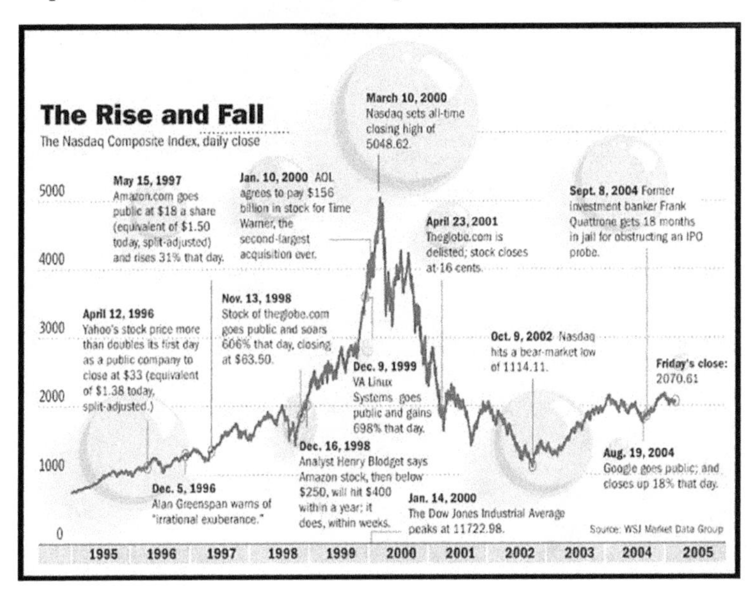

The Internet 1.0 Bubble. Courtesy of the *Wall Street Journal.*

Twenty-five years—plus a couple of business adventures, marriage, kids, and a few more gray hairs—since Todd and I first met at Cornell.

INDEX

D

E

F

L

M

N

O

P

R

S

T

U

V

W

X

Y

ABOUT THE AUTHOR

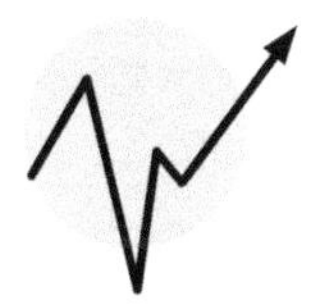

Stephan Paternot is co-founder and CEO of Slated, the world's first online film finance marketplace, where over 1,200 films have received over $1.25 billion in investor introductions as of 2018. Stephan is also co-founder of PalmStar, a film production and financing company that has helped bring to life over 30 films including *Hereditary* (2018), *Collateral Beauty* (2016), *Sing Street* (2016) and *John Wick* (2014). In addition, Stephan is the founder and general partner of the Actarus Funds, which have backed companies including LendingClub, SecondMarket, Indiegogo, AngelList, Digital Currency Group, and more.

Prior to these ventures, Stephan co-founded theglobe.com, one of the first Internet community sites, and the subject of this book. Stephan is a graduate of Cornell University, where he earned a Bachelor's degree in Computer Science, and now lives with his wife and daughter in Los Angeles.

CPSIA information can be obtained
at www.ICGtesting.com
Printed in the USA
BVHW030324061118
532237BV00001B/15/P

Latasha

and the *KIDD ON KEYS*

A novel by Michael Scotto

Illustrations by Evette Gabriel

Midlandia Press
Beaver, Pennsylvania

This book is a work of fiction. Any references to historical events, real people, or real locales are used fictitiously. Other names, characters, places, and incidents are the product of the author's imagination, and any resemblance to actual events or locales or persons, living or dead, is entirely coincidental.

Midlandia Press
An imprint of NNDS Corporation
1000 Third Street
Beaver, PA 15009

Visit us on the web at http://www.midlandiapress.com.

Edited by Ashley Mortimer
Typography by Kent Kerr

ISBN-13: 978-0-9837243-9-1 (ISBN-10: 0983724393)

Library of Congress Control Number: 2012948512

2 4 6 8 10 9 7 5 3 1

Printed in the USA.

As always, for J & L, my family

Table of Contents

Prologue

It's always been a mystery how I wound up with Ella.

I know where Momma and I found her—that's no mystery at all. We'd plucked my dog from a roomful of yipping strays at the Lucky Paws animal shelter two summers back. I also know how Ella came to Lucky Paws. A dog catcher for the city had discovered her on the streets. To be more specific—and if I want to be a good writer, I've learned, I should always be specific—they'd found her in a parking lot out behind a Dairy Queen on the South Side of Pittsburgh. The store manager had caught her trying to steal leftover Blizzards from the garbage. Ella didn't have a collar or any tags, so he reported her to Animal Control.

Momma and I learned about that episode from the file folder that came with Ella, which is kind of like the permanent record you get in school. It also had her vaccination papers, her weight (nineteen pounds then, fifty-four pounds now), and her fur color—as if you could possibly miss the short red hairs she leaves on every surface she touches.

But everything that came before the Dairy Queen is a blank. The shelter didn't know how long Ella had been on the streets, just that it had been a long time. They could only guess her birth month—April, they picked. They didn't even bother guessing what breed Ella is. The shelter put down "mix," which might as well have been "?" I understand why the folks at

Lucky Paws did that, though. Each part of Ella looks like it came from a different kind of dog.

But here is the biggest mystery of all. I just don't get who could have abandoned Ella in the first place. I can't understand how someone once looked at this mixed-up little cutie and thought, *I don't want her.*

I wanted Ella the moment I met her. I remember every detail about that day. It was Saturday, June thirteenth, and I had just graduated from first grade the day before. At my school, Cedarville Elementary, that's the year students start to get letter grades on their report cards, and I'm proud to report that I had received all "A"s!

"Put on your sneakers, my straight-A star," Momma told me that morning.

"Where are we going?" I asked. *Not far*, I remember hoping. It wasn't too hot yet, but it was very sticky—the kind of day where it seems like the weather can't decide if it's spring or summer and your hair shoots off your head like broken bedsprings. The only traveling I wanted to do was through my new stack of library books, next to the living room fan.

But when Momma answered, I forgot all about Chewandswallow and Klickitat Street. I must have forgotten how to close my mouth, too, because Momma laughed and said, "Pick your jaw up off the floor, silly. Let's go before the day really heats up."

I knew Momma had always had dogs growing up. But for most of the walk over, I simply refused to believe that we were actually going to adopt one.

"Can we really afford a puppy?" I asked. We didn't have a lot of money then. We still don't, really, but back then, when Momma was a hotel cleaning lady instead of a nursing aide, we had even less.

Momma glanced down at me with a grin. "That's a Momma problem," she said, "not a Latasha problem." That was her way of telling me, *I've got it covered.*

"And Mrs. O really said it was okay," I said skeptically. Mrs. Okocho is our landlady, an old Nigerian woman who lives on the first floor of our house.

Momma gave me a believe-it-or-not nod.

"But where will it go to the bathroom?" I asked. We only had a tiny square of grass behind the house. And as for the front yard...I couldn't imagine that a serious gardener like Mrs. Okocho would let a dog make number two on the same *block* as her flowerbeds.

"There's an old saying," Momma replied evenly. "'Never look a gift horse in the mouth.'"

I had no idea what gift horses had to do with dogs, but Momma's tone convinced me to hold my tongue the rest of the walk over.

When we came into Lucky Paws, the girl at the front desk led us back to see the holding area. That was where all of the dogs lived.

The holding area was lined with grated pens on either side. I held Momma's hand as I looked at each dog. Some were panting, tongues out like pink streamers. Others were barking. Others were pawing at their cage doors. I felt like Goldilocks from that fairy tale. None of the dogs seemed just right.

But then I spotted her. In a pen near the back of the room, I saw a bony red puppy lying on a folded-up Pittsburgh Pirates beach towel. "Poor thing ate her bed," the handler explained.

That ratty towel with the nibbled-on hemline was all she had; no toys, no nametag—even her tail looked as if she'd borrowed it from some other, much larger, dog. Something about her wide, quivery brown eyes made me want to pet her and tell her everything was okay. I asked the handler to open her gate.

The moment the handler unfastened the latch, the sickly puppy sprang with a sudden burst of life. She shot out of the pen, paws clicking, tail whipping against her sides, and she leapt chest-high a foot in front of me. Momma gasped and stepped back, but I reached out and caught the puppy in my arms. I felt her ribs against my forearms, her heart pounding. And when she licked my nose, I knew inside that she was mine and I was hers.

I named her right then, after a jazz singer Momma liked to play for me. I whispered her name like a prayer into the fur on her neck: three words…

Chapter One

Gifted

"Ella Fitzgerald Gandy," I warned, pointing my pencil at her.

I was sitting at the kitchen table in our house on Graham Street. A drawing of half a dog waited in front of me, aching to be finished—if only a certain little red beast would sit still for it!

At the moment, though, Ella had no interest in posing. She was intent on eating her own tail. She kept hopping up with her forepaws and twirling her bendy body on her rear leg, like a pinwheel in a wind storm.

"Please sit," I instructed. I hoped that I sounded firm and in charge, and not nervous like I really was. Ricky Jenkins's birthday party was less than three hours away, and this gift of his wasn't even finished, let alone wrapped and ribboned.

You might think, since I was making Ricky's present on the day of his party, that I hadn't put a lot of thought into it. But you'd be so wrong that it's not even funny. I'd been thinking about Ricky's present for a whole month, ever since we had finished third grade. I'd figured that it would be easy to pick the perfect gift. After all, Ricky isn't just some boy who lives across the street from me. He's my best friend—my best *human* friend, that is. But Ricky turned out to be very difficult to shop for.

Part of the trouble was that Ricky is a boy. Who knows what silly things a boy is going to like from one week to the next? A boy's brain is like one of those Magic 8 Balls. He'll think one thing's his favorite thing in the world, but if you give him one good shake, he'll completely change his mind.

On top of the whole boy issue, Ricky wasn't having just any birthday. He was turning ten. You'd never guess it by his height or his goofball sense of humor, but Ricky is a full six months older than me. He's actually the oldest kid in our grade. That's because he did kindergarten twice—"because I loooooved nap time!" he says.

But the hardest part wasn't that Ricky is a boy or that he was turning ten. The real problem was that best friends have to get each other the best presents. It's basically a rule. But every time I thought up an awesome present for Ricky, he either already had it or Momma and I couldn't afford it. Or both, like when I thought of getting him a signed jersey of his favorite Pittsburgh Steeler, Casey Hampton.

After a lot of thinking, I realized that I did have one thing that Ricky didn't: Ella. Ricky loves Ella almost as much as I do. He thinks it's awesome that she's a mutt and that she only has three legs and is a tripod dog. He even invited Ella to his party today. She got her own invitation and everything—which, of course, she ate.

I knew that Ricky's dream was to have a dog of his own, but I wasn't about to give Ella to him for his birthday. So I did the next best thing: I wrote about all the fun times he's had with her. To be extra creative, I pretended that I was Ella and wrote it from her point of view. I called it *Wild Days with Ricky*.

Which I would've gladly written down, if I could ever finish this drawing! "You are ruining your portrait," I scolded as Ella spun.

"Portrait?" asked Momma from the doorway. She was fastening her pink nametag to her scrubs. Momma usually didn't work on Saturdays, but she liked to pick up an extra shift at Children's Hospital whenever she could. "I thought you wrote Ricky a story."

"I wrote him a book," I corrected. "This is the cover. You can't have a book without a cover."

Momma slipped past my whirling pup and

fetched some cold cuts from the fridge. "I don't know where it comes from," she said. "So gifted…"

I smiled as I waited for the rest of the sentence. "And talented," Momma added as she fixed herself a sandwich for her lunch break.

All this summer, Momma had been going out of her way to call me "gifted and talented." She'd started it at the end of school. That was when Mr. Harvey—my third-grade teacher and the coolest grown-up in all of Cedarville Elementary—invited me to join our school's Gifted and Talented Club. Its nickname is the Talent Pool, and Mr. Harvey runs it. The club is all fourth and fifth graders, and it meets in his classroom once a week after school.

When Momma had started her whole "gifted and talented" kick, I'd thought it would get old fast—but it hadn't yet. What *had* worn out its welcome, though, was Ella's bad behavior. She'd abandoned her tail-chasing and was now wiggling in front of my shins, begging me to play.

"Sit," I told her again. I just knew that I should have drawn this picture while Ella was asleep. My girl is the cutest sleeper. She kicks her back paw off to the side and stretches her forepaws ahead, crossing them like a dainty little lady.

When Ella's awake, she is anything but dainty.

As I tried to sketch her floppy beagle ears, she was butting her sinewy shoulder into my calf so that I might stand up. *Sinewy* is this nifty word I found in my pocket dictionary. It means muscular, but not like a weightlifter—more like a sprinter. I love finding just the right word. Momma might say it is both a *gift* and a *talent* of mine.

"No play," I told Ella, rooting my foot to the kitchen floor. I usually loved our playtimes together, but I could almost hear the stove's clock ticking toward party time.

Momma zipped her roast beef sandwich in a plastic baggie. "You try her usual bribe?" she asked.

Momma meant Teddy Snacks, which are a tasty, bear-shaped cracker that Ella will basically do anything to get. I shot Momma a grumbly look that I hoped said, *Of course, that was the first thing I tried!*

She shrugged her eyebrows. "Just trying to help," she said, and she turned to pack her lunch into a brown paper bag.

"It almost worked," I said, feeling guilty for my attitude. "I just couldn't hold the treat up, hold the paper in place, and draw all at the same time. I need three arms."

"Or an assistant," Momma suggested.

I pushed my pencil aside. "You have time?"

Ella, who'd been whipping back and forth to watch us talk, turned to pant in Momma's direction.

"Not me," Momma replied.

I frowned. She meant Mrs. Okocho downstairs. "No way," I said. "Not today."

It's not that I don't like Mrs. Okocho. I actually like her a lot. She's more than our landlady. She's like the grandmother I never had—even if she does get cranky about Ella sometimes. But today was supposed to be a special day. Today, Momma's work started at eleven, Ricky's party started at one—and for the two hours in between, for the first time ever, Momma was letting me stay in the apartment by myself! I'd been fighting for that privilege for a year, and I wasn't about to ruin it by inviting Mrs. Okocho up.

Momma pointed two fingers at Ella and me. "You make a heck of a pair," she said. "Stubborn One and Stubborn Two. C'mere."

I set down my pencil and went over to Momma. She smoothed a curl of hair back on my head. She had that *Aw, my little baby* look in her eyes, and I worried that she would change her mind and send me downstairs to be babysat. But then she asked me, "What are the rules?"

I smiled in relief. I'd practiced this test in my head

dozens of times. “No answering the door,” I began. “No using the stove. No phone calls.”

“And tell Mrs. O when you leave for the party,” Momma said.

“I will,” I promised. I noticed that the room had gone quiet. That was rarely a good sign with Ella.

“And go straight to Ricky’s and then straight home,” Momma added.

“Straight across the street and straight home,” I agreed. I looked back and spotted my pup sitting near the table. Now that I’d stopped trying to draw her, she was perfectly still, right down to her tail. It just figured.

“Go ahead,” said Momma, slinging her bag over her shoulder. “Finish your present.”

I gave Momma an extra big hug. “Be good!” I told her.

“Hey!” she said in mock surprise. “That’s my line.”

Momma kissed me quickly on the crown of my head, opened the door, and left for work.

I waited a few seconds, listening as the hall stairs creaked with Momma’s footsteps. I heard her knock on Mrs. Okocho’s door and let her know that I was upstairs. Finally, the front door downstairs opened, then shut.

I couldn’t hold it in any more. I pumped my

fists and wiggled my hips. I didn't care how silly I looked—I had the apartment to myself!

"*Home, home on the range*," I sang, spinning around on the ball of my foot. "*Where a girl and her little dog—*"

As soon as I faced Ella, she popped up and tore out of the kitchen. My arms dropped to my sides. "Aw, girl!" I moaned. I followed her into the living room just in time to see her leap onto the couch, spin around, and dash toward my bedroom.

"No zoomies!" I pleaded as I heard the books on my bedside table crash to the floor.

Ella bounded back into the living room. "Careful!" I winced as she banged her left hip into our little coffee table. I always felt nervous and a bit guilty when Ella ran her scar into things.

It didn't faze her, though. Ella leapt again and bashed into the couch like she was at football practice. The couch slid half a foot toward me. I leaned over it and wrapped my arms around the wriggling beast. "We have to finish this present, or else…" I struggled to keep my grip as I thought up a threat. Only one thing came to mind: *Or else we'll both be terrible friends.*

In the kitchen, the phone rang. I looked away from Ella and she wriggled free.

The phone rang again. I knew that I wasn't supposed to answer it—but I really wanted to know who was calling. It rang a third time. Was it a telemarketer? Or was it something important? Maybe it was Momma with an emergency.

As Ella wreaked more havoc in my bedroom, I went for the phone. I took a deep breath and answered.

"Gandy residence," I said with a smile.

"You are not supposed to answer," said an accented voice. It was Mrs. Okocho.

"Then why did you call at all?" I demanded. I hate being set up.

Mrs. Okocho paused. "Your mama says you are making a portrait," she finally said. "But it sounds like you are making a war zone."

My skin tingled as I imagined what Ella's rampage sounded like downstairs. "Sorry," was all I could say.

"I will come and help," Mrs. Okocho said.

I heard Ella dash back into the living room, growling like a car engine. I'd really wanted to handle this myself, but there was no time to be prideful. "Thank you," I replied.

"Then it is settled!" our landlady declared. "I will bring for us a moofin to eat."

"A moofin?" I asked with dread. Was that one of

those smelly Nigerian stews she was always cooking?

"Yes! I went this morning to the bakery, for something to have with my coffee," she said. "This blueberry moofin is bigger than my foot!"

"Oh, a *muffin*," I said. Mrs. Okocho's accent made certain words sound so unusual. I loved that about her.

"See you in a flash," she said. We hung up the phone, and moments later I heard the hall stairs groan beneath Mrs. Okocho's bunny slippers.

An hour later, Mrs. Okocho was still upstairs bribing Ella to sit still for her portrait. Mrs. Okocho had not wanted to risk being licked by Ella—"Think of the germs, child!"—so she'd refused to hold the Teddy Snack in her fingers. But with a yardstick and a pack of dental floss that I hoped Momma wouldn't miss, I'd been able to devise a clever solution.

Mrs. Okocho sat on the couch dangling a Teddy Snack above Ella's head. I had tied dental floss around the snack's little ankle and then taped the dental floss to the yardstick, making it kind of like a fishing pole.

"Soon, my darling, soon," Mrs. Okocho told Ella as she shook the yardstick gently. She turned to me.

"Right?"

I nodded. I was so close to finishing! I'd drawn her broad mastiff chest and her stout pit bull forelegs. I was just working on her back half, which was long and lean like a greyhound's. I'd drawn her rear right leg, but there was one part that I couldn't decide on.

The trouble was this: Ella hadn't always had just three legs. When Ricky had first met her, she'd had all four. She lost her left hind leg nine months ago when she got away from me and ended up being hit by a car. The car broke Ella's leg. Dr. Vanderstam tried to do an operation to save it, but it was too badly hurt to ever heal right, so he'd had to take it off.

Ella doesn't miss her leg one bit, but I couldn't decide—should I draw her with three legs and her scar, or draw in the fourth leg that she had when Ricky first met her?

"You are upset," Mrs. Okocho observed. "What is your trouble?"

I told her what was bothering me.

"Draw her as she is now," she said. "Your Ella is very pretty, you know."

I smiled. Mrs. Okocho was goofy most times, but other times she knew just what to say. I finished the picture and carefully printed the book's title on it. Below that, I wrote: *by Ella Fitzgerald Gandy.*

"All finished!" I announced.

Mrs. Okocho lowered the Teddy Snack to Ella, who carefully broke it away from the dental floss and ate it.

"Good girl!" I said in surprise.

"Yes, yes," Mrs. Okocho said. And then she did something very unusual: she petted Ella's back. She did it lightly at first, like she thought it might feel gross, but then she petted her more firmly. "Very good girl." The sight of it made my insides all warm, like a drink of cocoa on a snow day.

Ella must have enjoyed it, too, because she spun around, put her paws on the couch, and licked Mrs. Okocho right on the face. The landlady let out a screech and bolted to her feet. "Oh, disgusting!" she cried, blinking rapidly. "Oh, the germs."

Mrs. Okocho waved her hands at me. "Child, child, fetch me the *roobing* alcohol."

Wouldn't you know that after all my fuss and worry, Ella and I still ended up being the first to arrive at Ricky's. I didn't mind, though. It gave us time to talk before Ricky had to pay attention to all of his other friends. "She's been so great with Ella," I told him. "I've got to do something extra nice for her."

"You could dust her apartment," he suggested.

"Never again," I said. I'd tried to dust for Mrs. Okocho once, in exchange for a ride to the library. "That lady has two feather dusters—one to dust her furniture, and another to dust off the first duster."

"Crazy," Ricky said. "Go get it!" He hurled a tooth-marked Frisbee across the yard and Ella raced after it. Ricky's yard was her favorite outdoor place because it was all fenced in, which meant no leash. She liked it even better than Friendship Park down the road. Since Ella's accident, Ricky's parents had let her come here to play so that we didn't have to make the long walk there. And also, I think, so Ricky would quit asking for a dog of his own.

Ella launched herself like a pogo stick and caught the Frisbee in her mouth. "Good catch!" Ricky shouted. "Now, bring it back!"

Ella trotted away to the corner of the yard. She was great at the *go-get-it* part of playing Fetch—but awful at the *bring-it-back* part.

I grinned at the pup as she whipped the Frisbee from side to side in her mouth.

"Ricky?" Mrs. Jenkins called from the back door. "Help me set up the snack table." She was awkwardly holding a long folding table up by one corner.

Ricky turned heavily and slumped his shoulders.

"On my *birthday*?" he moaned. He might have turned double-digits, but it certainly hadn't changed him much.

I thought about giving him a quick punch in that ticklish spot on his side for whining, but I didn't like to get too feisty in front of Mrs. Jenkins. She's one of those ladies who always looks like she stepped off the cover of *Essence* magazine—so I try to be my most proper around her.

"Gosh, Ricky, show some dignity," I said. He threw me a smirk. "I can help you, Mrs. Jenkins!"

"Sweet music to my ears," she sighed.

I jogged to the sliding back door and grabbed the table's other end. Mrs. Jenkins and I carried it out to the grass together. "Can I ask you a favor?" I asked as we pulled out the table's legs.

"Sure, Latasha, what do you need?" Mrs. Jenkins replied.

"It's about my present for Ricky," I confided. "Can you make sure he opens it last?"

Mrs. Jenkins smiled. "Got something special, huh?"

We glanced over at Ricky, who was trying to wrestle the Frisbee away from Ella. "I can't throw if you don't let go," he was saying.

"It's one of a kind," I replied.

"Well," Mrs. Jenkins began, "let's play it by ear. Mr. Jenkins kind of wants *his* present to be the grand finale. But he's still out picking it up."

I had to admit, if anyone could edge me out for "best present," it was Mr. Jenkins. He worked as a lawyer at a firm downtown, and he always got cool things through his job, like box seats for the Steelers and tickets to plays.

Ricky's mom and I flipped the table onto its legs. "You go ahead and play," she told me. "I've got it from here."

Mrs. Jenkins went into the house and I returned to Ricky and my pup.

"I'd been wondering where your dad was," I said. Mr. Jenkins almost never missed things that mattered to Ricky. I'd been surprised that he wasn't home when we arrived. "Any idea what he's getting you?"

"I hope it's a drum set," Ricky said. "He tried to go today without me noticing, but I totally saw him take the SUV."

On top of being the year that you can join Gifted and Talented at our school, fourth grade is the year you get to join the band. Ricky really wanted to play the drums. He'd been scheming all summer to get a set. If Ricky's dad had finally given in, I was *definitely* okay with him going last.

"Jeez, I hope I'm not interrupting your date!" yelled a boy from the door.

I scowled. It was Ricky's dopey friend, Dante Preston. Ricky ruffled the fur on Ella's back. "Go get him!" he told her.

When Ella gets excited, she doesn't run to you—she swims. On Ricky's command, my pup wagged her tail frantically and did a wiggly, floppy skip toward Dante.

Dante's eyes bulged and he clung to the door handle. "Jenkins, c'mon," he cried, his voice cracking. "Don't!"

I almost felt bad for the kid, even with those "date" cracks he was always making. I clapped my hands and said, "Ella, come!"

Ella sniffed behind Dante's knees and then returned to me. Dante's shoulders sank in relief.

Mrs. Jenkins came to the door behind Dante with a pair of snack bowls. When she tapped on the glass, he yelped in surprise. Ricky doubled over in hysterics. Ella twirled on her hind leg.

Dante moved aside so Mrs. Jenkins could carry out the Doritos and Skittles. "Not cool, bro," he told Ricky. "I almost died, for real."

"I'll put her on her leash," I huffed. "Don't pee your pants."

That made Ricky lose it all over again. I saw Mrs. Jenkins raise an eyebrow at me as she walked back to the house and my cheeks got warm.

I clicked Ella's leash onto her collar. "She's really nice," I told Dante. "She just loves meeting people."

We heard the glass door slide open again, and out came another one of my old classmates, Darla Robinson. "Happy birthday, dear Ricky!" she sang.

Ella wiggled and tugged at her leash. I looked to Dante. "See?"

More kids arrived and the party got rolling. We played all kinds of games, like Tag and Back-to-Back Balloon Pop. We also had a three-legged race, which I didn't want to do at first because I thought Ricky was making a joke about Ella. But then I learned that a three-legged race is actually a real thing. It gets its name from the way the runners have to race in pairs, with one of each runner's legs tied to the other person's. I didn't do so well, because I got paired up with Darla. You have to work in perfect sync to win a three-legged race, but we each tried to lead the way.

After a while, Mrs. Jenkins brought the presents and yellow cake out and set them on the snack table. We all agreed to do the cake first in order to give Mr. Jenkins more time to get back with his present.

Everybody sang "Happy Birthday," but Ricky

seemed glum. "What's going on?" I asked while he cut the cake.

Ricky looked me. "He's going to miss the whole party."

"No way," I replied. "You'll see."

Ricky nodded and handed me a slice so huge that it barely fit on my plate.

"I can't eat all that cake!" I cried.

"It's not for you," Ricky retorted. "It's for her." Ella clipped my calves with her wagging tail.

We all ate our cake—don't worry, I only gave my pup one little bite—and then Ricky's mom carried out the presents. She set mine on the folding table first so that it would be on the bottom of the pile. I gripped Ella's leash. "This is going to be awesome," I whispered in her ear.

As Ricky opened his gifts, each guest called out which one they'd given. "That's mine!" yelled Darla as he grabbed a box wrapped in yellow-and-blue striped paper. Ricky tore off the paper to reveal a trivia board game.

"That's from me," called Dante as Ricky opened an envelope and pulled out a prepaid debit card. "So you can get whatever you want."

At some time during the gift opening, Ella finally ran out of steam and flopped down in the grass. I was getting more and more pumped, though. Ricky had gotten some cool presents, for sure—but mine would be the most unique.

Only a couple others' gifts and mine were left to open when we heard a familiar voice at the back door.

"I hope you didn't eat all the cake," Mr. Jenkins said. He was leaning around the side of the door frame, just a head and half of a chest.

"Dad!" Ricky shouted.

"Hi, Mr. Jenkins," a few of us said.

Mrs. Jenkins gave her husband a smooch on the temple. She peeked past him into the house. "Think we can hold off until we open the other presents?" she asked.

I hope so, I thought. I didn't know what could be in there—but Mrs. Jenkins sure looked excited when she saw it. Ella just shifted her head in my lap and huffed.

"Ooh, I don't know if it can wait," Mr. Jenkins replied, shooting Ricky a gleaming grin.

"What is it? What is it?" asked Ricky.

I couldn't see too well because the folding table was in my way. I craned my neck as Mr. Jenkins stepped slowly out of the house.

When Ricky saw his present, he didn't even say words. He just sprinted over to his parents, repeating over and over, "Oh...oh..." He hugged his dad tight, right in front of everybody.

Then he knelt down to pet his brand-new puppy.

The dog was gray—almost blue—with oversized paws, wrinkly knees, and a head shaped like a road worker's shovel. "He's a Great Dane," Mr. Jenkins said.

"He's the best Dane ever!" Ricky cried, hugging the puppy. His parents squatted down to welcome their new family member.

I felt a whole swarm of things at the same time. Part of me was so happy for my friend, who had all but given up on getting a dog of his own. And part of me wanted to hide my present for Ricky, which didn't feel like such a big deal anymore. And another part of me was eager to plan some play dates for Ella and this new pup.

But there was another thing, too, underneath all that. It was a feeling I have sometimes when I watch all of the Jenkinses having a great family moment together. I couldn't find the right word for it. It was like my heart was being held underwater. I closed my eyes and scratched the scruff of Ella's neck, hoping it would go away before anyone noticed me.

"Latasha!" Ricky said. I opened my eyes and saw him peering through the crowd of kids. "Bring Ella over!"

I smiled too hard at him, and then moved Ella's head so I could stand. I jingled her collar. "Come on, sleepy," I said. She lifted herself and we walked together around the table. I might have felt a bit gloomy, but I really was glad that Ella could make a new friend.

But she didn't make a new friend. She did something I'd never seen her do before. The instant we rounded the table's edge, the fur on Ella's back spiked up like a mohawk. Her lip curled and she let out the scariest snarl I've ever heard. Then she rushed so hard at Ricky's dog that her nails tore chunks from

the grass. Guests leapt out of the way. The Great Dane tensed up and growled. I yanked Ella's leash and Mr. Jenkins pulled back on theirs.

"Ella, no!" I screamed. Ella looped her leash around a table leg and flipped the whole thing, smashing cake and snacks and presents in a messy pile. I wrapped the leash around my hand, praying she wouldn't pull free. When I was sure of my grip, I pulled sharply and marched us off. I heard Ricky call my name, but I was too ashamed to look back. I just dragged Ella away at top speed—away from the party, across the yard, and out the side gate without even a glance.

Chapter Two

The Tangled Tree

"Why did you do that?" I asked Ella. I'd been asking that question for hours—sometimes in frustration, sometimes in tears. In one snarling move, my pup had threatened Ricky's dog, wrecked his party, and probably ended our friendship.

All of that was bad enough. But the worst part was that I couldn't talk to anyone else about it. If I told Momma what had happened, she might not trust Ella to sleep in my room anymore. If I told Mrs.

Okocho, forget about my room—she might not want my pup in the house at all.

And that was everybody I trusted. The only one I could talk to was Ella, even though she'd caused all of this trouble and made me so upset that I could barely look at her.

The pup didn't have any answers, though. She was curled up on my bed, tucked into a round, red lump. She did that when I got upset, because she knew I thought it was cute. How could a dog that knew how to cheer me up and snuggle just right to keep my toes warm at bedtime also be a mean, growly beast?

The thought kept me up that night, and it stayed in my mind while Momma and I ran our Sunday errands. It didn't take long for Momma to notice.

"What's dragging you down?" she asked me as we climbed off the city bus.

"These canned veggies," I said, hefting my doubled-up plastic grocery bag. "They weigh a ton."

"Really, honey," Momma said. "You haven't seemed like yourself since last night."

I shrugged coolly.

"Latasha," she said. "What kind of family are we?"

"A no-secrets family," I replied. That was a deal Momma and I had made this year. We started it because I always try to act tough and grown-up, even when I'm upset—kind of like right now, actually.

Most times, I think it's a great idea to be "no-secrets" with Momma. Most times.

I focused on the road. If I looked Momma in the eyes, I wouldn't be able to keep it in. "I'm just thinking of a story," I replied.

"Well, then," Momma said, shifting her grocery bags in her hand. "I'll leave my gifted and talented girl to her thoughts." We walked up the hill toward our block. "If you want to talk, though…about your story…I'm right here."

I glanced at Momma without turning. I felt a little bad being dishonest, but it was only a half-lie. I actually was thinking of a story: Ella's story. When I really thought about it, there were so many important parts that I didn't know.

I didn't know what she'd been through before we'd adopted her. Maybe she'd had a fight with a Great Dane when she was living on the streets and Ricky's dog reminded her of it.

I also didn't know where Ella had gone the time she got away from me last fall.

The time you let her go, my brain told me. *The time you let her get—*

I blinked my eyes a few times, like I was flicking the lights on and off in my head. I couldn't start beating myself up about Ella's accident. I still feel guilty about it sometimes, and Momma says that's normal—but last year's accident and yesterday's freak-out probably had nothing to do with each other.

We entered the apartment to the usual Ella greeting of eyeball-high pogo hops. If there was one upside to Ella's accident, it was this: her remaining hind leg had gotten as strong as a bull's.

A dancing bull's. Ella hooked her forepaws on my arm and tickled my cheek with her nose. "Down," I said, but I was already laughing.

Momma turned from Ella to shield our shopping bags, but she was smiling, too. "Take her out for a potty," she said. "I'll handle the groceries."

I didn't have to be told twice! I clipped on Ella's leash, looped it around my forearm and wrist, and led her downstairs to the back grass. I refuse to call it a backyard—the Jenkinses have a backyard. We just have back grass, because Ella can literally jump from one end of it to the other.

Which she did quite joyfully as soon as we got out there. Watching my little mutt hop across our tiny patch of green, I thought about Ricky's massive yard. I remembered all of the fun times Ella'd had there, sprinting free like a racing dog, her ears flapping like sails. A new thought entered my mind.

Ella had all sorts of different dog breeds in her background. What if one of Ella's parents or grandparents was a mean dog? Would that make her a little bit mean, too? There were too many questions—I needed to talk to a dog expert. Luckily, I had one on speed dial.

"Vanderstam Veterinary, how can I help you?" Miss Simon at our vet's office always answers the phone the exact same way. Just hearing her greeting made me relax a little. I eased my death grip on the cordless phone and reclined against my bedroom wall.

"Hi, Miss Simon," I said.

"Well, hello, Latasha!" She knew my voice because I always call her when Ella gets into mischief—in other words, pretty often. "Congratulations! You're our first call of the week."

I thought I might be. It was Monday at exactly 9:05 in the morning. I would have called right at nine, when the vet's office opens, but I'd waited until Momma got in the shower so that I could talk in private.

"I need a little help," I explained. Actually, I

needed more than a little. I was glad that Momma likes her showers extra-long on Mondays, so I'd have enough time to ask all of my questions. I could hear the water running and Momma was doing a cross between humming and singing behind the closed door.

"Uh-oh, what did Ella eat this time?" asked Miss Simon, her voice knowing and friendly.

"It's not what she ate," I said. "It's what she almost ate."

"Okay...what did Ella *almost* eat?"

"It's pretty bad," I said, my nerves tensing up. I knew that she wouldn't overreact like Momma or Mrs. Okocho might, but Miss Simon liked Ella a lot. I didn't want her to think less of my pup.

"It's probably not the worst," she replied.

I guessed that was true. My eyes ticked from left to right as I considered the best way to tell Miss Simon what Ella had done. "Well..."

Have you ever tried to pour a little milk into your cereal from a big gallon jug? If the jug is too full, it can slip out of your hands and spill all over the place. That's exactly what it was like once I started talking. I flooded the phone with every detail of Ella's afternoon—even the stuff that didn't matter, like how Darla Robinson gets on my nerves with her perfect little braids and her barrettes that match her shoes, and how Ricky's family makes me sad sometimes for no reason at all.

"And I hurried her home, and on Saturday I cried, and on Sunday I felt sorry for us both, and now it's Monday and I want to make Ella better, so I'm calling you." I sucked in a breath. I felt like Ella probably does after a bout of the zoomies. She was watching me curiously from the throw rug on my bedroom floor. "Sorry," I added.

"Don't worry about it," Miss Simon told me.

"So, what I want to know is..." I listened for the sound of running water, to make sure Momma wouldn't overhear. "Do you think Ella is part mean-dog?"

"Ella's a little sweetheart," Miss Simon replied.

"She didn't look like it on Saturday," I said doubtfully.

"Well, did she show her teeth or growl at you?"

"No."

"Did she do that to any other people?"

"No," I repeated, wondering where Miss Simon was headed.

"That's good," she said. "It would be a problem if she was aggressive—do you know what *aggressive* means?"

I'd known that word since the first week I had my pocket dictionary. "It describes someone who is forceful or attacking," I answered.

"I thought you might," Miss Simon said. "Anyway, it would be a real problem if Ella was aggressive toward people, but she didn't pick a fight with a person. She picked a fight with another dog. Some breeds aren't good with other dogs. Others just have a strong prey drive."

I peered at Ella on the floor. "What the heck would a dog have to pray about?"

Miss Simon chuckled. "Not *pray* with an 'a.' *Prey* with an 'e.'"

"Like a bird of prey?" I asked. I'd learned about hunter birds on a class trip to the Pittsburgh Zoo last spring.

"That's right," Miss Simon replied. "In dogs, prey drive shows up in different ways. It makes a sheep dog want to round up sheep. It makes some dogs want to follow a scent, and others want to chase a ball."

"Or a turkey," I said, looking at Ella. Believe it or not, that was how she had gotten away from me last fall. We were on a walk together when we'd spotted a wild turkey, right in the middle of the city! I was so surprised that I let my guard down—and Ella was so interested that she ripped free from my grip and chased after it.

"Prey drive in action," Miss Simon agreed. "It can make certain breeds of dogs very sensitive around other dogs."

"How can I figure out if Ella's got one of those breeds in her?" I asked.

"There are blood tests that'll tell you all about a dog's breeding," Miss Simon said. A smile crept across my face. I could find out Ella's whole history, all with a simple test! "But they're not exactly cheap," she added.

My smile melted into a smirk. Momma wouldn't like *not exactly cheap*. We were still on a payment plan from Ella's leg surgery. That's why Momma was taking extra Saturday shifts.

Miss Simon must have sensed my disappointment through the phone. "But don't worry about the test," she said. "It won't solve your problem. There's really only one way to make Ella calm around other dogs."

The shower turned off—I only had another minute to talk. "I'll try anything," I whispered.

"You have to work on her socialization," Miss Simon said.

Socialization. I pictured each syllable in my head—that helps me sometimes when I meet a new word. “Is that like Ella’s social skills?” I asked.

“Bingo,” Miss Simon replied. “Social skills take training. For dogs and people, really. You should slowly introduce Ella to your friend’s dog. Take them for a walk together—work your way up to playtime. The more you get Ella used to this new dog, the less sensitive she’ll be. Who knows? Maybe they’ll really get along!”

I loved the idea of Ella having a new dog-friend. But what if it was too late? What if Ricky’s parents didn’t want to give Ella another chance? Or, even worse, what if Ricky didn’t? What if Ella’s outburst had given him a good hard shake and his Magic 8 Ball mind had decided *I don’t want to be friends*?

“Did you hear me?” asked Miss Simon.

I shook the questions out of my head. “What?”

“I said I need you to promise me—when you start socializing the dogs, make sure you have adults around. Deal?”

The bathroom door opened and Momma stepped out. “Deal,” I said. I thanked Miss Simon and clicked off the call.

“Who was on the phone?” asked Momma as she dried her ears with a towel.

A wrong number, a telemarketer, a prank caller— “Miss Simon,” I admitted.

Momma only raised an eyebrow. "Uh-oh, what'd Ella eat this time?"

I really wanted to take Miss Simon's advice. I wanted Ella to become best friends with that Great Dane. But I was nervous to even talk to the Dane's owner.

So I kept finding excuses to stay in the house until I felt ready to face Ricky. Most of those excuses involved playing games with Ella and reading picture books to her. But since Momma was away at work during the week, the rest involved Mrs. Okocho.

We watched two hours of cartoons together one day, and the next day she taught me how to sew a button back onto one of her cardigans. "Someday," she said, "I will teach you to play cards."

On one clear, not-too-hot afternoon, Mrs. Okocho suggested that I pick the weeds in her garden for her. "I would do so myself, but my knees," she said, giving each one a gentle tap. "They are conspiring against me." I would have been fine with helping—especially because Mrs. Okocho offered to pay me a dime for every weed I picked—but if Ricky came outside to shoot hoops in his driveway or walk his dog or something, he'd surely stop over and I'd have to face him whether I wanted to or not.

Instead, we ended up having "drawing class." Mrs. Okocho explained that she would bring out an object and we would draw it in pencil exactly as we saw it. I just hoped it would be less boring than it sounded.

"This I studied some years ago, at the community college," she told me. "We drew a bowl of fruits. But all I have are yams. I hope you do not mind."

She gulped down the bottom of her coffee mug and went to the kitchen to fetch them. This did not sound promising. Not only are yams deadly dull, but they're gross. They're slimy and way too sweet and they make a slurping, *floop*-y sound when you dump the chunks out of the can. I don't even like their pale orange color—they're like carrots that caught the flu.

But when Mrs. Okocho returned, she didn't have the canned yams I was picturing. She carried a mixing bowl that held a heap of what looked like oversized potatoes covered in tree bark.

"Feast your eyes on these beauties!" Mrs. Okocho said. She cautiously lowered the bowl to the table. I was amazed she'd made it without the pile spilling to the floor.

"So that's what a yam looks like?" I guessed I'd never seen a whole one before.

Mrs. Okocho looked at me as if I'd asked for a

ride to Mars. "Are you for real?"

My cheeks got hot. "Well," I sputtered, "why on Earth do you have so many of them?"

"Because they taste heavenly," she replied, like I should have been born knowing the answer. "Also, I can only find the true African yams some of the time. I must keep a reserve." Her eyes flashed with inspiration. "Latasha, you must try one!"

"I'm…not hungry," I said uneasily.

"Oh, but you must!" she exclaimed. "There are so many ways to prepare a yam. Boiled yams, stewed yams, fried yams in pepper sauce…or I could make for you my homemade sweet purple yam jam!"

Mrs. Okocho had grown on me over the last year, but I was pretty sure that her food ideas never would. "You go ahead and have a snack," I said, slipping out of my chair. "I'll check on Ella."

"Suit yourself," she said, already scanning the bowl for the perfect yam—if there is such a thing. "But soon, the aroma of my sweet purple yam jam will fill this house and your mouth will begin to water."

More like my eyes'll start to water, I thought. I could just imagine the sickeningly sweet smell of the cooking yams drifting up through our floor vents. There was only one place I could go to escape it:

outside. And if I wanted to go outside, I knew what I'd have to do.

I trudged across the street toward Ricky's. When I reached the door, I wasn't sure whether to knock or ring the bell. The strangest noises can make dogs go wild—for example, Ella's terrified of our oven timer and also of the sound Momma's cell phone makes when it gets low on battery. I didn't want to make Ricky any more upset with me by getting his puppy all riled up. To be honest, I really wanted to run back home and hide in Mrs. Okocho's flowerbed.

Knock, ring, or run? I wondered. In the end, it didn't matter. Just as I settled on knocking, the front door flew open and Ricky charged smack into me. "Oof!" I stumbled backward and fell in the grass on my rear end.

"Hey, perfect timing!" Ricky said, breaking into a grin. He was holding an envelope in one hand. He offered his free one to help me up.

I instantly forgot about my nervousness and slapped his hand away. "Why don't you watch where you're going?" I said, pushing myself to my feet.

"Says the girl who just hangs out on other people's

doorsteps," he replied. "This is for you."

He handed me his envelope. Written on the front in very fancy, very neat cursive were the words *Thank You*. "Or I guess I should say it's for *Ella*," he told me. "After all, she wrote that book for me, right?"

I had to think for a moment before I remembered that I'd given Ella author credit on Ricky's birthday present. "She's a pretty great writer, huh?" I asked.

Ricky smiled widely. "The best writer I know."

I put the thank you note in my back pocket. I didn't want to open it until I could share it with my pup. "So..." I began, hooking my thumbs into my belt loops. "You don't hate us? For wrecking your party?"

"I was ticked about the cake at first," Ricky admitted. "But Dad said that dogs tussle sometimes. We'll work it out."

Part of me felt relieved that Ricky was being so nice. But another part was annoyed that I'd spent so much time worrying over nothing. "Why didn't you come by and say something sooner?" I demanded.

"I've been super busy," Ricky replied. "You know, with Ham."

Yams, ham—what was it with food today?

Ricky's eyebrows went up. "Oh, man," he cried, "you haven't met Ham!" He yanked his front door open and hurried in. I guessed that was my cue to follow him.

I closed the door and slipped off my shoes. "I'm back!" Ricky shouted. "Latasha's with me!"

Mrs. Jenkins poked her head into the hallway from the dining room. "Hi, Latasha," she said, and then she ducked out of sight.

Ricky cupped his hands to call up the stairs. "Ham!" he exclaimed. "Ham, boy! C'mere!"

As Ricky whistled, I realized what was going on. "You named your Great Dane *Ham*?"

Ricky shook his head. "His name's Hamlet," he explained. "I wanted to name him Casey Hampton, since Great Danes get so big and all. But Dad said I ought to name him Hamlet." Ricky shrugged. "I figure, as long as there's 'Ham' in it. Ham! Come down, Ham!"

"Honey?" asked Mrs. Jenkins. She had returned to the hallway. "I don't think he's really learned his name yet. How about you go get him?"

Ricky did his trademark dramatic sigh. "You wait down here," he said to me. "This could take awhile. Lazy guy likes naps more than I do!" He bounded up the stairs.

Mrs. Jenkins gave me a head shake that said one word: *Boys*. "Well, back to work," she said, and she retreated into the dining room again.

I waited a few seconds, and when Ricky didn't return, I padded over to see what Mrs. Jenkins was up to.

I found her leaning over a large sheet of off-white poster board that was spread across the table. She was carefully drawing a line on the sheet with an odd-looking pen. Once Mrs. Jenkins had finished the line, I spoke. "I'm sorry about the trouble with Ella."

Mrs. Jenkins looked up and smiled warmly. "It's all right," she told me. "But thank you for the apology." She drew another line.

"What kind of pen is that?" I asked.

Mrs. Jenkins held the pen out for me to see. It had a feather at one end and a shiny, needle-sharp tip at the other. "It's a calligraphy pen," she explained. "*Calligraphy* means 'beautiful writing.'"

I would have to jot that down in my special vocabulary notebook when I got home: *calligraphy – a beautiful word that means beautiful writing*. Then I remembered the beautiful *Thank You* written on the envelope in my back pocket. I picked it out by a corner and held it up for Mrs. Jenkins to see. "Yours?" I asked.

"Well, the note on the inside is all Ricky," she said. "I did some envelopes to warm up for my little project here. I haven't used my pens in a while, so I was kind of rusty."

"I do arts and crafts sometimes with Mrs. Okocho," I ventured. Except that Mrs. Jenkins's project looked a lot more interesting than sketching a bunch of icky yams.

"Then maybe you'll appreciate this," she said. Ricky's mom moved her leather pen case aside and spun the large poster board for me with a grainy *whoosh*.

"It's for Mr. Jenkins's parents," she said. "It's their fiftieth anniversary this fall."

"Gosh," I said. I studied the poster board—which I realized when I touched its edge wasn't poster board at all, but some kind of cloth or canvas. At its top was a single line, with a single name written beside it in Mrs. Jenkins's fancy script: *Crafton Jacob Jenkins (1836 - 1874)*. From the top line, three more lines branched out in a row, each with a name beside it. From those, more lines and names spread across a third row. Some lines died out, but most of them continued to blossom, getting more and more complicated.

"This is the complete Jenkins family tree," Mrs. Jenkins said, "starting with Ricky's great-great-great-great grandfather, Crafton. Mr. Jenkins gathered up all of the records, and I'm putting them on this nice vellum so we can get it framed. That's what you call this fancy paper—vellum."

"I bet they'll like that," I said quietly. I stared at the clusters of names, with their clean lines and beautiful labeling. It was so big, though, that my eyes couldn't hold it all at once. The longer I looked, the less the picture looked like a tree. It turned into a maze.

"I hope so," Mrs. Jenkins replied. "It took Ricky's dad forever to track it all down. Family histories can get kind of messy."

Something felt wrong inside me. That heart-underwater feeling was inching up again, but something else had come with it—something spicy, even angry—and it was all pushing against my ribs. I didn't understand what was making me so upset. It was just a dumb picture.

Except that it wasn't dumb. Not even a little.

"Latasha?" asked Mrs. Jenkins.

"I'm sorry, I just remembered something," I said, fumbling for any excuse. "I have to run home." And for the second time in two visits to Ricky's, that's exactly what I set out to do.

When I reached the door, Ricky came down the stairs with Hamlet walking slowly beside him. "Where are you going?" he said. "I just got him out of bed!"

"I'm sorry," I said, and I hurried out the door.

I sat in our apartment, my legs stretched on the couch, Ella curled at my feet. I was looking at the scribbles I'd made in my vocabulary notebook.

My notebook had started as a way to keep track of words I learned. But after Ella's accident, I'd started using it to keep track of my feelings, too. It really helped me on tough days, when my pup felt extra sore and I felt extra guilty.

I'd planned to write about Ricky's family tree, but when I opened the book, I realized that I didn't want to write. I wanted to draw.

I started to make a family tree of my own. I began mine in reverse, working back from me. I wrote my name at the bottom, *Latasha Esther Gandy (January 21, 2003 –)*, and a dotted line beside me pointed to *Ella Fitzgerald Gandy (April Fool)*. Above my name, I drew a big "T" shape. On the left of the "T" I wrote down Momma—or *Stephanie Gandy (February 13, 1982 –)*, to make it official. I went back along Momma's side to label her brother who lives in Las Vegas, and her parents, who I never got to meet because they both passed away while Momma was a teenager. I also filled in a few great-aunts and uncles from Momma's family down in Atlanta. "That's where the Gandys originally lived," I explained to my pup.

Then I went back to the "T" above my name so that I could start my dad's family on the right. I wrote my father's name: *Patrick Kidd.* After his name, I added a *?* That was where his birthdate would have gone if I'd known it.

That was all I had. And that hurt so bad that it made my face twitch.

"Why am I worried about where you came from?" I asked Ella, my voice breaking. "I don't even know where I came from."

Chapter Three

New Dog

This might sound bad to admit, but honestly, I don't much miss my father. I think about him sometimes—a lot, lately—but I don't miss him. You have to know somebody to miss him, and I know the look of Dad's handwriting better than I really know him. I've only met him a few times, but he sends me a funny birthday card every January and a manila envelope with money in it that matches my age. This year, he gave me $12.69—or nine one-dollar bills, nine quarters, and nine each of dimes, nickels, and pennies. That's how I know that my dad is not a bad person. Nobody who makes me smile just by the way he puts money in an envelope could be bad. But other than that, I know very little about him.

He works as a musician, but I don't know what instrument he plays. He lives in a place called Ambridge, which is forty-five minutes north of Pittsburgh—but usually he is traveling all over for different gigs. That's the word musicians use for their concerts. His looks are fuzzy to me. But he's very tall, and I could never forget his blazing red hair—redder than Ella's, even—which makes his skin seem even paler than it really is. Pale like a ghost.

"Wait a sec, wait a sec," Ricky interrupted, holding Ella at arm's length to escape her frantic licking. "Your dad's *white*?"

I glared at him. "And?"

"And nothing," he said quickly. "Just didn't know, that's all. You look like your mom."

I guessed it would be surprising—if my dad and I were walking down the street together, no one would assume we were related. And Momma's very pretty when she's not tired from work, so that could even be a compliment. But Ricky's voice felt like a punch in the stomach. "Okay," I replied. I sat unmoving on the porch.

It was the day after I'd fled Ricky's dining room. After Momma left for work, he'd stopped by to make plans for how we would introduce our dogs. We quickly decided that since tomorrow was Saturday, and Momma wasn't picking up any extra shifts for a change, we would have her and Mr. Jenkins bring the dogs out to the street. Then, with lots of encouragement (and even more treats), we'd try to get Ella and Hamlet to walk nicely next to each other.

I wasn't sure why I'd brought my dad up. Maybe I

wanted to try to explain why I'd run away yesterday. But I hadn't even gotten that far before Ricky had shut me up with, "Your dad's *white*?" Like that was all that mattered. Now I sat in stony silence, wishing I hadn't said anything—wishing my friend hadn't even come over.

Ella, on the other hand, couldn't have been happier to see Ricky. At the moment, she'd tangled herself in her leash with her wild pinwheeling, and Ricky's face and shirt were wet from her slobbery tongue. She was sniffing him all over, too, poking him in the side with her nose.

I was dead-set against smiling, no matter how cute Ella got. But then Ella's nose jabbed Ricky's ticklish spot and he let out a girly "Ooh-hooh!" I covered my mouth with my hand, pretending that my nose itched.

"What has gotten into her?" he sighed. "She's even crazier than usual."

I lowered my hand and cracked a sly smile. "It's probably because you stink like Ham."

"He doesn't stink," Ricky muttered. He shifted his weight. "I don't think he likes me."

"Impossible," I said without a pause.

"He doesn't like me like she does," he said, scratching Ella under the collar. "He doesn't even run to say hi when I come into the house. He just walks."

"Ham probably just has...a slower motor," I said. "Maybe if Ella gets used to him, she'll slow down a little, he'll speed up a little, and they'll both be normal."

Ricky smiled as he imagined our pair together. "We'll see tomorrow, huh?"

"How about two o'clock?" I suggested. I figured that would give Momma time to go to the Laundromat and handle whatever other Saturday chores we had lined up.

Ricky stood and said, "See you two at two!" He leaned in and rubbed behind Ella's ears, adding in a weird voice, "Won't I, girl!"

"Get out of here, goofy," I laughed.

"It's not Goofy, it's Scooby-Doo!" Ricky retorted. He cocked a thumb at my pup. "Ella got it."

Her tail was wagging so hard that it bent her body like a crescent moon. I got up to take her inside.

"Hey," Ricky called after me. "I'm sorry about— you know..."

"Thanks," I said, and I meant it.

"Why don't you just ask your mom to tell you about him?"

The thought of that sent a chill through me. "You know that saying," I replied, "if you can't say something nice, don't say anything at all?"

Ricky nodded.

I choked up on Ella's leash to bring her closer. "Momma never, ever says anything about my dad."

Our little Saturday dog-date almost didn't happen at all. That was because of Momma. She wasn't too busy or anything—it's just that when I asked her to help, she made me start at the beginning and explain precisely why we had to be so careful introducing the dogs.

Looking back, I probably shouldn't have gotten so detailed.

"Oh," she said, pressing a hand to her neck as I described the snarling and the charging. "Oh, that's embarrassing."

Honestly, I'd forgotten how much it might upset Momma to hear about it all for the first time. I'd gotten so used to the fact that the scuffle happened that it just felt like another story to me. By the time I reached the table-flipping and the flying presents and the cake-smashing, Momma'd had enough. "Latasha *Esther* Gandy," she said, her voice getting louder and higher, "why did you not tell me about this before?"

This is exactly why, I thought. I hate it when Momma uses my middle name like that. I'm not a fan of the name *Esther* even on a good day, but when Momma's mad, she spits it out like a curse word.

Rather than bring that up, though, I told her, "I wanted to protect Ella." The pup watched us from my bedroom's doorway, belly flat on the floor. "I didn't want her to get punished."

"And I guess you forgot our deal about keeping secrets?" Momma scolded. "This is a—"

"No-secrets family," I said along with her. "I'm sorry."

She looked at me, the fire in her eyes slowly cooling. "I hope you apologized to the Jenkinses," she told me.

"I did," I said, nodding sharply. "Mrs. Jenkins said everything was okay."

Momma pursed her lips at Ella. "And you," she said, shaking her head. The pup seemed to sink even farther into the carpet.

"She didn't mean to start trouble," I insisted.

Momma tucked her chin and shot a look at me from under her brow. As soon as the spotlight was off of her, Ella scrambled into my room, out of sight. I could hear her paws scratching the carpet as she shoved herself under my bed.

"See how bad she feels?" I said. "She messed up, Momma, and she knows it. I just want to give her another chance."

Momma didn't respond. I crossed over to her and gripped her hand. "Doesn't everybody deserve a second chance?" I asked.

"Everybody?" Momma squeezed my hand back. She sighed. "They want to meet at two, you said?"

At two o'clock exactly, the whole Gandy family stepped out onto the porch. I held a baggie of Teddy Snacks and Momma clutched Ella's leash, double-wrapped around her hand.

"Sit," Momma said as Ella danced in the hot, dry air.

But before Ella could even decide whether to obey, Ricky's front door opened and he stepped out by himself. When he waved, Ella wagged so hard she nearly made herself hover.

"Ouch!" Momma said as Ella's happy tail snapped against her calves. "Watch that thing!"

"It hurts even worse in the winter," I said, grinning.

"They'll be out in a minute," Ricky yelled from his front steps. "Ham's being fussy."

Momma glanced at me, then down at Ella, who was struggling so hard to go to Ricky that it was making her cough. “Let’s get to it,” she said doubtfully.

Ella’s tags jangled as we slowly let her down the stairs. She dragged Momma straight toward Ricky, not even stopping to sniff the gutter or the base of the tree out front.

“Hi, Miss Gandy,” Ricky said.

“Hot enough for you?” Momma replied, wiping her forehead with the back of her free hand. It always feels about fifteen degrees hotter than it is when you’ve got to hold onto Ella.

Ricky knelt to scratch behind Ella’s ears. “So where are we doing this?” he asked me.

“Sidewalk,” I replied. “No yards. The sidewalk is like neutral ground.”

Ricky pointed a finger in agreement. “Got your treats?” he asked.

I held up the baggie of Teddy Snacks and shook it. Ella instantly spun back and sat for me.

“Very good!” Momma exclaimed.

“This won’t be so hard,” I replied, feeding Ella a crunchy treat.

But then, Ricky’s front door opened once again. Mrs. Jenkins led the way out, followed by Mr. Jenkins—followed by Hamlet, who plodded behind them.

In an instant, Ella's fur jutted up and she was tugging and barking meanly. No, she sounded worse than mean—she sounded ferocious. "Girl, no!" Momma said sternly, wrapping the leash another time around her wrist. She looked at Ricky's parents. Mr. Jenkins was holding Hamlet back, because the Great Dane was growling now himself. "I am so sorry about her," Momma said.

I was so embarrassed by Ella's behavior that it made the back of my neck tingle. But I refused to let it scare me off. Not this time. I pushed my brain to come up with a solution—anything to help Ella calm down. After a few seconds, two words entered my mind: *New Dog*.

"How about we take her for a lap around the block?" I suggested to everyone. "She can cool off and we'll start over."

"Good idea," Mr. Jenkins said.

I took Momma's arm and led her and Ella off. Once we'd passed a few houses, Ella stopped straining and walked along with us. I fed her three Teddy Snacks as we moved down the block. "Good girl!" I said.

"Should you really be rewarding her?" Momma asked me.

It was one of those questions that isn't really a question at all, but I answered anyway. "I have a plan."

"I just don't think Ella's ready to make a friend," Momma said.

Almost like she understood, Ella stopped so short that Momma nearly crashed into her. The pup shook herself until her spiky fur settled, and then she darted onward, all floppy tongue and wagging tail.

"Look at her," I said as we marched along. "She's already forgotten about what happened. It's like New Dog at home."

"New Dog, huh?" Momma replied.

New Dog is the name we have for this odd thing Ella does at dinner. Every night while we eat, Ella sits and waits next to one of us for a scrap. Except she doesn't really wait at first—she cries, she begs, she even demands by putting her paw on someone's knee. None of that works on us, of course. She only gets her treat once she stops begging and sits patiently.

On most nights, one bit of pork chop gristle or a single piece of broccoli is enough to satisfy her. But on some nights, one treat is simply not enough. That's where New Dog comes in.

When Ella wants another treat, she doesn't immediately start begging again. Instead, she gets up, trots around the whole table, then sits back down in her exact original spot. As if that would somehow convince us that she's not the little red cutie we just treated—that must've been some *other* dog. So that's what I say when Ella returns: "Oh, look, Momma! It's a new dog!"

The crazy thing, though, is this: when she comes back around, Ella really does behave like a new dog. And each New Dog version of her is better behaved than the last. A round-two New Dog doesn't demand a treat with her paw—she'll only whimper. The round-three version won't even cry—she'll just sit. A round-four doesn't sit—she lies down without even being asked.

I guessed that we'd need Ella to be at least a round-seven-or-eight New Dog before she could walk nicely with Hamlet.

We reached the corner at Coral Street and crossed back to our side of the road. "We'll go a few houses past Ricky's," I said, "then cross back over and try again."

"You're the boss," Momma replied. I sure liked the sound of that!

We passed the Jenkinses, Graham Street dividing us. I fed Ella a whole fistful of treats to keep her attention off Hamlet, who was lazing at Ricky's feet. Then we looped back around for a second try.

"New dog!" I told Ella.

Same old dog. We got about one house away from the Jenkins family before the fur shot up and the barking began. Ella growled and cried as she tried to tug Momma over toward Ham, but Momma and Mr. Jenkins kept them apart pretty easily this time.

"One more try?" I asked as we hustled our noisy pup past.

Mr. and Mrs. Jenkins both nodded kindly.

Ricky followed us for a few steps. "You're not fooling anyone with that tough girl act," he called out. "Everybody knows you're just a big softie."

I decided he meant Ella. My girl shook herself calm and I petted her from neck to tail. "You're doing so well!" I told her. "You shook that prey drive right out!"

I looked up at Momma. "We need to both tell her how great she's doing," I said. "If we make her feel good about herself, she'll try even harder next time."

Momma gave me an amused smirk. "Oh, yeah?" she asked. "Where'd you pick up that idea?"

I was stunned that she had to ask. "From you!"

Momma finished our lap around the block with one hand grasping Ella's leash and the other on my shoulder.

On the third pass, Ella didn't lunge at Hamlet—she just growled and cried and yipped. "That was awesome, Ella!" Momma said.

"You're doing better every time," I added, feeding her more Teddy Snacks.

It was true. By the fifth round of New Dog, Ella had stopped growling. And in the seventh round…

The two dogs walked side by side for three whole houses.

"You're doing it!" Ricky exclaimed, clapping his hands.

"You'll get them riled up again," I warned.

But inside, I felt the same as he did. I was so proud of Ella that I could have shouted the news from the top of Mount Washington.

"What do you think?" Momma asked me after we'd circled around once more.

Ella and Hamlet were sitting just a couple of feet apart, both panting heavily. "I think that's enough for today," I replied, beaming.

"Sounds right to me," Mr. Jenkins agreed. "I think these pups are wiped out."

Mrs. Jenkins poked him with her elbow. "Them or you?"

"Don't worry, I'm still grilling tonight," he said, hooking an arm around his wife's waist.

"Hamburgers for Ham!" Ricky promised his dog.

I turned away from the Jenkinses and focused on giving Ella my last few Teddy crumbs.

"But if you two are around tomorrow," Mr. Jenkins told Momma, "we can train some more."

I bounced back up to my feet.

"You're the best, Dad!" Ricky said.

"Really? Are you sure?" asked Momma.

I thought about that gift horse she'd once told me about and nodded for encouragement.

Mr. Jenkins smiled at me. "Definitely."

"Perfect!" Mrs. Jenkins said. "Latasha, Ricky—let's get a photo. Puppies and their trainers."

After learning the Jenkinses' dinner plans, Momma and I were both in the mood to run the grill ourselves. The only trouble is that we don't own a grill, or even have a good space to use one anyway. So instead, we improvised our own barbecue.

Juices sizzled in the frying pan as Momma turned our hot dogs with metal tongs. "You did a great job with her today," she said, glancing back at me from the stove.

I was seated at the kitchen table, one bare foot resting on Momma's chair, the other on the floor. In front of that foot, for the first time since Ricky's party, Ella lay totally exhausted on her side. Our training session had gone better than I could have hoped—but the other thing I had on my mind had started to slink back in. I needed to talk to Momma about it, but what if it ruined our perfect night?

"Grab the buns," Momma instructed.

I went to the bread drawer at the counter and fetched the hot dog buns. "Can I toast them?"

"*May* I," replied Momma. Then she winked. "And it wouldn't be a barbecue without toasted buns."

I pulled a handful of buns from the plastic bag and opened them flat. Then I popped a pair into the toaster. I returned to my chair and settled down again in front of Ella.

Momma hummed as she turned the hot dogs once more.

We're a no-secrets family, I reminded myself. That meant I owed it to Momma to tell her what I was thinking.

"So, Momma…" I began, trying to sound as casual as can be. "What do you think of Mr. Jenkins?"

She shrugged without turning. "He's nice."

"I think he's a really good dad," I replied.

Momma threw a smile back toward me. "I'll bet he is."

The toaster went off and our browned bun-tops popped into view. I tucked my toes under Ella's warm belly. "Ricky's…pretty lucky to have him around."

Momma's back stiffened. She turned off the stove

burner and faced me.

"Momma..." I said, pausing to wish the shakiness away. "Do you think Dad ever wonders about me?"

She stepped toward me slowly, as if the lights had gone out and she didn't want to trip. "Are you thinking about him?" she asked.

There was no more dancing around it. "I want to call him," I replied. "I want to talk to him."

Momma sat in the chair beside mine and didn't say a word.

"Are you mad at me?" I asked.

"Not at all," she said firmly. "Why would I be mad?"

My stomach tightened like a pulled rubber band. "Because you hate him."

Momma let out a low sigh. "I don't hate your father, sweetie."

"Then why don't you want me to know him?" I demanded.

Under the fluorescent kitchen light, Momma's eyes looked almost like they were glowing. Quietly she replied, "It's not that."

The rubber band in my belly snapped and I felt myself sinking into the chair. "He doesn't want to know me."

"It's not that, either," Momma told me. "Your

father is a…" She flexed her hands like she wished to grab the words. "Your father made a choice. Years and years ago. And that choice was to not be part of this family."

Something dripped onto my hand and I realized that I was crying. Before I could even sniffle, Momma reached over and wiped my cheeks with her thumb. Her palm was still warm from handling the frying pan. Once the tears stopped, Momma went on.

"I don't hate your father," she repeated. "I'm not even mad at him anymore. I feel sad for him sometimes, because he is missing out on something wonderful."

She pressed her pointer finger gently to the tip of my nose. It made my whole body relax. Ella must have felt it, too, because from below the table I heard a loud, heavy huff of breath. I peeked at her and tickled her ribs with my toes.

"Honey," Momma said, "what brought all this on?"

"I'm tired of being jealous of Ricky," I said. "Best friends shouldn't be jealous of each other."

"People get jealous sometimes," Momma replied. "It doesn't make you a bad friend."

I nodded, but I wasn't sure I believed her.

"Can I try calling Dad?" I asked. "I think it would help."

Momma touched her chin as she thought. Her mouth opened to speak, but the wrinkles in her brow had already told me everything.

"Momma, please?" I interrupted. "If he says, 'No, I don't want to talk,' fine. But…don't I deserve a chance?"

Momma hung her head and smiled to herself.

I couldn't tell what kind of smile it was. It made me nervous—had I pushed too hard? "What?" I asked.

"You've definitely got one part of him," she said. Her hand fell on top of mine. "You're both very hard to say 'no' to."

My heart began to thump like a drum. "Does that mean…?"

Momma rose from her chair and, for a moment, she looked twice her age. She moved like Mrs. Okocho does after she's been in her rocking chair for too long.

"I'll call him tonight," she told me. "I'll try to set something up."

I almost had to check the floor to make sure I hadn't started floating. Momma looked toward our dinner at the counter and said, "Our hot dogs turned into cold dogs."

Chapter Four

Common Grounds

The next weekend, Momma and I came home from our first round of back-to-school clothes shopping to find the phone ringing. Ella couldn't decide which excited her more—our return or the ringing phone—so the moment we entered, she began to spring to and fro across the kitchen.

"Settle down, wild thing!" Momma said, holding our Goodwill bags high out of reach. "Honey, grab that, would you?"

I swung a bag that held my light green first-day-of-school jumper onto the table, and then swiped the phone off the wall mount.

"Gandy residence!"

"Uh-oh," the voice on the line said. "I think I might have the wrong number. I'm trying to reach my little girl, Latasha...but you sound *way* too grown up to be her."

My eyes became platters. "Daddy!"

"Hey there, jelly bean," he said. And just like that, Dad was back in my life.

Except it wasn't really just like that. It had been a whole week and a day since Momma promised to get me in touch. A week and a day, and a turn of the calendar from July to August. A week and a day, and a calendar turn, and three more Ella and Hamlet play dates—and one call between Momma and Dad that I couldn't help but overhear.

"No email," I'd heard Momma say. "An honest-to-goodness phone call."

"Oh," she'd snapped, "I'm sure you've got *plenty*

going on."

"I ask you for very little, Patrick."

I hadn't been trying to listen in. It's just that when Momma gets cross, her voice cuts through doors, walls, and even pillows.

But none of that mattered now—my dad had finally called, and he'd called just for me.

"You still there, kid?" he asked.

"I'm here, I'm here," I said quickly. I cupped my hand over the receiver. "Momma, may I take the phone to my room?"

Momma gave me a nod. "But leave your door open for me," she added.

I trotted off to my room. Ella stayed behind to bat at Momma's bags and beg for treats.

"Sorry about the noise," I told my dad as I settled onto my bed.

"No worries," he replied. "Sorry it took me a little while to call."

"It's okay, Daddy."

"So, my girl," he began. "What's the latest news in the world of Latasha?"

I thought for a few long seconds. Dad's question was a totally normal way to start a conversation, but it felt life-and-death important to answer it just right.

Out in the living room, Momma walked toward

her bedroom with some of our shopping bags, Ella sniffing behind her. Momma slowed down to glance at me as they passed.

"Momma and I just did back-to-school shopping," I said eagerly. That definitely fit under new, if not exactly exciting.

"Ugh," Dad replied. "I remember those days with my mum...and I do *not* miss them."

"What do you mean?" I asked. I loved shopping for new school outfits. And I was extra excited to start fourth grade at the end of the month. I couldn't wait to meet my new teachers and wrap my books in clean brown paper that I could write my name and draw little designs on—and most of all, I looked forward to the first meeting of Talent Pool with Mr. Harvey.

"I always hated school," Dad said. "Band was okay...but everything else? Gag me with a spoon."

"Oh." It was like a cloud of disappointment had settled down around my head. I almost didn't add the next part. "I kind of really like school."

"Well," Dad replied, pausing, "that's probably better."

More seconds that felt like minutes passed by. I saw Ella leave Momma's room and walk a lap around the couch.

"So aside from going out and, you know...buying

new pencils and whatnot," Dad said. "What else have you got going on?"

"I've been training my dog a lot," I said. I snapped my fingers to get Ella's attention. I hoped that she would come and make a warm little nest against my side.

"That's hard work, huh?" he replied.

Instead, the pup looked at me and then walked off to the kitchen. "The hardest," I sighed.

"Sounds like it," Dad said with a laugh.

"Did you ever have a dog growing up?"

"No way," he said. "I'm definitely not patient enough for a puppy. They just…*need* so much, you know?"

"…Oh." I wished I could have a do-over with this whole phone call, one that went more like the great calls I'd imagined all week.

"I did have a guinea pig once," Dad added hastily.

"Really?" I asked. "What was its name?"

"It was silly," he replied.

That sounded promising. "Come on, what was it?"

"Thelonious," he replied.

"What the heck kind of name is that?" I blurted it out before I could think of a nicer way to ask.

"Like I said!" Dad replied, laughing. "I named

him after this piano player I really liked. A jazz guy."

My face lit up. Finally—this was the sort of thing I'd been hoping to learn! "That's awesome," I said. "And it's kind of funny, too—"

"—Yeah," Dad cut in, "but I fed him cauliflower one night and he died."

I sighed so hard it flushed the air out of the room.

"It was pretty horrible," Dad said. "And gross, too."

I was totally out of words.

"Hey, kid..." Dad said. He chuckled, which actually made me really angry. "This whole...'us talking on the phone' thing?"

"It's okay, Dad," I murmured, clutching the edge of my mattress. I felt foolish for pushing to have this call—I just wanted to drop it. "If you have something you've got to do—"

"—No, it's not that," Dad replied.

I heard the crinkly slap of a plastic bag hitting the kitchen floor. *Great*, I thought bitterly. *Now Ella's eating my new dress.*

"It's just..." Dad went on. "It's a little awkward."

"Hang on," I grumbled. I hopped off the bed and marched toward the kitchen. I heard more thrashing of my Goodwill bag—I could already imagine my chewed-up, slobbery dress.

"I don't know how this stuff is supposed to work," Dad said. "You know?"

But when I reached the doorway, I didn't find a chewed-up dress. It hadn't even left the bag. Instead, Ella had somehow managed to knock the bag off the table and get its handles caught around her hind leg. She was whipping the bag (and my dress) from side to side against herself, trying to get free.

"Ella!" I laughed. I shielded myself from her frenzied tail and freed her leg from the bag. I petted Ella's neck and her wiggling slowed. "Oh, Ella Fitzgerald Gandy," I told her, "what am I going to do with you?"

"Everything all right?" I remembered that the phone was still clamped between my ear and shoulder.

"Yeah, it's just Ella, being her crazy self," I said. I stroked Ella's ears with my free hand and gave them each the gentlest little pull, like she likes.

"Wait, your dog's name is Ella Fitzgerald?" asked Dad. "Like the singer?"

"Yeah. Mom loves her."

"I know," Dad replied. "It was her idea, then?"

"No," I said, "it was mine."

"And it was your idea," he echoed, as if the words tasted like dessert. "That is...incredibly cool.

Actually, that might be the best dog name I've ever heard."

"Definitely beats Hamlet," I agreed.

"...Sure," Dad replied. "Hey, listen. I have a proposition for you. You want to hear it?"

I had to smile—I love when adults use big words around me and just assume I'll know what they mean. "What's your offer?" I asked.

"The past couple months," Dad said, "I've been sitting in here and there with this jazz band in the city. I don't know when they'll need me next, but when they do...I'd love to come in early and take you out for a coffee. What do you say?"

If I wanted our coffee date to go well, I needed to prepare. As far as I could figure, there were two things I needed to do to be ready.

First, I had to come up with some conversation starters. I thought it might take a while since it was so hard for me to do over the phone. But actually, it was easy. I just got my notebook, opened to a clean page in the back, and listed things I wanted to know. I stuck to simple questions—facts I really did want to learn, but nothing that would be awkward. I asked about little things, the kinds of details that I would want to know if I were to write a story about my dad. Like: *What's your favorite city to visit?* And: *When did you start playing your instrument?* Which led to something even more basic: *What actually is your instrument?* I'd wanted to ask on the phone, but when I got nervous I completely forgot.

I finished my list less than an hour after I'd started it. But the second thing I had to do for our coffee date wasn't so simple—I had to learn how to like coffee!

Momma only drinks tea at home, so I'd never had a chance to try coffee. To be honest, I'd never been interested before. But I didn't want to embarrass myself, like the time I tried grapefruit juice at Ricky's last winter and spat it all over the kitchen counter. Who knew that a drink with such a pretty pink color could end up tasting so nasty?

After Momma left for work on Monday, I decided to have coffee practice. I knew just the person to help me.

"Welcome, sit!" Mrs. Okocho led me to a chair at her huge dining room table. "You are timed perfectly. I am just about to fix a fresh pot." Mrs. Okocho is the biggest coffee drinker I know, even more than my teachers at school. It's her favorite drink, and she'll have it at any time of day—even an hour before bed, which makes absolutely no sense.

Now that I think about it, the fact that Mrs. Okocho loves coffee so much might be the reason I never cared to try it.

As I waited for the coffee to brew, I felt myself starting to sweat. I was a bit nervous, but mostly it was because Mrs. Okocho had all of her windows closed. The August heat had turned the dining room into a tropical jungle, and the potted plants that decorated the room didn't help that image.

Mrs. Okocho peeped around the doorframe. "You are sure that you would like a coffee?" she asked. "The flavor is very strong."

"Oh, I know," I bluffed.

"I can make cocoa with the cute little marshmallows," Mrs. Okocho offered. "Or by the look of you...perhaps a nice cool iced tea?"

Iced tea actually sounded perfect—but I was on a mission. "Thanks, Mrs. O," I replied, "but I could really go for a fresh cup of coffee. The hotter, the better."

"Ha-ha!" she cackled. "That is what I say as well!" She returned to the kitchen.

No kidding, I thought, dabbing at my neck with a napkin from the table holder.

Mrs. Okocho carried in a small bowl of sugar

cubes. "It is brewing," she said. "You *did* ask first your mama about this, yes?"

That was the one thing I hadn't done. I hadn't even mentioned that Dad wanted to take me for coffee—only that he wanted to visit me. I wasn't trying to break our no-secrets rule, exactly. It's just that I only got that far before a look crossed Momma's face. The look said *I'll believe it when I see it*. It made me not want to tell her anything else.

"It'll be fine," I said.

That seemed to satisfy Mrs. Okocho, because she continued fetching items from the kitchen. By the time our coffee was ready, she'd brought out three kinds of artificial sweeteners, a shaker of cinnamon, and two small ceramic jugs—one with cream, one with skim milk. I'd had no idea that coffee was so complicated!

Finally, Mrs. Okocho shuffled in with a pair of steaming mugs. "Here we are!" she announced. She set my cup in front of me and I let the steam waft up my nose. The smell was sharp, but not exactly bad.

Mrs. Okocho sat down and told me, "Go ahead, child. Fix it up however you like!" I watched her shake some cinnamon into her mug, add about four cubes of sugar, and then stir in some cream.

I liked all the things Mrs. Okocho was adding

into her coffee—but at the same time, it *was* Mrs. Okocho adding them. She had very odd tastes when it came to most foods. What if nobody but her put cinnamon in their coffee and it made me look weird?

"Is there something missing?" asked Mrs. Okocho. "I have nutmeg if you would like."

I had no idea what nutmeg was, but I guessed that I would probably *not like*. I decided to keep things simple and normal. "Thanks," I replied, "but I like my coffee plain."

"You mean black," Mrs. Okocho replied. "That is the name for plain coffee."

"Right," I replied, glancing at my inky beverage. "That's what I meant to say."

"Let it cool some, first," she suggested.

Once my mug got a little less steamy, I lifted it and took a drink. The moment I swallowed, all the saliva dried up in my mouth. My eyes and my lips scrunched toward each other like they wanted to trade places.

"Latasha," Mrs. Okocho said, "are you all right?"

I nodded, sucking on the sides of my tongue to try to get some moisture back.

"Are you sure you do not want something else to drink?"

I couldn't believe that my father wanted to take

me out for this disgusting, awful stuff!

"It's fine," I replied, trying not to gag. But my next sip was even worse than the first. All I could taste was bitterness, a hundred times worse than grapefruit—like I'd bitten a Tylenol in two.

"That is enough, I think," Mrs. Okocho said as she moved my coffee cup to her side of the table. "I refuse to let you suffer."

I hung my head in defeat.

"Would you like some water?" she asked.

I shrugged and Mrs. Okocho left the room. So much for not embarrassing myself—I was just glad it had happened here and not in front of my dad.

Mrs. Okocho returned with a glass of cold water. I took a mouthful of it and swished the terrible taste away. "Better?" she asked.

"Thanks," I said. "I don't know how people drink this stuff."

Mrs. Okocho waved an arm at the many sugars and spices on the table. "Most often, with help," she said. "What inspired this little…experiment?"

I hesitated for a second. I didn't want to go through the details—I'd done that enough in my head lately. After thinking, I landed on an answer that was simple and true. "I just want to be cool."

Mrs. Okocho smiled at me. "You, my child, are

already the coolest."

I smiled back and took another gulp of water. I'd never noticed how delicious it was.

"Mrs. Okocho," I finally said, "if someone wants to meet for coffee…I don't *have* to actually order coffee, do I?"

That night after dinner, I sat on our couch to read a novel from the library. Ella curled up at my feet like usual.

Momma came in with two small bowls of ice cream. "You want a dessert break?" she asked. Before I could even turn, Ella sprang from her slumber and draped her head over the back of the couch to stare at Momma.

"Not you, silly," Momma told her.

"Do we have blueberries?" I asked, replacing my bookmark.

"I'll put some on top," Momma replied.

Ella stared after Momma as she returned to the kitchen. "Dessert," I said. Ella's head whipped toward mine, her ears perked and alert. "Dessert," I repeated, and her ears jumped and flopped in response. It amazed me to discover what words Ella could learn when she thought they were important.

Momma returned with our fruit-topped ice cream and sat with me. For a minute we enjoyed our desserts in silence—except for Ella, whose tail quietly thumped the couch cushion as she waited for leftovers.

Momma wiped the corner of her mouth. "Sorry I don't have any…coffee to go with it," she said.

I couldn't believe that Mrs. Okocho had blabbed! She must have caught Momma before she came upstairs. "You heard about that, huh?" I said.

"What's going on?" she asked.

There was no sense trying to be cute about it. I explained about Dad's visit, and how important it was to be ready. When I finished, Momma took a bite of ice cream and I waited. She finally replied, "So your father wants to take his nine-year-old out for coffee."

I stuck my spoon into my ice cream and swung my feet to the floor. "I'm full," I replied. "May I be excused?"

"Latasha," Momma said, "wait. I'm not trying to pick a fight."

"I'm going to have a mocha latte, anyway," I simpered, leaning back into the couch. "Mrs. Okocho taught me how to order one."

Momma gave me a small, sad smile. "Listen," she

said. "About your dad saying he'll visit?"

"He's going to," I replied. "It might be a while, like he said. But he will. He wasn't lying."

"I'm sure he wasn't," Momma said. "When he promised he'd take you out, he probably really meant it. But it's one thing to make a promise and another to keep it. I will not watch you waste the rest of your summer waiting for your father to turn one into the other."

"I'm not going to waste—"

"—Just make *me* a promise," Momma said, holding up her pointer finger.

I exhaled slowly. "What?"

"If your dad comes, great. I'll be happy that he did," she began. "But promise you won't plan your whole life around it. Play with Ricky, care for Ella…I don't know, be nine! Deal?"

As if she had to chime in, Ella settled her head across my lap and turned on her side. Her look took the fight right out of me. "Deal," I agreed.

"Good," Momma said, standing. "After all, you're a Gandy. And us Gandy girls? We don't sit around waiting for some man to call on us. No matter who he is."

Chapter Five

Talent Pool

Momma's talk about Dad had been frustrating—but the worst part was that she'd been completely and totally right. Weeks went by, all without a word from him. In fact, Momma and I seemed to hear from everyone *but* him.

A letter arrived from Miss Simon, reminding us to schedule a check-up for Ella. It had been almost a year since she'd lost her leg, and Dr. Vanderstam wanted to check the strength of the joints in her remaining three. We also got a packet from Mr. Harvey about his plans for this year's Talent Pool. Most of the packet was about this competition that the club entered every year. I'd heard of it around school before, but I didn't know much about it. It sounded neat, even if the name for the competition was a little silly.

"'The Innovation Conversation,'" Momma read to me. "'A problem-solving contest for exceptional students. Participating teams will work together to respond to open-ended challenges with creative thinking and style.'" Momma bumped her knee against mine. "Well, you've got plenty of both of those."

I looked away, blushing. "What do they mean about an open-ended challenge?"

Momma skimmed the flyer. "Ah!" she said. "After school starts, the folks who run this thing will give everyone three basic ideas to pick from. Then each team will use one of those ideas to inspire a performance project."

"Like a play?"

"Sure," Momma replied. "It says here: 'Team performances can include original videos, artwork, dance, skits, or live music.'"

After reading about the Innovation Conversation—or the I.C., which was a lot less silly-sounding—I was really excited to start Talent Pool. But I couldn't feel all the way excited. It was weird how quickly two little words like "live music" could bring Dad back to mind, along with the sad, lonely feeling that always followed. That never used to happen to me.

At least I had Ella, and Mrs. Okocho, and even goofball Ricky to keep me occupied. A week before school, on a day that had been especially rough, I spent a whole afternoon watching Ricky try to look cool while he showed off his latest toy—a drum pad.

Except he insisted, "It's not a toy."

Ricky's not-toy was a little mini snare drum, only the head was quiet when you hit it, like a pen slapping on a book cover. It was actually kind of cute.

"It's not cute, either," he said. "It's awesome. Right, Ham?"

Hamlet walked in a circle and flopped onto the carpet in Ricky's room.

"I thought your folks were getting you a drum set," I said.

"They will," he told me, absently clicking his drumsticks together. "This is just for practice. Maybe next year I can get the real thing."

I started to wonder if my dad had learned on a fake instrument when he was our age. But the next thing Ricky did pushed that thought away.

"Besides," he said, giving the drum pad a tap. "I can still rock out on this."

Watching Ricky rock out is like watching Ella try to catch her tail—it *almost* actually happens.

Before I knew it, the calendar turned again and it was September. "How do I look?" I asked Momma, smoothing out my dress. It was Tuesday morning and we were standing on the sidewalk outside Cedarville Elementary about ten minutes before the start of fourth grade.

"You look ready to take over the world," Momma replied. I glanced down at myself. I didn't know if anyone had conquered the world while wearing a bright green jumper—but I took the compliment anyway.

I slung my backpack high on my shoulder, careful not to whack any of the kids or adults who were milling past us. I watched all of the parents and guardians escort their kids to the steps. One mom gave each of her twin sons a rib-crushing hug. I saw Darla Washington from my grade laughing with her grandma, who winked at her and handed over a lunchbox with a picture of Ray Charles on the front. One dad lifted his kindergartner—I figured kindergarten because she'd worn a can't-miss-it pink ballet tutu—up above his head. That dad held her high above the crowd, like she was a prize he'd won and he wanted everyone to know.

I tried to imagine what that little girl felt like, but nothing came.

"Mrs. O will be waiting here at three," Momma said from behind me. She placed her hands on my shoulders and rubbed each one. "Knock 'em dead, sweetie."

The first day of fourth grade was the same as any other grade—except that Ricky wasn't in my homeroom. He was in the other fourth grade class, with Mr. Loch. I had Miss Prooper, who looked like a raisin but had a loud, mean, truck driver voice.

"Everything she says sounds like a threat," I told

Ricky when I met up with him at lunch. "Like, 'I know you'll do your best this year'...*or else*!"

"Her actual threats sound worse," said Ricky's friend Dante, who was also at our table. A bunch of us who'd had Mr. Harvey last year were sitting together.

"Dude," Ricky laughed. "How were you late to the first day of school?"

Dante puffed out his cheeks before he replied. "I don't know, man, I just was."

When the first bell rang, I'd thought that nobody I knew had ended up in my class, but then it turned out that Dante had. He just came in fifteen minutes late. When he entered, Miss Prooper went off on a rant about how disrespectful it was to be tardy, and how she would not tolerate it under any circumstance. She made Dante say who he was three whole times, and then she wrote his first name on the board—"So I'll *remember*."

"I know why she's so mean," Ricky said. "My friend Bud in fifth grade? He says the kids in his class called her Prooper-Scooper."

That was kind of gross, but it got a laugh out of me.

"I can't believe her parents named her Prooper," Dante said, shaking his head.

"That's her last name, doof," Ricky sneered.

"Nobody picks their last name."

"Whatever," was Dante's witty reply.

Ricky was wrong, though—some last names did get picked. In a way, my dad picked my last name. If he'd stayed, I might have wound up being Latasha Kidd. Latasha Esther Kidd, with my little mutt, Ella Fitzgerald Kidd. But these were the kinds of thoughts I'd been trying to stay away from. I needed to change the subject, and fast.

"So how's Mr. Loch?" I asked Ricky.

"He's no Mr. Harvey," he said with a sigh.

On the plus side, I didn't have to wait long to see our old teacher. That's because on Thursday, we had our first meeting of Gifted and Talented! Usually, our meetings would be held right after school, but this first meeting was for both the kids and our parents, so it took place in the evening. Even Momma was able to make it—except she hadn't had time to change all the way out of her work clothes. She'd switched to slacks but couldn't find a shirt to match, so she'd had to put a zip-up fleece on over her scrubs top.

"You can't tell, right?" asked Momma as we entered the school.

I looked her over. "Except for your ID," I said.

Momma saw that she'd forgotten to remove her bright pink nametag. "Very wise," she replied, and she unpinned the tag and stuffed it in her pocket.

We reached Mr. Harvey's classroom just in time, at one minute before eight o'clock. Half the seats were already filled with kids and parents. I saw Darla and her grandma, and a couple kids from my new class with their parents, but there were a lot of people I didn't recognize. One thing was for sure—adults look *weird* sitting at third-grader desks.

The front of the room, though, looked normal as ever—the "Classroom Star" chart hung next to the blackboard, announcing the students who had done good deeds that week; the little classroom library stood in the corner; Mr. Harvey's "Wanted: Read or Alive" recommended reading list was taped to the wall above it. And, of course, there was Mr. Harvey himself, with his thick-rimmed glasses and big, broad smile, sitting at his desk.

"Latasha! Ms. Gandy," he said, standing. "Great to see you both. Grab a snack and have a seat. We're waiting a few more minutes to start."

Behind the crowd, I spotted a handful of desks that had been pushed together with a tablecloth draped over them. They held a display of cookies and fresh fruit, plus a coffee urn.

"Oh, look!" Momma said. "Your favorite drink."

I responded with a playful scowl.

"Good thing Miss Prooper isn't running this show," I said quietly. I broke a cookie in half for Ella and folded a napkin around it. "She'd probably lock all the late people in the supply closet."

After a few more families arrived, Mr. Harvey stepped in front of his desk. "All right, it looks like everybody's here," he said. "Ladies, gents, hello and welcome to the Talent Pool. Some of you were part of the program last year, and some of you have had me for class, but for everyone who's new, I'm Mr. Harvey. I'm glad everyone could make it out this evening. In fact, kids, let's give our parents and guardians a big 'thank you' for making the time. And…a one-two-three!"

"Thank you," I chanted with the other kids.

"Perfection," Mr. Harvey said. "'Thank you's are important, because the Gifted and Talented team is not just made up of fourth and fifth graders. Your parents and guardians are part of the team, too. It's the grown-ups in our lives who give us rides to and from our events, who provide supplies, and who chip in for the snacks at our weekly meetings. By the way—a special thanks to Darla Washington and Mrs.

Washington, who provided our cookies and fruit tray tonight."

I glanced back at Darla and her grandma, who smiled and shrugged in unison as if they'd practiced it.

"To have the most successful year we can," Mr. Harvey continued, "we need everyone to work together. That's especially true when it comes to our big project: the Innovation Conversation. Now, the first round of judging—that's the regional round—takes place on Saturday, December fifteenth. That's the week after our Winter Band and Chorus concert, and the week before holiday break, so I hope we won't have any conflicts."

"I'll make sure I stay off the schedule," Momma whispered in my ear.

"December fifteenth might sound a long way off," Mr. Harvey said, "but anyone who was here last year can tell you: the I.C. adds up to be a whole *lot* of work."

The fifth grade families murmured in agreement.

"Last year, we *just* missed the cut to move on to the state round," Mr. Harvey said, holding his fingers an inch apart. "But the team did such great work. I think this could be our year, as long as we all stick together and do our part. What do you say, guys?

Who's ready to get started?"

I knew I was! My hand shot up as high as I could reach. I saw other hands go up around me.

Mr. Harvey shook his head. "Uh-uh, we're not in school tonight," he said with a smile. "I want to hear you loud and proud! Who's ready?"

We all hollered together, even the grown-ups. Momma gripped my hand and grinned like she'd just been waiting for an excuse to shout. She looked so pretty when she lit up like that.

"All righty-roo!" Mr. Harvey said with a clap.

"Then onto our first order of business." He lifted a stack of stapled papers and passed them out.

"The contest judges just released the list of challenges we can choose from," he explained. "They all look interesting to me…but it's not up to me, or any of the other adults in the room. Whatever you kids pick to inspire your project is entirely up to you. So read everything over, and at next week's meeting I want to hear which challenge interests each of you the most. Then we'll vote on a winner."

"Latasha," Momma said as we walked, "you'll strain your eyes."

"The streetlights are super bright," I assured her, peering at the pages. We weren't even halfway home from the Talent Pool meeting, but I was already squinting at our challenge list.

"Our house lights are brighter," Momma said, taking the papers from my hands.

I huffed through my nose. Honestly, home was only ten minutes away, but I was just so psyched to get started!

When we got to our apartment, I grabbed the challenge list back from Momma. She went to the phone to check our voicemail, and Ella followed me to the kitchen table. I tried to read the papers over, but the pup kept nudging my side with her nose, sniffing and wagging.

I looked at Momma, who was listening to a message on the voicemail. "Momma," I said, "can you call her over?"

Momma held up a finger and kept listening on the phone. Something she heard made her roll her eyes and smile just the tiniest bit.

Ella kept prodding me, her tail whacking a table leg. "What!" I demanded, laughing. I patted the pocket she'd been sniffing and realized what she wanted. "Oh, sorry girl!" I'd totally forgotten about the half-cookie I'd set aside for her. She whined hungrily as I pulled the paper-wrapped treat from my pocket.

"I know, I know," I told her. "Your life is so hard." I broke up the cookie and fed Ella one nibble at a time as I studied the list of challenges. Mr. Harvey was right—they all looked interesting. One challenge was about planning a trip to the moon, but we could only bring certain supplies. Another one wanted us to put on a show about an old explorer and his adventures. The third one especially caught my eye. For that challenge, we had to put on our own musical where all of the characters were animals.

"How about that one?" I asked Ella as she chewed a cookie bite. "Maybe I could play you!"

Momma set the phone down in front of me on the table.

"You have a message," she said, walking toward the living room.

"Who, Ricky?"

"Oh, no," she replied, exaggerating each word. "It was *the president*!"

I looked after Momma as she left the kitchen. The president? Of what? And what had gotten her so grumpy all of a sudden?

I turned on the phone and went to our voicemail. Its lady-robot voice told me we had one new message. When it began, though, I didn't hear anyone speaking—I heard a piano! It took me a moment to recognize the song. It was "Hail to the Chief," except it sounded quicker and jazzier than when we'd listened to it during social studies. Then the song stopped and a voice began to speak.

"Hello," it said, "this is the president of the United States calling for Ms. Latasha Esther…"

My mouth opened in a wide O. The *actual president?* What on Earth was going on? I stared down at Ella, but believe it or not, she wasn't much help. I pressed the phone close to my ear.

"Latasha," the president said, "on behalf of the United States government, I would like to personally offer you an apology. You might think that your father has forgotten about you, but I assure you, that is not at all the case. He has been busy this month working for me, the president, on a top-secret musical mission. Sadly, the details are classified. But now that your dad—who, by the way, is one of the bravest and most handsome men I've ever met…"

I began to realize that this voice sounded not at all like the president, and a whole bunch like someone else I knew. "Daddy…" I said, groaning and laughing at the same time.

His message went on, "Now that the world is once again safe, I've given your father permission to visit you. He will be coming to Pittsburgh this Saturday. Latasha, if you would still like to see him, he would very much like to see you. Please call him at home. God bless you, and God bless the United States of America."

And then "Hail to the Chief" picked up again until the message ended. I was smiling so hard that my cheeks tingled. I set down the phone and looked at Ella. "I tell you what, pup," I said, rapping my fingers against the challenge list on the table. "He gets a 'ten' for style."

Chapter Six

Kidd On Keys

"Latasha, don't get me wrong," Momma began. "I'm happy you wanted to clean the house. But did you really need to clean Ella, too?"

"First impressions are very important," I replied, wrestling with my towel-clad pup.

Ella hadn't been dirty or stinky—actually, her dog food makes her fur smell like a corn chip, and, for whatever reason, her paws always smell like buttery popcorn. But I wanted her to look groomer-fresh when Dad came over today.

That's right—it was actually going to happen! After I'd heard Dad's message on Thursday, I talked to Momma and she called him that very night. They agreed that he would come by at two p.m. on Saturday so that we could spend the afternoon together. I'd been counting down the hours ever since.

Counting down the hours and cleaning every inch of our apartment. I'd dusted the ceiling fans, cleared every cobweb, and I even had Mrs. Okocho come upstairs to teach me her "secret floor-mopping technique" for the kitchen. It turned out her "big secret" was just to do it twice—boring! At least it kept me busy, though. Waiting around is the worst.

That was my other reason for bathing Ella, even though she doesn't much like baths—I knew that with bribing her to climb into the tub, actually washing her, and drying her off, that last hour until two o'clock would zip right on by.

Ella's bath had gone as planned, except for one detail that I'd forgotten. Maybe our towels are scratchy, or maybe it's static buildup—but whenever I try to dry Ella off, she goes bonkers! So now, right at the time Dad was supposed to arrive, instead of an adorable, sort-of-corn-chip-smelling cutie, I had a drippy, wriggly beast on my hands.

Or, to be more precise, in my arms. She was struggling with all her might to break free from my towel grip and zoom around the whole house. That was the way she preferred to dry off.

"Settle!" I insisted as I rubbed her coat. "What will your grandpa think?"

"Grandpa, huh?" asked Momma from the door.

"Sure," I replied. "He's my dad, and she's my girl… so, Ella's his grand-pup."

"I'm sure he'll love that," Momma said with a chuckle. She paused, thinking. "Do you…tell her that I'm her grandma?"

I shot Momma a *Really?* kind of look. "Well, yeah."

Momma backed out of the doorway, waving her arms like she was running away. "Oh, I feel old."

"Let's keep that grandma-grandpa talk just between you and me," I told Ella. I stroked her side and her wriggling slowed.

But then the doorbell rang. "He's here!" I exclaimed. Ella tore free and raced for the door. She was so excited, though, that she tried to run out sideways and banged right into the doorframe.

"You poor little simpleton," I giggled as she shook the water from her coat and rushed out of the bathroom.

I followed Ella's damp paw prints into the kitchen. I found her next to Momma, flapping her ears against her head to dry them. "I'll go down for the door," Momma said. "Put her on the leash or something!"

That seemed wise. I didn't want my pup jumping all over Dad until they knew each other better.

I hooked my fingers under Ella's collar and let Momma slip out the door. "Come on," I pleaded, clipping on her leash. "You want a Teddy Snack?" No response. "Dessert?" That at least got me a pause. But then two sets of feet thumped up the hall stairs and

Ella set right back to dancing. To be honest, though, I really couldn't blame her. If I had a tail, I'd have been wagging it like crazy, too!

Momma reopened our door. And there he was behind her. He wasn't quite as tall as I remembered—taller than Momma, still, but not like the picture in my head. Everything else was the same, though. He smiled, thin-lipped, like he was thinking of a joke. His brown eyes took in every detail of the room as he entered. His thick, wavy hair, orange-red like a fireball, peeked out from under his hat brim.

His eyes fell to me and his thin smile grew until his teeth began to show. I recognized that smile—it looked like mine.

"Hey there, pumpkin," he said.

I barely noticed Ella bumping the side of my knee. I wanted to run over screaming and wrap my dad in a huge hug—and I also wanted to give him a good punch in the thigh for making me wait so long. Instead, I just stood my ground and smiled back, hoping he'd notice that we matched. "Hey, Daddy," I said quietly.

He looked down at Ella and purposely widened his eyes. "Well now!" he said, stepping past Momma. "This must be the infamous Lady Ella!" He glanced at me. "May I say hello?"

I nodded eagerly and loosened my grip on Ella's leash. She pranced toward him, spinning and hopping, and Dad dropped to one knee to pet her. "She's a little wet," I warned.

"That I can handle," he said, offering the back of his hand so she could learn his scent. Then Dad removed his hat with a grand gesture. "It is a sincere pleasure and honor to be in your presence," he told Ella, bowing his head almost to her eye level.

Ella twisted around and whacked him right across the face with her tail. Dad flinched back in shock and I yanked Ella away as quickly as I could.

"Well," he said, blinking the sting away, "that smarts."

"You okay?" asked Momma, laughing. I wasn't laughing, though, not one bit. I wanted to run to my room and hide under the covers until my father gave up and went home. I didn't know if I could feel any guiltier than I did in that moment.

Then a drop of blood fell from Dad's nose and onto the twice-mopped floor.

"Still get these when you're nervous?" asked Momma, glancing at the tissues up Dad's nostrils.

“Sometimes,” Dad replied, watching the ceiling. With those tissues stuffed in his nose, he sounded like he was half-man, half-kazoo. “Not so often anymore.”

“I am so, so sorry, Daddy,” I said. I was doing everything I could not to cry. Our whole afternoon together had been ruined before it could even start. Because of Ella, he'd spent the last fifteen minutes stuck staring at our kitchen ceiling. I'd have drunk a whole pitcher of icky black coffee if it would take back what she'd done.

But Dad just looked over at me and winked. “It's only a trickle.”

“Keep your head back,” Momma ordered, guiding him by his forehead.

“Yes, Nurse Gandy,” he said with a flare of his eyebrows.

“Not quite,” she corrected, and then she looked over toward me. “Hey, honey? Why don't you go check on the pup? I'll bet she feels terrible.”

Ella had done exactly what I'd wanted to do: run away and hide in my room. I found her curled up at the head of my bed, tucked into the corner behind my pillow. It was almost cute enough to make me forgive her on the spot.

But not quite. “Ella Fitzgerald Gandy, I am very

disappointed in you," I told her, my voice heavy and slow. "You almost broke your grandpa's face. That was bad. Very bad. Don't you want to have a grandpa?" For a second I forgot what I meant to say next, but then it came back. "You will sit here while I'm gone and think about what you did."

And then I grabbed my notebook off my desk and left the room. Ella must have realized how serious I was, because she did the unimaginable and stayed right where I'd told her to.

Before I entered the kitchen, I heard Momma and Dad talking, so I waited outside to listen.

"Am I all cleaned up?" asked Dad. His voice had returned to normal, so I guessed his nosebleed had stopped and the tissues were out.

"Yeah, you look good," Momma replied. The sink turned on for a second, then back off.

"So do you, you know," Dad said.

"Oh, you drop that nonsense, mister," Momma told him, but she didn't sound mean.

"No fooling," Dad said. "You look great. Both of you."

I smiled beside the doorway. Maybe the day wasn't ruined after all.

"And come on in, Latasha," Momma called out. "I know you're out there."

Rats—how did Momma *do* that? I came in and saw my parents standing beside each other at the sink. Dad stepped forward, took a deep breath, and put his hat firmly on his head. "So, kiddo," he said, "we ready to hit the town?"

"As long as you're not mad," I said uncertainly.

"You kidding?" he replied. "I got beat up by Ella Fitzgerald! That's like a badge of honor."

Some people call Pittsburgh the City of Bridges, because we have about a million of them. But I think it should be called the City of Neighborhoods. Pittsburgh isn't one big place—it's really a bunch of little places. Within the city limits, there are ninety different neighborhoods. I'm not even exaggerating that number. I counted it once, right on a map in the library. Just don't ask me to list all of their names.

Anyway, that's the reason a real Pittsburgher won't tell you she's from Pittsburgh. She'll say she's from Lawrenceville. She'll say she's from Polish Hill. As for me, I'm from Friendship. The cool thing about having so many neighborhoods, with all their crooked lines and one-way streets, is that every time you leave your own, it feels like an adventure.

The only problem is that if you don't know exactly where you're going, it's super easy to get lost.

Like Dad and I were now.

"We're almost there," he insisted. "I can feel it in my bones." We were rumbling in Dad's powder-blue station wagon down a street I'd never heard of.

"Where are we going again?" I asked.

"This cool coffee shop my buddy brought me to last year," he replied. "It's in…Beltzhoover…near the park."

I sighed. Describing a place as "near the park" was about as helpful as saying it was "near the bridge."

The brakes squeaked as we stopped at a light. Dad looked at me. "What do you say?" he asked. "Left turn?"

I shrugged. "Could be," I said, nervously tapping my vocabulary notebook in my lap. I had listed so many questions for Dad in it, but if the day kept up like it had been, I wouldn't get a chance to ask any of them.

Dad noticed my drumming. "What do you have there?" he asked. "Diary?"

"Sort of," I said. I explained how I used the notebook to write down my thoughts and cool words that I wanted to remember for later.

"It's funny," Dad replied. "I used to do something

a lot like that."

I perked up in my seat. "Really?"

"Sure," he said, "except mine was all rhymes. Big lists of rhyming words, you know, for when I'd write lyrics? Except my notebook didn't have a cool little strap like yours to keep it shut."

I smiled. I liked how Dad noticed little details about things, just like I did.

"I write other things in here, too," I said. "Like, I wrote a whole page of questions I wanted to ask you."

"Oh-ho," he said, chuckling. "So our little get together was going to be a—what? An interrogation?"

I blushed. "No, not like that," I said. "More like an interview."

"Ah, I get you." He turned onto another street. "Well, since we are hopelessly lost at the moment, why don't we start the interview now?"

I happily opened my notebook, pulling the strap an extra bit so it would make the little *snap* that I liked. I flipped through the book to my interview page. "All right," I said. "Question one—"

"Lay it on me, sister!" he shouted.

"Question one," I repeated firmly, hoping to keep the silliness in check. "What instrument do you play?"

Dad looked at me like I'd spoken in Japanese.

"Your mother never told you?" he asked.

The hurt in his voice made me nervous. "No…" I said cautiously.

"Well," he said, pausing for far too long. I watched his jaw muscles flex. "Well, why would it come up, I guess? Never mind. Just, uh, look behind you—under the blanket."

I turned my head. On the backseat, a dark blanket covered a large, rectangular object. I strained to grab the blanket, but my seat belt held me in place. "I can't reach," I told him.

"Don't tell your mother I did this," Dad said, and before I could reply, he unclicked my seat belt. "Just a quick peek."

I swiftly leaned and yanked the blanket. Underneath was a huge, shining keyboard that reached from door to door. "Whoa!" I said. I wanted to give it a long look and figure out what all of the knobs and buttons up above the keys were for—but I was nervous about not wearing my seat belt, so I faced front and re-buckled myself. "So was that you playing 'Hail to the Chief' on that message?" I asked. "You're good!"

Dad half-smiled, but I could tell that he was thinking about something else. He was squinting like he was trying to make out something very far away.

"Daddy?" I asked.

His head jerked toward me. "Listen," he said. "Let's put this coffee shop on hold."

I didn't even know what had gone wrong. "But…" I couldn't let the day end like this, I just couldn't. My breath caught in my throat and I felt the corner of my lip quiver.

"How about french fries instead?" asked Dad.

My heart started beating again.

"Do you like french fries?" he asked.

I had to think for a second so that I could remember how to speak. "Yeah, I do!"

"I know a place," Dad told me. He pulled into a gas station to turn the car around. "And even better…I actually know where it is."

"Welcome to the Dirty O," Dad announced as we entered through the door. Then he saw the look on my face and burst out laughing. "Relax, kid, it's just a nickname. It's perfectly safe."

Looking around the shop, with its scuffed-up tile and the grubby college kids at almost every table, I understood the nickname completely. What I didn't understand was why we'd come here.

"We're here for the best fries in town!" Dad explained. "I used to come here when I was at Pitt." He meant the University of Pittsburgh, the biggest college in the city.

Dad took me to a counter in the back. A lady with bushy gray hair and a huge mole beside her nose asked us for our order. "You want to split a small?" Dad asked me.

"Can we get a medium?" I asked. I'd been so busy cleaning the house that I'd totally forgotten about lunch.

"Look up before you decide," he said. He pointed to the wall above the counter, which had different-sized paper food boats nailed to it. "Those are the sizes."

I stared at the writing on each boat. *Small* was the size of a paperback novel. *Medium* was the size of an encyclopedia. And *Large* was the size of the Carnegie Library.

"Small's okay," I said.

Dad laughed hard—he has this great, really-real laugh that shakes his head and his shoulders—and then he ordered us a small. After we paid and got an order number, Dad picked a table for us in the corner. "After you, madame," he said, holding out my chair. I could definitely get used to that.

"So," Dad said, dropping into his seat, "want to move on through the interview?"

I scanned through my notebook past the questions we'd covered. Such as: *How old are you?* (Thirty-two.) *When's your birthday?* (June third.) *Do you have any siblings?* (I'm an "only," like you.)

"Here we go," I said, touching my pen to a new line. "Do you have a band?"

"Not exactly," Dad replied. "I like to play all over. So I just sit in wherever I'm needed. It's good being the guy who fills in—you're like the hero of the band."

"Is that what you're doing tonight?" I asked. "Filling in?"

"With this jazz and soul outfit," he agreed. "They're called the Ministers. Their piano player's an older guy—got some problems with his health. So to the rescue, here I come…" His fingers danced across the table's edge and flashed up like they were taking off in flight. "*The Kidd on Keys.*"

"Is that what people call you?"

Dad shrugged. "It's what *I* call me, anyway," he said. "My nickname with most folks is, *Hey, you're late!*"

We both laughed—but I could kind of see their point.

"What's next?" he asked. "This is fun."

I moved on to my next question. “What are your parents like?”

Dad pulled in a big breath through his nose. “Pop died when I was a kid,” he said. “I was in junior high.”

“Just like Momma was,” I said quietly. The thought made my eyes sting.

“Well,” Dad jumped in, “I do still have my mum.”

I had a grandma! “Does she live nearby?” I asked eagerly.

“Oh, no,” he said, “not for a few years now.”

I huffed in disappointment.

“She got remarried a while back, retired down to South Florida,” he said. “I go down to see her for a few days every Thanksgiving. And *that* is about enough for the both of us.”

I gaped at him—I couldn’t imagine seeing Momma only once a year.

“Mum is—” Dad said, pausing. “I love my mum. But she always thinks she knows what’s best, and she always takes the time to *tell you*. She has this way of talking down that makes you feel smaller—like she shrunk you with her words. I’d just as soon keep my distance.”

I wanted to ask why she was like that, but a glass-shattering screech cut me off.

“Number fifty-eight!” shouted the lady with the

mole by her nose. For a half of a second, it killed every conversation in the restaurant.

"Was that us?" Dad said in a fake whisper. "I didn't hear her."

I liked the way Dad laughed, but there was something I liked even better—the way he made me laugh.

He handed me our order ticket. "Grab that, would you? And napkins. We'll need 'em."

I got our fries from the counter and when I came back, Dad's fingers were dancing along our table's edge again like it was a keyboard. He was nodding and his upper body swayed to a soundless beat. It made me think of this one lady in our church choir who gets all the solos—when she sings, she does it with her whole body.

"Are you working out a new song?" I asked.

Dad's eyes opened. "All the time," he replied.

"That's how I feel about stories," I said. "Everywhere I look, I see one."

Dad smiled. "You got anything cooking right now?"

"I'm kind of wondering about the fry counter lady," I said. When I'd gone to get our food, I'd spotted her near the fryers, talking with the cook—he was this bone-skinny guy with a gray ponytail tucked into his hairnet. "I think she and the cook are having a secret romance."

"Is that so?" he said with a laugh. "How'd you pick that up?"

It was all in how the lady was acting with him. "They were laughing and then she touched his arm," I explained. "But when she did it, she glanced around like she hoped no one else had noticed."

Dad grabbed the brim of his hat and tipped it toward me. "I like your brain, kid, you know that?"

That might have been the best compliment I'd ever gotten.

He shifted his hat back into place and leaned across our tray. "I have a little tale for you," he said offhandedly, "and it's absolutely true. If you're interested."

I nodded fiercely. "Tell it!"

Dad pointed at me in agreement. "This story takes place about eleven years back, on a chilly October evening," he said. "My senior year at Pitt. First semester, just past midterms. The setting? Right…here."

"At the Dirty O?" I asked.

Dad flashed his eyebrows devilishly. "At this very table."

I pulled my chair in until I could feel the table

against my ribs.

"The characters of this tale are: myself—"

"*—the Kidd on Keys—*"

"—and, believe it or not…the lady at the fry counter."

"The secret romance?" I asked, glancing back. She was leaning against the cash register, still chatting it up with the cook.

"Well," Dad said, "she looked a lot different back then. She was a lot more slender, for one. Young, with a beautiful face—and the smoothest skin you ever did see."

I smirked at him. To be honest, it made me a little queasy to hear him talk like that about some random stranger.

But Dad went on. "She had a much deeper tan back in those days," he said. "And the sweetest voice. Honey-sweet."

That left me baffled—the counter lady's voice was all vinegar.

Dad tucked a strand of hair behind his ear. "And she had a cute…perfectly round…afro."

"Dad!" I burst out. "What kind of weird story is this?"

He shot me a crafty grin. "This is where I met your mother."

In an instant, the Dirty O was transformed. Its looks were unchanged, but it somehow felt like an entirely new place. I'm not sure what expression I was wearing—but it must have been the right one, because Dad leaned back in satisfaction and went on with the story.

"Like I mentioned, it was my last year of school. I took classes during the day and played with anyone who'd let me on stage at night. And in between, I was coming here a few times a week for a nice, balanced meal of…french fries." I snickered—Dad knew just how long to pause to give his jokes a punch. "Speaking of! Have some. They're good as leftovers, but better fresh."

We each popped a salty fry in our mouths. Dad was right—they were the best I'd ever tasted.

"So I'm coming here pretty regular," he continued. "Then one night, that cold October night, there's a new girl working the counter."

"Momma," I said.

"She doesn't pay me much mind at first," he said, dipping a fry in ketchup, "but I sure notice her. She's always humming songs behind the counter. Old stuff—*good* stuff. Dusty Springfield, Etta James—and, of course, the indispensible Ms. Fitzgerald."

He jabbed our table with a pointer finger. "I start

sitting here in the corner so I can hear her better. And, I'll admit, so I can see her better, too. Soon, I start giving her flyers for the shows where I'm playing. Every time I'm in here, a new flyer. A basement party on Atwood, a club gig at the Upstage. And she's always got an excuse for why she can't make it. One time, she tells me she doesn't have money to throw away on a show. So I try to play it all cool and I tell her, 'I'll get your name onto the list.' You know what she said?"

"What?" I asked.

He raised the pitch of his voice and said, "*How about I put you on the list? The list of white boys who come in here pestering me for a date.*"

That was Momma, all right—he'd even cocked his head like she does when she's annoyed.

"But that didn't stop me," Dad said. "I just realized I'd have to be a bit more creative."

"So what'd you do?" I asked.

"I made her a CD," he replied. "A CD with all the songs I'd heard her humming at the counter."

"You remembered them all?"

He looked me right in the eye. "How could I forget?"

Why hadn't Momma ever said anything about all this? It was more romantic than any of those silly fairy tales we used to read together. "Did she like the CD?" I asked.

That grin that matched mine spread across Dad's face. "Oh, yeah," he said. "And that was that. She was done for."

We talked for another hour as we finished our fries. Dad didn't share much more about Grandma, but he told me all about his adventures playing on the road. I told him about school, and Mr. Harvey, and how I wanted to put on that animal musical for the Innovation Conversation. And we laughed a whole year's worth of laughter.

On our ride back to Friendship, though, it was Dad's story about Momma that really stuck with me. It made me wonder, *If they were such a good match, why'd they ever split up?* Only one reason came to mind—and it made me feel so bad that I pushed it away before my brain could really think it.

We pulled up to the curb on Graham Street. "Wish me luck tonight," Dad said, and I did.

"Can we do this again soon?" I asked. "Like, really soon?"

"Without a doubt, my dear," he said. "If you do end up doing that musical project for the..."

"Innovation Conversation," I chimed in.

"If you do that," he said, "maybe I can give you some song tips."

That settled it—I'd fight for that project even if it meant taking on the whole Talent Pool!

"Do you want to come up and say hi to Momma?" I asked.

"Not today," he said. "But I've got something you can take with you." He reached back under his keyboard and grabbed a recordable CD in a plastic case.

I stared at the disc. "Is that...the mix you made for Momma?"

"I made this one for you," he replied.

My eyebrows shot all the way up to my hairline!

"I didn't know before if it would fit you," he went on, "but I think I did all right. The playlist is in the back of the case. It's all female singers. Check the title."

Dad had written it on the disc in marker: *Tough Ladies for My Tough Lady.*

I raced up into the house so that I could listen to my new CD. But first I had to contend with my crazy leaping dog. She was so excited to see me that she wrapped her forepaws around my arm and wouldn't let go.

"I'm here, my girl, I'm here," I told her, holding the disc out of her reach.

"Thank goodness," Momma said as she entered the kitchen. "That dog cried for an hour after you left!"

"She did?" I asked, instantly guilty.

"She must've thought you weren't coming back or something," Momma replied. "She was inconsolable."

I knelt and embraced Ella around the waist with one arm. "Poor simple girl," I whispered to her. "The loneliest dog in the world."

"So how'd it go?" asked Momma.

I sped through a summary of our afternoon. Momma's face was tough to read through it all—but to be honest, I wasn't trying very hard. I just wanted to listen to my mix!

"He made you a CD," Momma commented.

"Just like for you," I replied.

Momma sucked her cheeks in, just nodding to herself.

"I'm going to my room to listen," I said. "You want me to leave my door open?"

"Closed is fine," she said.

Even better! Ella and I went to my room and shut the door. I had an old CD player that used to belong to Momma in my desk drawer and a pair of small speakers for it—not too loud, but definitely good enough. I hooked everything up, popped Dad's CD in, and let it play.

From the first song on, I was hooked. Some of his "tough ladies" I'd heard of, like Mary J. Blige and Adele. But most of the names on the playlist were new to me—someone named Mavis Staples; some super-sad, super-beautiful singer named Nina Simone; another called Janis Joplin. The songs' styles were all over the map, but each singer had one thing in common: it was like each one was talking straight to me.

Ella watched me from the bed. "He's not a musician," I told her as I swayed on my feet. "He's a magician."

Chapter Seven

Ella's Anniversary

Anyone who's spent five minutes with Ella knows that she can be a handful—or an armful, or a lapful, or a licky-face-tail-whack-to-the-knees-ful. But there is one place where she behaves like a regular angel: in Mrs. Okocho's Oldsmobile. As soon as she climbs onto the bedsheet Mrs. Okocho always spreads across the back seat for her, Ella just curls up in a ball and doesn't stir until we reach our destination. I never trained her to do that. I don't know how she picked it up.

What I do know is this: as we all rode to Dr. Vanderstam's office, I found myself wishing that Ella's calm was contagious.

It was the third Saturday in October, and Mrs. Okocho, Momma, and I were taking Ella for an important check-up. A year ago this week, Ella had had her accident and her surgery. Now it was time for Dr. Vanderstam to examine her and learn how the rest of her body had held up.

I always got a little nervous when we took Ella to the vet, but today I kept finding new things to fret over. What if Dr. Vanderstam said I was giving her too many treats and making her fat? Or what if he told me I wasn't giving her enough exercise? Or that I was giving her *too much* exercise?

"You can't give a dog too much exercise," Momma assured me, looking over her shoulder.

"You totally can," I replied. It was true—I'd looked it up online. "And for a dog with three legs, it can lead to this horrible thing called…arthritis."

Momma and Mrs. Okocho shared a glance and a smirk, which I did not appreciate one bit!

"It's a serious condition!" I cried. "Your joints wear out and feel all swollen—"

"—Honey, please," Momma cut in. "Everything will be fine, I promise you."

"Listen to your mama," Mrs. Okocho said. "She is a wise lady."

"And then later today," Momma added, "you'll have a nice visit with your father, and you'll wow him with your world-famous meatball hoagies."

I lowered my eyes to my lap, grinning. "They're not world-famous."

"Give it time," Momma replied with a wink.

I had to admit, meatball hoagies *were* sort of my specialty—even if they made up a full one-quarter of the things I knew how to cook. I couldn't wait to see the look on Dad's face when he tried one. As long as Ella's check-up went well, I knew that today would be a perfect day.

I reached over to my round fur ball and stroked her shoulders. Now that I thought about it, I'd had a lot of great days lately. The last six weeks had been a breeze—all along the way, things had just seemed to find a way of working out how I wanted.

It all started with Talent Pool, that first week after Dad's visit.

"Hear ye, hear ye!" Mr. Harvey announced. "The first official meeting of the Cedarville Elementary Gifted and Talented Club is now in session!" He leaned back against his desk and clapped his hands together. "Let's pick a challenge."

Each of us had a turn to argue for our favorite idea. I got to go first—"Since you've got your hand a mile in the air," Mr. Harvey noted. I quickly explained why I thought the musical challenge would be best. I talked about all of the different creative skills we'd use to make costumes and backdrops, and what fun it would be to tell a story with songs, and how our show would have the most style in the whole competition.

"Plus," I added, "I've already got an idea for an animal song—it's called 'The Lonely Dog Blues.'"

You can probably guess who'd inspired that.

Sometimes I get nervous talking in front of a group like that, but I felt great once I'd finished. A few kids hopped on board with me right off the bat.

But still, some kids had other challenges in mind. Two boys especially—these fifth graders named Russell and Gautam—had their hearts set on doing the Mission to Mars challenge. In true science fair style, they'd even made a poster board about why it was the strongest choice. It was nerdy—but I wished I'd thought of it!

"The last three teams to win our region did projects about science," Russell argued.

"We could act out a skit about landing on Mars," Gautam said.

Then they did their big finish—they unveiled a slow-motion walk they'd invented that made them look like they were in low gravity on Mars.

I worried that those boys might win the group over—but then I got backup from an unexpected place.

"May I speak, Mr. Harvey?" It was Darla Washington.

"Miss Washington has the floor," he declared.

Darla cleared her throat in her usual dramatic way. "I've had a lot of hobbies," she said, "and I'm pretty good at most of them."

Oh boy, I thought. Darla has this habit of talking very highly of herself—sometimes for minutes at a time. I slid down in my seat and tried not to sigh too loudly.

"But my favorite hobby is playing the piano," she said. With that, I straightened up in my chair and leaned forward. "My grandma's had me in lessons since I was three, and I've gotten first place ribbons at my last two recitals. It would be so much fun to play for a musical. I'll bet that between my playing and Latasha's writing, we could put on a show that no one would forget!"

My cheeks were burning hot—partly because I was flattered, and partly because I felt guilty for thinking she only wanted to brag.

Darla wasn't done, though. She went on to tell each other kid in the club how his or her talents would help make a great musical—how Donnie Yerba could paint scenery, and how Rachel Kwan could make animal ears for our costumes.

"And science could be important, too," she said. "We'll have to do lots of studying to make sure we get each animal just right. Maybe we'll even find one that moves like this!"

And then she did a perfect imitation of Russell and Gautam's Mars walk.

Darla basically saved the day—when it came time to vote, only Russell stuck with the Mission to Mars challenge. In the end, Gautam jumped spaceship to give the animal musical a total of eleven votes.

Well, twelve votes if you count both of my hands.

We came up with a story idea very quickly. It was all about what happens when the owners go away and their pets get left home alone. Our characters were some hamsters who want to eat all of the cereal in the house, two cats who think that the humans are *their* pets, a tattletale parakeet—and, of course, one very lonely dog.

Since we didn't have a ton of time, we decided to take the team's favorite songs and just change the words to be about animals. That made it easy for me to come up with lyrics and for Darla to learn each tune. But when it came to "The Lonely Dog Blues," I didn't want to copy a song that was already out there. I wanted to do something unique. And I knew just who I needed to help me.

Fortunately, Dad seemed really excited to teach me about music. "That sick keys player is going to be taking a long rest," he said, "so I'll already be down your way quite a bit. You've got great timing, kid!" I always got a happy little smile when he called me *kid*—it was different from how Dad's name is spelled, but sometimes I pretended that it was the same.

Over the past six weeks, Dad had come to see me three times. The first day, we went out to do what he called "invaluable musical research." Really, all Dad did was take me to his favorite used record store in town. It wasn't just called a record store, either—it actually sold real records, like the vinyl kind that you have to play on a turntable. It was fun because I got to listen to strange songs over the store's crackly speakers, and I learned a bunch of new words—like *sleeve*, which is the thin paper case for a record, and *platter*, which is what people used to call records because of how big they are.

Dad even promised he'd buy me anything I wanted that was under ten dollars—which would have been awesome if we actually had a record player at home. I tried to take it as one of those it's-the-thought-that-counts moments, like the time Mrs. Okocho made me a Christmas sweater with a puff-paint snowman on it.

That afternoon had been fun, but Dad's other two visits had been more useful. On those days, we didn't go anywhere—Dad came to the house, lugged his keyboard up the stairs, and gave me music lessons. Momma hadn't exactly been thrilled by the idea at first, but she gave in once I explained how much it would help the Talent Pool.

Our first lesson was about chords, which are the note clusters you use to build a song. Our second lesson was about the ways you can arrange chords next to each other, which are called *progressions*. Dad had a great way of explaining it to me. "Chords are like words," he said. "They only tell a story if you put them in the right order."

At the end of that lesson, we'd made plans for today. "Next time I come down," Dad had told me, while collapsing his keyboard stand, "I'll reveal to you the secrets of the jazz universe. We're going to learn the twelve-bar blues."

Even though I was worried—sorry, *concerned*—about Ella's check-up, I could hardly wait to see Dad. I really wanted to show off all the work I'd done for our animal musical. All of the lyrics were written, from "The Lonely Dog Blues" to Darla's personal favorite, "Hamster" (in the style of Aretha Franklin). But even more, I was excited because today's visit was different from all the others.

Until today, Dad and I had only met up when he already had a gig in town. But this afternoon he didn't have a gig, with the Ministers or anyone else. He was driving down just because I'd invited him. He was supposed to arrive at one for our lesson and then stay all the way through dinner. When I'd asked him to join us, he gave me the best answer. He'd said, "There is no place I'd rather eat." That even made Momma smile.

But before I could enjoy our perfect family dinner, I had to survive Ella's check-up.

Ella's tail slapped the doorframe as she led Momma, Mrs. Okocho, and me into the waiting room. At the desk, Miss Simon set down the magazine she was reading and smiled at us. "There's that happy tail!" she said. "And how've the Gandys been?"

"Fabulous," I told her.

"Did you ever get things worked out with that neighbor dog?" she asked.

"It's all okay now," I replied.

"I'm quite glad to hear it!" Miss Simon said. "Dr. V will be ready for you in a minute."

We sat in chairs along the wall. Mrs. Okocho unfolded the comics section from her morning newspaper. I petted Ella to keep her settled. And Momma put a hand on my shoulder—almost like she was settling me.

While we waited, I thought about my pup and Hamlet. I'd told Miss Simon the truth—those two got along now almost as well as Ricky and I did. But lately, I hadn't been the best about setting up play dates. Between Dad's visits, homework, and especially Talent Pool, I hadn't had any time to bring her over. Thinking back, I hadn't even sat at Ricky's lunch table much in the past few weeks—I'd been eating with Darla and some other Talent Pool kids so we could brainstorm song ideas. I wondered if Ella missed her easygoing pal.

Before I could think more about it, though, a lanky figure in a white lab coat entered from the exam area. "Come on back to room one," Dr. Vanderstam said.

Momma and I stood, and I took her hand as we walked Ella back. "I will stay here and read my funny papers," Mrs. Okocho said.

Ella wiggled along as we went back. She liked Dr. Vanderstam a lot—which was good, since he had to poke around all over while he examined her. He was able to check places that Ella didn't even like me to touch, like inside her ears. My pup just smiled and panted as she stood on the metal exam table. As Dr. Vanderstam studied Ella, I studied him, trying to figure out what every nod, *hmm*, and *ahh* really meant.

Within a few minutes, the exam was over. Dr.

Vanderstam smiled and announced, "Miss Fitzgerald is in perfect health."

I blinked in disbelief. "She is?"

He patted Ella's back, which set her to wagging. "Her coat has filled in nicely around her scar, her muscles are strong, her weight is healthy, and her joints are in fine condition," Dr. Vanderstam said. Ella's tail caught his lab coat, whacking a flap into the air. The vet flinched and laughed at the same time. "I can tell she's in wonderful hands."

Momma kissed me on the top of the head.

We all left the exam room and Momma went to Miss Simon's desk to write a check for the visit. "All is well?" asked Mrs. Okocho.

"That's right," I said, relieved and surprised at the same time.

We rode home in the Oldsmobile, Ella's body on the bedsheet and her head in my lap. I rubbed my jaw—it felt all hot and worn out, like I'd eaten a whole bag of beef jerky. "My mouth kind of hurts," I said.

Momma glanced back. "Well," she said, "you *were* grinding your teeth that whole visit."

"I can't believe I worried so much over nothing," I muttered.

"Don't beat yourself up," Momma replied. She turned toward me like she had a secret to share.

"Worrying over nothing is half a mom's job."

I cuddled against my pup. When Momma treats me like we're partners, I feel like the most important girl in the world.

At home, I did one last check in the kitchen for all of my dinner supplies. Once I was double-sure that we had everything, I grabbed our fresh hoagie buns from the counter and tucked them away on a high shelf. "Don't even think about thieving," I told Ella.

And then I waited for Dad. I flipped through a couple of books on my shelf. I tried singing my girl the opening I'd written for "The Lonely Dog Blues":

"*If you want to stay smiling,*
Then don't you look at me.
I'm the saddest little puppy
That you ever did see..."

At a quarter past one, Momma poked in to check on me. "How are you girls holding up?" she asked.

"He's always a little late," I told Momma.

That was true—but as the minutes ticked away, Dad became more than a little late. Soon enough, it was two o'clock, and we still hadn't heard a single word from him. My antsy feet had practically tapped a hole in the floor—and I was feeling more foolish by the second. Ella paced across my legs on the bed, brushing against me like she did when a storm was coming.

It made sense for Ella to behave that way. Though the sky outside my window was clear and brilliant blue, I could see a storm coming. And its name was Momma.

Her grumbles were like distant thunder as she stalked past my door.

"…Same old Patrick…"

"…no-account fool thinks…"

"...another thing coming!"

I knew Momma just wanted to stick up for me, but seeing her angry only made me feel worse. It was such a relief when the phone rang a few minutes later.

I hurried to the kitchen, but Momma beat me to the receiver. "Hello?"

"Is it Daddy?" I asked.

Momma held up a rigid finger. "Oh!" she said, breaking into an icy smile. "You want to speak with your *daughter*. I'm so glad you didn't forget about your *daughter*."

I turned my head away as she handed over the phone. I hated how Momma looked when she got mean. It made me nervous that someday she'd point that look at me.

I put the phone to my ear. “Hey, Daddy.”

“Kid,” he began, and from the careful, sighing way he said it, I knew what would come next.

“You can’t make it,” I replied.

“I am a Class-A jerk,” he said.

I sank back against the wall. I saw Momma standing in the living room. She was pinching the bridge of her nose and shaking her head slightly.

“I should have called before now,” Dad said. “I should have called this morning, the moment I got the gig. But I got wrapped up and—”

“—What gig?”

“This wedding out in central PA,” he replied. “Buddy of mine called me to help out, last minute. I’m driving over now. I’m really sorry to do this to you.”

Then don’t! I wanted to scream.

“But we had plans,” I said instead. I sounded like a mouse.

“I have to take whatever comes, whenever it comes,” he replied. “It’s just how this line of work is. Do you understand?”

I didn’t understand, not the littlest bit. How could he drop me, just like that? I held the receiver away from my mouth so he wouldn’t hear me sniffle.

"I'll take a rain check on our lesson," Dad went on. "I promise."

"And dinner, too?" I asked, my voice all wobbly.

"Sure, definitely," he said.

I breathed out slowly, hoping that would make my heart stop racing.

"I need you to know," Dad said, "I'd really rather spend time with you right now."

"You mean it?"

"Heck, yeah!" he cried. "Don't you know how much fun you are?"

That didn't lift my bad feelings away, but it made them lighter—light enough that I could smile.

"But it's like I said," he added. "If I want to keep my head above water, I've got to grab on to whatever little driftwood blows my way. Even a rinky-dink wedding gig in"—he sighed in disgust—"Cow-Pie, Pennsylvania."

Something in Dad's voice made me wish that I was riding out with him, or that I could pay him for my lessons so he didn't have to worry about money—or that I could at least find the right words to cheer him up. "Well," I said, pausing to think. "Do you at least get a little wedding cake?"

That got me a chuckle. "I like a girl with her priorities in order," Dad said. "How about this? I'll snag *you* a piece if I can. Anyway, kid, I've got to watch the road. Give Ella a big honkin' smooch on the nose for me, would you?"

I was still upset when I hung up the phone, but it was hard to stay mad at Dad. He'd sounded tired and lonely, like he was heading all that way just to play in a big, empty room.

When I returned to the living room, I found Momma sitting on the couch with her back to me. "Are you all right?" she asked. Her voice didn't match the question at all—her words came out as dark as coal.

"I'm okay," I replied, though that wasn't all-the-way true. "A gig came up and Dad really had to take it."

"That's what he does best," Momma said. "Why would I expect anything different?"

I wasn't even sure if she was talking to me anymore. What I did know was that between Dad's disappearing and Momma's turning into a black cloud, I just wanted to go to my room and lie down for a long nap.

Then Ella's tongue smacked me on the palm of my hand. I looked down and saw her staring up beside me. She kept licking my hand, her eyes locked on me—and I knew that giving up on the rest of the day simply wasn't an option.

I knelt down and hugged Ella around the neck. "I bet I know what you'd like to do," I told her.

"Ready, pups?" Ricky said, shaking a knotted rope toy. "Go-go-go!" He hurled the rope across the length of his backyard, and Ella and Hamlet dashed after it. Well, it was more like Ella dashed and Hamlet lumbered. I couldn't believe how big Ham had gotten. Back in July, he'd just been a little heap of wrinkly skin—and now, only three months later, he was already bigger than Ella.

And he was stronger than her, too. I had to laugh as they played tug-of-war with the rope. Hamlet stood there like an anchor while Ella yanked on the other end without any luck.

"Look at those two," Ricky commented. "Crazy and Lazy."

"Is that fun for him?" I asked.

"Pretty sure," Ricky replied. "He plays the same way with me. He brings me the rope and then makes me do all the work."

"Sounds kind of smart when you put it that way," I said.

We watched the dogs struggle over their toy. A gust of wind swirled the fallen leaves on the ground, and I zipped my jacket up to my neck.

After a minute, Ricky glanced over and spoke. "He's really missed her, you know."

"Really?" I asked.

"Well, yeah," he replied, shoving his hands into the pouch of his hoodie. "It's been about a hundred years since you came over."

I rolled my eyes and grinned. That was Ricky-speak for anything that took longer than he wanted. "It hasn't been that long."

"It's been a whole month," Ricky said. "Ham was getting worried."

"I don't think he worries much about anything," I said. Ham was sitting in the middle of the yard, gripping the rope in his teeth as Ella tugged away at the other end.

"Fine," Ricky sighed. "I was worried."

I turned in surprise. "About what?"

Ricky frowned and stepped ahead of me. "All right, guys!" he called out to our pups. "Bring it here; I'll throw it again!"

Ella and Hamlet didn't even look at him.

"Why were you worried?" I asked again.

Ricky turned sharply. "Because you made a new best friend and forgot all about us!"

I had to stare at him for a moment. "He's not my best friend," I cried. "He's my dad!"

Ricky squinted. "What do you mean, your dad?" he asked. "I'm talking about Darla."

A laugh sputtered out of me before I could catch it. "Darla Washington?" I asked.

"It's not funny," he murmured.

"Darla's not my new best friend," I said.

"Could have fooled me," he replied. "You're always hanging out with her anymore."

"Because of Talent Pool," I told him.

"Just forget it," Ricky said. He headed toward our dogs, but I grabbed onto his arm.

"Wait," I said. "Did you really think I didn't want to be friends anymore?"

He looked down at one of his sneakers.

"I could help you with that musical if you want," he offered. He reached into his hoodie pouch and pulled out a pair of drumsticks, which he always seemed to be carrying ever since he'd joined band. "Like, you could come over here to practice the songs. And I could be your official beat keeper."

"You don't have to do that," I said. "How about I just do a better job at hanging out?"

He hesitated. "…Yeah?"

"Come on, Ricky," I said. "Darla's all right, but I only have one best friend."

He took a deep breath and as he let it out, his lips spread into a smile. "Your songs sound funny," he said. "I've heard you guys practicing."

"Thanks," I replied, tightening my cheeks to pinch my grin back.

"What's the one Darla's always mumbling?"

"The hamster song?"

"Yeah," Ricky said, "do that one!"

I rolled my eyes, but I was actually glad he asked. "Count me in, beat keeper," I said. Ricky patted a drumstick against his leg as I tapped my foot. Then I sang:

"*H-A-M-S-T-E-R,*

Riding in my hamster ball.

Cereals are what we eat.

Grains and nuts, they can't be beat."

Then I began to punch the air in front of me in time with the song. "*Gottaeat'em, gottaeat'em, gottaeat'em, gottaeat'em…*"

We both broke up in giggles. "I can't believe Billy Cutler's going to sing that," he said. Billy was a fifth grader who always wore dress shirts and suspenders to school.

"He's pretty good," I replied. "You'll see."

"Hey," Ricky said, "I have a music trick. Want to see it?"

I nodded in agreement. Ricky raised his drumsticks above his head and clicked them together four times. "One, two, three, four!"

Immediately, Hamlet dropped his end of the rope and strolled toward us. Ella hurried along with him, whipping the rope against her side, running circles around the big dog as they approached.

"When'd you teach him that?" I asked, impressed.

Ricky shrugged. "About…ninety-nine years ago," he said, rubbing the crease of Hamlet's brow. "Let's go in and get them a treat."

Ricky clicked his drumsticks and Hamlet followed him to the sliding door. I hooked on Ella's leash and brought her along.

As we entered the kitchen, Ricky shouted out, "Mom, where are those sweet potato thingies?"

"Whoa, whoa!" Mr. Jenkins said. He was standing at the counter with a slow cooker lid in one hand and a big spoon in the other. "How about an inside voice, bud?"

"Sorry, Dad," Ricky said. "Are you sneaking into Mom's chili?"

Mr. Jenkins quickly wiped his mouth with the back of his hand. "You'd never prove it in a court of law," he said, and I had to grin. "Latasha, has my son invited you to dinner yet?"

I really wanted to stay. In that moment, I wanted nothing more than to be part of Ricky's family—his just-right family where Mom never looked mean, the worst thing Dad did was sneak a bite of dinner early, and nobody ever got forgotten. I wanted that, even if it was just for a meal.

But I wasn't a Jenkins. I was a Gandy.

"I can't," I replied, the words more bitter than coffee. "I promised Momma I'd cook."

I trudged up the stairs to our apartment with Ella at my heels. I couldn't think of a single thing I wanted to do less than make a meatball hoagie dinner right now—but that had been the plan, and Dad's skipping out didn't change that.

I opened the door to find Momma already in the kitchen. She was listening on the phone. "See you in forty-five," she said, and then she hung up.

"Who was that?" I asked flatly.

"Pizza Franco," Momma said. That perked me up—Pizza Franco is my favorite restaurant in the whole city. "I thought you might not feel like cooking tonight."

I was so grateful it made my knees weak. "Thanks, Momma."

She took Ella's leash from my hands and unhooked her for me. "Can we talk for a second?" she asked as Ella darted off to the living room.

I dropped into a chair at the table and Momma stood in front of me.

"I owe you an apology," she said. "For earlier."

My brow crinkled. "Momma—"

"—Hang on, I want to be honest with you," she told me. "No secrets, right?"

I nodded.

"When your father called…" she said, halting. She sat beside me and started over. "Before you were born—when you were a baby—your father pulled that disappearing act a lot. Even when I really needed him here. Especially then."

I finally had to ask her. "Is that why you split up?"

"There wasn't just one thing," Momma replied. "But...it mattered. It made me feel like I was nothing."

I knew exactly what she meant.

"When he did that to you today," Momma continued, "all I could think about was how lousy that used to make me feel. But I shouldn't have been hung up on me. I should have been there for you. I'm sorry for not being right there, sweetie."

I bolted to my feet and clasped Momma in the tightest hug I'd ever given. Today might not have been the perfect day I'd planned, but she had rescued it from being a disaster.

Once I unwrapped myself from Momma, she stood up. "I hope you got that pup plenty of exercise," she said. "I ordered her a Franco's frosted cupcake for her anniversary."

As Momma gathered dishes for dinner, I remembered the talk I'd had with Ricky—how I'd been hurting his feelings without even knowing it. "Maybe if I sat Dad down and really talked to him," I said, "he'd be different."

Momma gave me a sympathetic smile. "You've got a good heart," she said.

I hate when Momma says things like that—things that sound like compliments but really mean, *Silly girl.* "I trained Ella to be nice to Hamlet," I insisted.

"Training dogs is hard work," Momma agreed. "But training people is harder."

Chapter Eight

The Lonely Dog Blues

I quickly learned that there is one major difference between teaching something to Ella and teaching something to Dad: Ella is always around to learn from me. The longer I waited, the less sure I became. What if I told him how I felt and he got mad at me? That was another difference between him and my pup—if my dad didn't like what I had to say, he could just pack up his keyboard and leave.

Or, even worse, what if I told him how he'd hurt me and he just didn't care?

That was my main worry as I waited for Dad to trudge up our front stairs. Well, that and Momma. She was standing with me in the kitchen and her arms were crossed so tight that her muscles showed, like that time in second grade when I'd painted Ella's toenails and let her run around before they'd dried. I'd waited another two weeks for Dad to come back around—I prayed that Momma wouldn't scare him right out the door. I reached down and gave my whirling pup a squeeze on the neck for courage. At least I knew how Ella would react. She was already bouncing in excitement.

I opened our door and when I saw my father, I had to smile. One of his hands gripped the underside of his keyboard, and the other held a bulging bouquet of flowers. He offered the bunch to me, its pink and white and yellow and red blooms bright enough to burst. "Hey, kid."

I clasped the bundled stems and turned to show them off. "Momma, *look*!"

Momma smiled at me, then shifted her eyes to Dad. "Glad you decided to come out of hiding," she said.

I wanted to throw her a smirk, but first I had to

raise my bouquet out of Ella's curious reach.

"Are these lilies?" I asked my dad. I'd been helping Mrs. Okocho tend to her garden for the last few weeks to earn money for Christmas presents—she was turning me into a regular flower expert.

"Good eye," he replied. "And they're just for you."

"None for Momma?" I asked, glancing back at her stern face.

"Well…" he said, "I've got something else for her."

He set his keyboard on the kitchen table and unslung its stand from his shoulder. "Down, girl!" I hissed as Ella put her paws up and nosed at the keys.

"She's okay," Dad said, and he pulled an envelope from inside his leather jacket. I watched Momma's face soften as he walked it over to her. Dad spoke quietly, so I had to strain to hear him over Ella's ruckus.

"It's less than all I owe," he told her. "But it's my absolute best."

"Patrick," Momma replied, her voice warmer than I'd heard in weeks. She took the envelope like she was afraid of breaking it. "What's this about?"

"I got some news today," Dad said. He turned to face the both of us. "I have been ordained!"

I felt like I knew that word, but it couldn't possibly mean what I thought. "You became a priest?" I asked.

"To be more exact," Dad replied, "I became a Minister. The bandleader called me up last night. Asked if I wanted to make things official and join his crew full-time."

Dad and I flashed our matching smiles. "That's awesome!" I cried.

"Good for you," Momma added, and I could tell she really meant it.

Even Ella got into the act, circling Dad's feet and poking at his knees for attention. "Don't you worry," he told her. "I didn't forget you." He reached into another pocket and removed a chew bone for Ella.

I watched him hand the toy to my girl and I had to wonder: how could someone be so thoughtless part of the time, and get things exactly right other times?

Ella seized the toy in her teeth and sprinted off to the living room with it. Then she dashed into my room. Then Momma's.

"Ella!" she grumbled.

My pup skittered back into the kitchen, wagging wildly, and darted out again. *Sorry, Mrs. Okocho*, I thought.

Momma sighed and took the flowers from me. "How about I get these in some water for you?"

"Thanks," I said. Then I remembered something

I'd learned while helping in the garden. "Oh, and cut the stems on a slant. They'll last longer."

Momma pursed her lips at me before she left the room.

"Well, it's true, you know," I muttered.

Ella bounded into the room a third time, whipping her head around with the bone between her jaws.

"Boy, oh, boy," Dad mused. "Does she get like that a lot?"

"You have no idea," I said, looking at the linoleum.

Dad chuckled as she dashed out again. "All right, that's it," he announced. "We'll never get any practicing done with her like that. How about we settle Miss Ella down with a nice, long walk?"

"You can let her snuffle around a little, but keep her walking," I explained. "She has to know you're in charge."

"Am I, now?" Dad commented. He jingled Ella's collar. "You heard it. Let's go!"

Ella stopped sniffing the bushes and we continued slowly toward Friendship Park. I hadn't taken Ella there in a while, and she seemed even more curious than usual about every sight and smell.

I stole a glance at my father as we walked. Dad's good news had been really exciting, but it hadn't been enough to make me forget last month. I had to say something.

"Daddy," I began timidly. "We need to talk about something."

"Uh-oh," he replied.

I felt my insides begin to tingle. "Uh-oh, what?" I asked.

"Conversations that start that way are never about good things," Dad said. "It's never like, 'We need to talk…about how great you are!' It's always bad news." Then he glanced at me with that sly grin of his. "Or is it?"

"It's…" I wanted to go on, but the words seemed to be stuck beneath my collarbone. Finally, I burst out, "We need to borrow your keyboard."

"My keyboard?" he asked.

"For the Innovation Conversation," I added. "Darla only has an upright piano at home. We need something for her to play at the competition."

"Is that so?"

I nodded insistently. It wasn't what I'd really wanted to talk about, but it wasn't a lie, either. Actually, Darla had been hounding me about it ever since I'd mentioned that my dad played the keyboard. She did it in her usual Darla way—by showing everyone her clipboard with our supplies list, and mentioning how "the keyboard is *not* crossed off yet, Latasha!"

Dad shrugged. "I have a second keyboard at my place," he said. "From my early days. It's only a sixty-one key, and, honestly, its carrying bag is fancier than the board itself. But it sounds fine. You can borrow it for as long as you need."

I smiled and hugged his arm.

We reached the loop of road that circled Friendship Park. Dad stopped at the corner as we took it all in. A few runners in sweats were jogging on the sidewalk, while a couple of little kids played Tag near the drinking fountain.

"Now, before we go and have a grand old time," Dad said, "how about you tell me what's really on your mind?"

I eyed him nervously. "What do you mean?"

Dad cocked his head. "Kid, I might not be Dad of the Year, but I've got eyes and ears." He choked up on Ella's leash to keep her on the sidewalk. "It's all right, really. Untrouble your brain."

I'd thought it would be tough to have a serious talk with a puppy wiggling between our shins—but once I started in, I barely noticed the distraction. I told Dad about how I'd waited for him, and how I'd gone from angry, to worried, to embarrassed and back. "And then you called, but it was like you almost forgot," I went on. "And Momma was super mad… and I felt like you didn't care about me at all."

Dad shook his head. "That's not true," he replied. "That's never been true."

"It's how you made me feel." I watched some cars pass as I worked up the courage to finish. "You can't go away without warning me," I told him. "You can't forget me. You can't."

My father watched me silently.

I couldn't stand the quiet. "Are you mad?" I asked.

Dad rubbed at a spot near his eye. "I'm proud," he said. "That was brave of you to tell me all that. And I promise—I won't forget you."

And then he took his hat off and fitted it on my head. I touched the brim and felt so relieved that I probably could have taken a nap right there on the corner.

"That's a loan," he said with a wink. "Now, what say we go and run your girl's battery out?"

I looked down, and when I saw Ella I had to hold back a laugh. "Daddy?" I pointed to the panting pup.

It seemed that Ella had felt like having a nap herself. While Dad and I were talking, she'd circled him twice, wrapping the leash around his ankles, and

then laid down to rest. "Ella," I called, almost singing. The pup looked at me, but just huffed and shifted her head to a more comfortable position.

Dad tried to lift his foot out of the tangle, but he couldn't wriggle free. "How about that?" he said. "She trapped me."

After our talk, Dad really did do better. He was still kind of late, but he came by to hang out every day he had a rehearsal. We talked about the latest news in our lives, like the new (old) band Dad had discovered at the record store, and the "weird lunch" contest I'd judged at our table at school. (For the record, Ricky gulped down a dozen deviled eggs and had to go to the nurse's office for the afternoon, but Dante won by making a Cheetos-and-Little-Debbies sandwich. And I *lost* by having to watch him eat it!)

Other times, we just traded complaints about the folks who were on our backs. For me, it was Miss Prooper, because I hadn't followed every single one of her silly instructions for our homework—as if it mattered whether I drew my map of the United States in purple pencil instead of black. For Dad, it was his bandleader, Joe—"For no reason at all!" he'd say.

The rest of our time together, my father worked with me to finish "The Lonely Dog Blues." He helped me find a good key to create a simple tune for Darla to play. After that, I just had to practice and practice until the song felt perfect. By mid-November, it seemed really close. But I had this pesky feeling that things could be a *little* better.

"No nerves allowed," Dad told me. "It's just you, me, and Sleepy McGee over there."

He meant Ella. We'd walked her before starting, so she was sprawled out on the couch, tongue almost to the floor. Momma had gone downstairs to play cards with Mrs. Okocho, so Dad and I had set up the keyboard he'd lent me in the living room.

"Here we go," Dad said. He played my song's little intro, and I began to sing:

"If you want to stay smiling,
Then don't you look at me.
I'm the saddest little puppy
That you ever did see.
You heard the news?
I've got the lonely dog blues.
What will I do?
I've got the lonely dog blues.
Clock tells me it's been an hour
Feels like it's been a year

Where, oh where, did my owner go,
And when will she come back here?
I'm chewing shoes.
I've got the lonely dog blues.
It's such a snooze.
I've got the lonely dog blues."

I stopped singing and looked at my father. He kept playing the song's twelve-bar progression, his eyes closed. "Dad?" I asked.

He opened his eyes and smiled at me. "You're good, kid," he said, resting his hands in his lap. "I really like it."

"That's it," I said with a smirk. "You really like it."

That's all any adult I'd sung for could tell me. Mr. Harvey, Mr. and Mrs. Jenkins, Darla's grandmother, Momma—no one had had a single comment for me except, "It's great! It's funny! It's wonderful!" The only one who'd had any suggestion at all was Mrs. Okocho—and her big contribution was, "You should bark like a dog after every verse." I needed advice—real advice.

"Well..." Dad said slowly. "There are a couple little places you could work on."

I swiftly flipped to a clean page in my notebook. "Now that's more like it!" I exclaimed, crossing to sit beside my pup. "What's off?"

"The first line," Dad replied. "I'm not feeling the rhythm of it. Is there a way you can change it so it matches the third line?"

I repeated those lines in my head. He was right—they were different. One had more syllables than the other. "What about…*If you want to keep your smile…*"

Dad clapped his hands together so loudly that it startled Ella awake. "Yes!" he said.

I scribbled down the change. "What else?" I asked.

"That bit about having the lonely dog blues is cute," he said, "but it needs to get bigger by the end. Like—" He played the last few chords and sang for me:

"*It's such a snooze.*

I've got the lonely dog blues.

I've got the left-me-all-alone-ly, all-locked-inside-my-home-ly dog blues!"

I added that note, too. I couldn't just copy his new line word for word—we had to write all the lyrics ourselves—but maybe I'd be able to use the general idea. "Thanks, Daddy," I said.

"Outside of that, I love it," he told me, standing up from the chair we'd dragged out of my room. He moved to the couch and plopped down with an arm around me. "If you guys don't win, the judges are crazy."

I hugged my notebook to my chest.

"I think we can wrap for today," he said. "Let's pack up."

I grabbed the keyboard's carrying bag. It was made from this shimmery nylon, and it had special lettering stitched on the side, like on Ricky's custom Steelers jacket. I ran my thumb across the letters—*The Kidd on Keys.*

"Daddy?"

"Yeah?"

I swallowed to keep my throat from going dry. "Do you absolutely have to go down to Florida for Thanksgiving?"

I felt him sigh next to me. "She *is* my mum," he replied. "I ought to see her once a year."

"I know," I replied. "It's just—couldn't she come up here instead?"

Dad shook his head. "We've talked about this before." He lifted his arm off me and stood again to stretch.

I knew Dad didn't much like the idea, but my friends and I had all been talking about Thanksgiving at lunch and it had gotten me thinking. The Jenkinses had plans to visit Ricky's grandparents and all of his cousins near Detroit. Darla and her grandma were having a big potluck with some families in their apartment building. And all I had was a little dinner with Momma and Mrs. Okocho. The only kid having a lamer Thanksgiving than me was Dante—and he said he was happy about it because he liked eating Boston Market better than turkey anyway.

But I couldn't just pretend like I was satisfied. "There's plenty of room," I insisted. "And I promise, Momma will do all the cooking. I won't let Mrs. Okocho make anything."

That at least made Dad grin a little. "Mum already got me a ticket down," he said.

I smirked—but not for long. "How about Christmas, then?" I suggested. "She could come up, and so could your stepdad."

"Jeez, Latasha," he moaned, "can we just drop it?" His voice felt like a jab with a long needle.

Dad must have seen the tears on their way. "I'm sorry, kid," he said. "It's not because of you."

"Then what is it?" I asked.

Dad knelt down to my eye level. "Do you remember that thing I told you about my mum?" he asked gently. "About how she can shrink you down with her words?"

I nodded.

He reached out and rubbed my shoulder. “I don’t want her to come up here,” he said, “and shrink what you and I have.”

I guessed that was supposed to cheer me up, because Dad stood again and exhaled in satisfaction. “So,” he said brightly, “let’s just forget about her, and stick to having fun, huh?”

If only it was that easy.

At every Thanksgiving dinner, we have this little tradition where we hold hands and list a few things from the past year that we appreciate. It’s Momma’s version of saying grace.

We sat at one end of Mrs. Okocho’s table—Momma at the head, Mrs. O to the left, me to the right. Mrs. Okocho went first, saying how she was thankful for how Momma and I had welcomed her into our lives, and a bunch of other nice stuff that normally would have made me feel all happy and full and loved. But I wasn’t listening all that closely. I wasn’t watching her, or Momma, or even the big spread of turkey and mashed potatoes and buttery rolls. My eyes kept drifting to the other end of the table, and all I could see was how much room we had left down there. And it made me want to hide in my bed, tucked safely under the covers like the way I'd left Ella before coming downstairs.

"Latasha," Momma said, squeezing my hand. I glanced over and forced out a smile. "Your turn, sweetie."

I realized that I'd missed what Momma had said altogether. "I'm…" I began, looking over the table. "I'm grateful for our dinner. And for Ella being okay. And—" I narrowed my eyes. "And I hope Daddy is having just as good of a Thanksgiving as I am."

I wasn't even sure what that meant, but it must have been good enough to fool everybody, because Momma smiled and we all let go of each other's hands. "All right," Mrs. Okocho said. "Let us feast!"

As she cut the turkey, I stole another glance at the foot of the table, and I gripped the edge of the tablecloth until my fingernails went pale.

Chapter Nine

Secret Weapon

On the Monday after Thanksgiving, my father called to check on me and share stories from his trip. "Three days of lectures," Dad griped. "'*When are you going to settle down? When will you get a* real *job? And take off that hat at the table!*'"

I doubted that my grandma really sounded like the Wicked Witch of the West, but Dad's impression made my frustration with him melt away.

"I'm a hat guy, what can I say?" he went on. "Not my fault I got this giant-sized noggin."

I giggled. "Your head's not that big."

"It's probably from all the brains up in there," Dad said. "Jokes aside, though, how about we do something together? You pick what it is."

I squeezed the phone in excitement. "Can it be anything?"

"Not anything," he replied. "It can't be inside the apartment. We have to go somewhere."

That was fine—I already had something in mind. "I want you to meet my friend, Ricky," I said. "And his family."

"Ehh…"

"It's our school's winter concert next week," I explained. "Momma's coming with me. Ricky's playing these huge drums—they're practically bigger than him!"

"Timpani?" he asked.

"That's the name!" I replied. "Will you come? You can have the aisle seat if you want."

"Okay, okay," Dad gave in with a chuckle. "It's a date."

"I wanted a clip-on," Ricky said, tugging on his necktie, "but Mom did *this* to me."

Momma smiled at him. "You look very dapper, Ricky," she said.

He just blinked at us. I leaned over and stated, "It's a compliment."

"Oh—thanks!" Ricky said. "Is your dad still coming?"

I patted the empty aisle seat next to me. "Any second," I replied.

"Cool," Ricky said. "I've got to get back to the band room. See you after!"

My eyes followed him as he ran past the few rows behind us and out the back of the auditorium. When I resettled in my seat, I noticed Momma watching me.

"I'm not worried," I told her.

"Good," she said. "There's still time yet."

It was 7:20 in the evening, which gave Dad ten minutes before he was officially late. I really wasn't bothered, though—it wouldn't even be so bad if he came in a minute or two behind. The chorus performed before the band anyway. And besides, it was the part that came after the concert that mattered most. I decided that I wouldn't look back again until he arrived.

To kill some time, I studied the stage for a moment and then shut my eyes and tried to recall every detail about it. The stage's curtain, a heavy, dark purple drape, was closed. Some risers were set up in front of it for the chorus. An upright piano stood off to the side. I knew it came from the band room, which is where we'd been having our rehearsals for the Innovation Conversation. It was for the chorus's accompanist—which is a fancy name for "piano player" that Darla insists I use on her.

I felt a tap on my shoulder. "Can I sit here?" said a voice.

I opened my eyes. It wasn't Dad—it was Dante.

"I'm holding it," I replied.

"Oh," he said with a frown.

"There's space on this end," Momma offered, pointing a thumb to her far side. "Here—I'll slide down one so you kids can talk."

I didn't really have anything to say to Dante, but Momma grabbed her coat and shifted over a seat anyway. "Sorry," Dante mumbled, stepping on my shoes as he crowded past me.

Momma smiled at Dante as he sat. "So, too cool to sit with your family?" she asked him.

Dante shrugged. "They had important stuff to do. They're picking me up after." He turned to me. "I just wanted to see Jenkins bang on those big old Tiffany drums."

"*Timpani*," I replied.

"What. Ever," Dante scoffed. "I heard he's got to stand on a ladder to play them, *heh-heh*."

I rolled my eyes. Outside, a bell sounded, and then the auditorium lights flashed a few times. A flood of families hurried in from the hallway to take their seats. I draped my coat across the one I was holding for Dad.

A minute later, the chorus filed out onto the risers. Then the lights went down and our principal,

Dr. DeSoto, came onstage to introduce the chorus director.

I sighed and wished Dante hadn't worked his way in between Momma and me. I could have used an arm to clutch onto.

Then I heard him next to me. "Mind if I join you?"

My whole face lit up with a smile—but Dante leaned over before I could speak. "Actually," he said, "it's *reserved*."

"Can it," I whispered. "This is my dad!"

Dad tipped his hat.

"Sorry, sir," Dante replied.

"Sir..." Dad repeated with a chuckle. He handed my coat back to me and ducked into his seat. "Sorry I'm running behind."

The audience applauded as Dr. DeSoto finished speaking. "You're just in time," I said.

"If I'm late to practice," Dad told me, "the bandleader fines me twenty-five bucks. But if he wants to run practice late—well, that's all fine and dandy."

I peeked over at Dad. "Does he really fine you if you're late?" I asked.

Dad shot me a *you'd-better-believe-it* glance.

On stage, the director gave a signal to his

accompanist. The piano sounded out and the chorus began to sing. It was different from our choir at church—a lot of the chorus kids stood kind of stiffly as they sang—but they still sounded good.

Dad was having fun, too. Through every song, he shimmied in his chair and tapped his feet to the beat. When the chorus wrapped up with "Jingle Bell Rock," I even caught him playing along with the accompanist on an imaginary keyboard in his lap.

As the chorus director guided his kids out a side door, Dad leaned toward me. "Thanks for inviting me," he said in my ear.

"Sure, Dad," I replied, trying to sound calm and not like I was so happy I could squeal.

"Were any of those kids in your Gifted and Talented club?" he asked.

"A few," I replied. "I'll introduce you to them during cookie time."

"Cookie time?"

"Yeah!" I said. "After the show, everyone's invited to the cafeteria for cocoa and these huge oatmeal cookies."

Dad scratched his chin with his thumb and gave a big nod.

"They're from the PTA," I explained. "Here's my plan. I'll get cookies for all three of us, and Momma can introduce you to the other grown-ups."

"Got it all figured out, huh?" he said, still watching the stage. Two custodians were up there, moving the last riser out of the way. When they finished, the purple curtain opened to reveal the school band. They were still finding their seats and fixing their music stands.

"Look, look!" Dante whispered to me.

At the back of the stage, we could see Ricky stepping in behind the timpani, which looked like two huge, shiny witch's cauldrons on wheels. He practically disappeared behind them, until he stood up on a stool. Dante couldn't stop snickering.

After another introduction from Dr. DeSoto, the band began to play. To be honest, they weren't as good as the chorus. All of their songs were slowed down to make them easier to play, so "Good King Wenceslas" felt like it was half an hour long. Then, on the next tune, the clarinets kept making weird squeaks as they played. At least Ricky sounded good. He was right on the beat with the timpani. And loud, too. I decided that's what I would say if Ricky asked how I liked the concert: *You were super easy to hear!*

But about halfway through the performance, something wonderful happened. My dad slipped his hand around mine and held it tightly. And he didn't let go. From then on, nothing on stage really mattered at all.

The band finished their last song and everyone applauded. Dad let go of my hand so we could join in. We all stood and I clapped hard—I was happy for my friend, but even more, I was excited about cookie time!

As the applause died out, Dad hugged me with

one arm. Then he told me, "I have to go."

I stared up at him.

He looked over at Momma. "Steph, I'm sorry, I've got to skip out."

"You okay?" she asked.

I tugged at his sleeve. "Daddy," I said quietly, "what's wrong? What'd I do?"

"It's not you, kid," he replied. Dad sniffled and then grabbed his nose with his thumb and forefinger. "We'll talk soon, okay? Promise."

I watched him push past the crowd in the aisle, holding his nose like he'd smelled something awful, and I just wanted to scream after him. How could he not understand how much this meant to me?

After a minute, Momma led us out to the hallway. "Let's go home," I said to her.

"I know, sweetie," she replied. "But we should find Ricky and say something nice first."

We went to the cafeteria. Inside, all of the kids were meeting up with their families for snacks. I had to blink my eyes for a second—the last thing I wanted was for anybody to see me cry.

We spotted a table where Ricky was laughing with his parents. "Hi, Latasha!" Mrs. Jenkins said with a wave.

Ricky looked around us. "Hey," he said, "your dad

didn't make it?"

"No, he came," I said, my voice quaking. "He had to go."

Dante stepped up next to me. "I saw him," he added. "She's not lying."

"Why would I lie?" I snapped at him.

Momma put a hand on my back to calm me down. "You sounded great," she told Ricky.

He beamed at us. "Yeah, I was pretty loud, huh?"

A few days later, I found myself staring at Ricky's timpani in the band room. We'd just finished another rehearsal for Talent Pool and I could hear the other kids gathering their things behind me. "And next time," Darla warned one of them, "you'd better know all the words to 'Pesky Pete the Parakeet'!"

"Let's cool off, Darla," Mr. Harvey said. "We've still got nine days and another rehearsal yet. Everyone is doing great work."

I wasn't so sure about that. Practice hadn't gone well today. I guess you could say that we sounded less like the chorus had and more like the band. We had a lot of work to do and not much time—but right then, I wasn't really worrying about it. I had other thoughts on my mind.

"Can I help you with that?" asked Mr. Harvey.

I turned and saw that everyone else was gone. Mr. Harvey pointed to Dad's keyboard. I'd been zipping it up in its bag before I got distracted.

I decided to just ask what I'd been wondering. "Mr. Harvey," I began, "how do you teach somebody who doesn't want to learn?"

"I think you and Darla are being a little hard on Gautam," he said. "'Pesky Pete' is a tricky song."

"I don't mean Gautam," I replied. "I just mean… anybody."

Mr. Harvey took a knee on one of the chairs across from me. "Having trouble with a friend?" he asked.

Just then, I thought of Dad's big, shoulder-shaking laugh. I zipped the case shut. "Sort of, yeah."

He studied my face for a second. "Do you want to talk about it?"

I shook my head and stood up. "Mrs. Okocho's waiting for me," I replied.

Mr. Harvey lifted the keyboard bag by its strap. "Gosh!" he said, tilting like the bag weighed a hundred pounds. "You carried this yourself? You are strong!"

"I just want to know really fast," I said. "What do

you do if someone doesn't want to learn?"

Mr. Harvey led me out of the band room. "You know," he replied, "I've never met a student who doesn't *want* to learn—only students who don't *believe* that they can. Does that make sense?"

"You mean like they don't believe in themselves?"

"Right."

We walked together down the empty hall. "So how do you fix that?" I asked.

"I can't tell you how many times I've asked myself that question," Mr. Harvey replied. "The trouble is, you or I can't force somebody to learn."

I let out a long breath as we pushed open the school's front doors.

"But here's what we can do," Mr. Harvey told me. "We can care. We can listen. And we can try to understand."

As soon as Mrs. Okocho got us home—and as soon as I could get Ella to stop hopping all over me—I grabbed our phone and called Dad's cell. After a few rings he picked up. "Hey there, kid," he said. "What's the buzz?"

"Can we talk for a minute?" I asked.

Suddenly, his voice sounded far away, like he was holding the phone away from his mouth. "Two minutes! It's my daughter," Dad said. "Joe, Joe, I know."

I winced. He must have been at band practice.

"Yeah, yeah, twenty-dollar fine, I'm shocked," I heard him say. Then Dad's voice got clearer to me. "Sorry, my dear. Everything okay?"

"Did I get you in trouble?" I asked.

"No, it's my fault," he said. "I left my ringer on. But it's actually great that you called."

"It is?"

"Yes, indeedy," he replied. "This Saturday, keep your schedule clear. We've got some very important business."

Dad didn't explain what our "important business" was—but it must have been a pretty big deal, because on Saturday, he pulled up outside our house exactly on time.

"Hustle! Hustle!" Dad said as I climbed into his station wagon. "We don't want to be late."

"Sorry," I said, fixing my second mitten. "When you said noon, I thought you meant more like...

Dad-noon."

He grinned at me. "Not today, kid," he said. "We've got an appointment to make."

"Where are we going?" I asked.

Dad started the car's engine. "You'll see. Wave to Ella."

I looked toward the house. Up in our apartment, Ella had pushed the living room curtains aside and put her paws on the windowsill. I waved to her as we rode away, and she wiggled back at me.

We reached the corner and turned onto Penn Avenue. Dad's car rumbled past the dollar store and the cemetery, and then we hit the stoplight by Children's Hospital.

"How cool is it that your mother works there?" asked Dad.

"Pretty cool," I replied.

"You should be proud of her," he said.

"Well, yeah, I am," I said—like I needed to be told! The light turned green and we moved on.

We passed by the 31st Street Bridge and then slowed to a crawl in the Strip District among the packs of Saturday shoppers who were lined up for their fresh breads and seafood and vegetables. As we waited for the van ahead of us to parallel park, Dad turned to me.

"I owe you an explanation," he said. "About the band concert."

I was relieved that I didn't have to bring it up. "What happened?" I asked.

"I..." he said with a frown. "I got a nosebleed."

I instantly remembered the last time he'd gotten one. "Are you still hurt from Ella?"

"No, no," he assured me. "I just get them sometimes. When I'm really nervous."

I squinted at him, trying to imagine my dad being nervous about anything. I couldn't picture it.

He drummed on the steering wheel with his palms. "It was the crowd, I guess," he said.

"You play for crowds all the time," I replied.

"I mean all those other parents," he said. "I kept thinking about meeting them, you know? Playing it in my head. I don't know any of them. What were we going to talk about? What would I say?"

"I don't know," I said. "How about, 'Hi, I'm Latasha's dad. When I was in school, I was in band, too. And now I have a career as a musician extraordinaire.'"

Dad glanced at me with a little smile. "You know what I like about you?" he asked.

"What?"

"When you look at me," he said, "you see a

different story than most people do."

We finally got past the Strip and into downtown Pittsburgh. We turned onto a side street and found a parking meter. "Can you at least give me a hint about where we're going?" I begged as we got out.

Dad fed the meter some quarters. "I'm going to show you my secret weapon," he said.

I stared at my father—he could be so weird sometimes!

"Let's march," he commanded, and we tramped down the block.

"What secret weapon?" I asked as we cut through the cold.

He looked at me and said, "Against feeling nervous."

Dad stopped us outside a building with a pair of spotless white doors and a brass doorbell beside them. A man's name was printed in big lettering on the doorframe. I couldn't tell if it was a store, or what.

"Ever been here before?" he asked.

I shook my head.

"Me neither." And with that, Dad rang the doorbell. A thin man with a gray mustache answered.

"Good afternoon," Dad said. "I'm Mr. Kidd. I have a twelve-thirty appointment."

"Please!" the man said, and he opened the door

wide for us.

Inside, it looked like a cross between a Macy's and a mansion. The walls were lined with displays of suits, shirts, and ties, but the floor was all dark brown hardwood, and scattered about were wooden chairs with fancy carvings and silky cushions. Right in the center of the room, a big chandelier hung from the ceiling.

"Will we be taking measurements today?" asked the man with the mustache. I realized he must be a tailor.

"Nope, I'm easy," Dad replied, unbuttoning his peacoat. "An off-the-rack kind of fellow. Let's pick out some options, and my lovely daughter here will help me make a final choice."

My cheeks got cherry-hot. "May I take your coat?" asked the tailor.

"Thank you," I replied. I stuffed my mittens in my pockets and handed it over.

The tailor went off with our jackets, leaving us alone in the showroom.

"So, we're going suit shopping?" I asked.

"What can I say? I love the way new clothes feel," Dad explained. "This is what I do when I need to feel better. When I'm nervous, feeling shrunk down…or working with a jerk…"

"You mean Joe?" I asked.

Dad held his hands up. "Hey, you said it, not me!"

I shot my father a playful sneer. The tailor returned. "Young lady," he said, "why don't you have a seat? Your father and I will go find some good fits, and I'll send him out to you."

I eased into one of the fancy chairs. The thing was more comfortable than my bed! And then I waited and thought about why we were here. I'd never seen Dad wear a suit before. How could he even afford to shop at a place like this?

I was able to wonder about all of that and then hum my way through "The Lonely Dog Blues" three whole times before Dad came back.

But when he returned, he looked like a totally different guy. Dad's hat was gone, his hair was pulled back, and he'd changed into a sharp navy blue suit with a striped pattern. His tie was red with tiny white diamond shapes, and a handkerchief peeked out of his pocket. His shoes were as shiny as black ice.

"So tell me," he said, "what do I look like?"

"Well…" I began. "You look great! But—kind of like a banker."

Dad stretched his arms so his cufflinks showed. "You think?"

"Yeah, definitely," I said. "A banker with a huge

office…with, like, an aquarium in it."

"All right, I get it," he laughed. "It's not quite right. Back in a few!"

I waited a little while longer, and then Dad returned with a brand-new look. This time, he had a brown sport coat and a stiff black dress shirt.

I shook my head. "Now you look like a professor," I said. "Who teaches…German, or something."

Dad straightened his back. "Vat makes you say zat?" he demanded.

He modeled a half-dozen more suits for me after that. Each suit's pattern had a weirder name than the last, like *tic weave* or *herringbone*.

"Sharkskin?!" I cried.

Dad was showing off this super-shiny blue suit with a matching hat, and talking with an overdone New York accent.

"It's just a name, kid," he replied. "It's not made-a sharks."

"I know," I bluffed.

"It's a blend. Wool, silk, mohair…"

"*What* hair?"

"*Fuhgeddaboutit!*"

And then I waited some more. I locked my hands together and rested my chin on them. This was our last weekend to practice my song before the

Innovation Conversation—and instead, we'd spent ninety minutes playing dress-up! I was having fun—Dad was always a lot of fun—but it sure didn't seem like "important business." This was goofy. Ridiculous.

Dad came out wearing one more suit, and the tailor followed a few steps behind. My mouth opened in a wide, toothy smile. "That's the one," I said.

His coat and vest were charcoal-colored, and underneath Dad wore a bold shirt that was blue like the ocean. He looked sharp, handsome, and mysterious—he looked like the Kidd on Keys.

"What do you say, sir?" asked the tailor.

Dad smoothed his lapels and checked himself out in the tall, three-sided mirror.

He glanced at me, and I nodded in encouragement. Then Dad faced the tailor. "I'm just…not sold on this," he said. "I just think today's not my day."

Dad changed back into his own clothes and the tailor gave us our coats. Dad tipped him, and then we left for the car empty-handed.

"Hey, next week," Dad said. "What time's your Innovation thing?"

"The first team performs at ten," I said. "We won't know the order we go 'til the day of, though."

"Then I'll be there at ten," he told me. Then he winked. "And dressed to the nines."

We reached the station wagon and climbed in—but my mind was still stuck at the tailor shop.

"Dad," I began, "didn't you like the suit I picked? You looked so cool."

He smiled. "I thought it was perfect."

I was totally confused. "Then why didn't you get it?"

Dad looked at me and grinned. "I never buy," he said. "I just like to try things on."

He started the car and we headed home. I really wanted to understand my dad, like Mr. Harvey said. But the more I learned about him, the harder it seemed to get.

Chapter Ten

Innovations, Conversations

"I'm so sorry!" I told Ella as I scratched behind her ears. "I wish you could come!"

The day was finally here—December fifteenth. It was just after sunrise, and in half an hour, we'd be heading up to a high school north of Pittsburgh for the first round of the Innovation Conversation. Mrs. Okocho was driving Momma and me, and since the host school was not far from where Dad lived, he was just going to meet us up there. My whole family would be cheering me on—everyone except for my pup, of course. I felt guilty that she was left out, especially since she'd had to listen to me practice every single night. I hoped that all the breakfast scraps I was feeding her would make up for it.

"How many sausage links has that been?" asked Momma.

"I'm just giving her the ends," I replied.

"You will make her tummy ache," Mrs. Okocho

cautioned as she scooped up some scrambled eggs with her toast. Momma had invited her to eat with us as a thank you for driving.

I swallowed my last bite and pushed my plate away. "May I go practice one last time?" I asked.

"Go ahead, Gifted and Talented," Momma said. "Not that you need it."

For the first time, I felt like Momma might actually be right. I knew "The Lonely Dog Blues" cold. And the rest of the team had stepped up, too. Our dress rehearsal on Thursday had gone so much better than last week. Maybe it was everybody's extra work, or maybe we all just felt surer of ourselves when we put on our costumes. I know that happened for me—even though my whole "costume" was really just a headband with a pair of felt dog ears glued to the ends. The way it changed me made me think of Dad and his weird suit-testing habit. Maybe he'd been onto something after all.

Ella followed me into my room, and I grabbed the dog-ear headband off my dresser. "You get a private preview," I told her.

My girl gave me the best compliment she could have: she sat right down to listen.

After we loaded the car, Mrs. Okocho drove us all the way up to a town called Moon. The high school there was hosting the Innovation Conversation in its gym.

We arrived right at nine—Mr. Harvey had told us to come early so we could get organized and practice. I lugged my dad's keyboard across the school parking lot with Momma and Mrs. Okocho at my sides.

"Sure you don't need a hand?" asked Momma.

"It's not so heavy," I replied. That wasn't totally true, but I was afraid that if I let go of the keyboard, the nervous tickle in my belly would come back.

When we entered the building, though, any plans I had to keep calm crumbled into dust. Mr. Harvey had told us there were a lot of schools competing, but this was too much to take in. The lobby and hallways were packed with team after team. Barely a few feet of space split each cluster. All of them were checking over props, practicing lines—near the corner, I even saw a pair of girls tap dancing in unison. "We don't have tap dancing," I told Momma.

"Don't worry about that," she said. "Let's just find your people."

By the time I spotted our team at the end of a hallway, Dad's keyboard case felt about three times heavier than when I'd pulled it out of the car. "If it isn't our playwright!" Mr. Harvey said. "Here, let me take that."

Mr. Harvey lifted the strap off my shoulder and I sighed in relief. He set it against a row of bright red lockers next to Darla, who was clapping a beat as Gautam practiced "Pesky Pete the Parakeet" for the four or five hundredth time.

"What time do we go on?" I asked.

"Eleven thirty-five," Mr. Harvey replied.

Perfect! I thought. That gave us plenty of time to practice, but it wasn't so late that we had to wait for hours and hours.

"What's the plan 'til then?" asked Momma. "Do the kids need any help?"

"I think we're all ready to rock," Mr. Harvey said. "I'd recommend finding a good seat in the gym. It's split with a divider. We're on the side with 'Tiger Pride' written on the wall."

I tapped Momma's elbow. "Can you call Dad and let him know where we'll be?"

"I'll tell him to find us in the front row," she replied. "Good luck!"

"It's *break a leg*," I corrected.

Mrs. Okocho inched past Momma and offered her hand to me. I took it and she gave me a firm shake. "Break your legs," she said.

Close enough, I thought with a grin. "Thanks, Mrs. O."

She and Momma worked their way back down the hall, weaving past a team of astronaut kids in puffy white snowsuits.

I turned around to find Darla standing half a foot behind me. "So," she said, "do you think we could practice just a little bit now?"

For the next hour, we huddled in the hall and held one last rehearsal. We worked through every bit of movement, every song, and every line of narration that came between. I'd added a narrator part to help explain what was happening—but also because everyone on the team had to participate and Russell refused to sing a single note.

A little before ten o'clock, the announcement speakers beeped loudly and a voice rang through the halls. "Round one of the Thirty-Third Annual Innovation Conversation will begin in ten minutes," it boomed. "Beginning teams, please head for the gymnasium and take your places."

I saw a team from our hall head out of sight. Other teams huddled together to have one last pep talk.

Mr. Harvey stepped into the middle of our group

and clapped his hands once. "All right, superstars, bring it in," he said. We formed a circle around him. "We need to meet back here at eleven-fifteen, on the button. I'll stay here to watch our props. If you want to stick around and practice more, let's respect the performers in the gym and do it very quietly. But personally…I think you guys are golden! I recommend that you relax, join your families, and enjoy some of the hard work the other teams have done."

I headed straight for the gym to check in with Momma. When I pulled open the doors, I spotted her and Mrs. Okocho in the front row of the bleachers like they'd promised. And they weren't alone, either.

"There she is!" Mrs. Jenkins cried. She was sitting beside Momma, applauding as I approached, and on her other side sat the rest of the Jenkins family.

"Thanks for coming," I told them.

"Like we'd miss our favorite neighbor's big stage debut," Mr. Jenkins said.

"I *told* you we'd be here," Ricky added, shaking his head.

I wasn't really focused on the Jenkinses, though. My eyes searched the rest of the gym—the basketball court, where the first team was setting up its backdrop, the upper rows of the bleachers, the entrances…

"Where's Dad?" I finally asked.

Momma shared a glance with Mrs. Okocho. "I couldn't reach him yet," Momma said. "He didn't answer his phone."

My heart began to rattle my ribs.

Mrs. Okocho smiled reassuringly. "He is probably driving here now and wants to be safe," she said.

"Can we call him again?" I asked. "Can we call right now?"

"Of course, sweetie," Momma replied.

But before we could leave the auditorium, a woman with horn-rimmed glasses and frosty hair stepped out onto the basketball court. She waved to the crowd with her wireless microphone. "Good morning, friends and families! My name is Edith Shapiro, head judge of…"

Momma took my arm and guided me to sit beside her. "We'll call again after this performance," she said.

"But Momma—"

"There's lots and lots of time," she promised. "You know how your father loves the last minute."

I nodded weakly. The head judge joined her partners at a table by the divider wall, and the first team began to perform. I barely even looked at their play. Instead, the whole time my mind raced through the different reasons Dad could be late.

Maybe he overslept.

Maybe he got mixed up and he's sitting on the other side of the divider.

Maybe he got another nosebleed and had to change his shirt.

Maybe he got lost on his way here.

Maybe he changed his mind—

I felt Momma shake my arm and applause sounded out around me. On the gym floor, the performers took a final bow. One kid was dressed as an explorer with a leather hat and a tan safari outfit, and four other kids were wrapped head-to-toe in Ace bandages. I felt really rude for zoning out during their whole play, so I clapped extra hard for them.

The second the applause died down, I led Momma out to the hallway so we could try Dad again.

"I'll do it," I insisted, and Momma handed me her phone.

I dialed Dad's number and waited. It never even rang—it just went straight to voicemail.

Momma could see it on my face. "I'm sorry, baby," she said, rubbing my back.

"Why is he doing this to me?" I demanded, my voice cracking.

Momma's gaze fell, and she just slightly shook her head.

But then she looked back up with calm eyes. "I'll do everything I can to get him here," she said. "I'll stand out here and call every other minute."

"What if he never turns on his phone?"

"Well…" Momma said, "his apartment isn't that far from here. If he doesn't answer in the next half hour, I'll send Mrs. Okocho there to get him."

I wiped a stray tear from the corner of my eye. "She'd do that?"

"Are you kidding?" Momma replied. "She'll tie him to her bumper if she has to."

A tiny smile fought its way onto my face.

"That's my beautiful girl," Momma said. "Just… try not to let it eat you up. This should be a great day for you. I'll take care of this."

I did my best to listen—but it was hard to stay in one place without looking at the clock every twenty seconds. So, I spent my time cycling between a few places. For a few minutes, I watched my teammates who were still rehearsing. When I got antsy, I went down the hall by myself and enjoyed all the craziness rushing by—the girl whose giant turtle shell costume kept getting caught on the locker handles, three boys who sprinted down the hall hefting a Styrofoam rocket ship above their heads.

In between all of that, I stopped by the gym to watch the other teams perform. The first time, I crammed myself in between Momma and Mrs. Okocho. But the second time I returned, Mrs. Okocho had stepped out.

"Did she really go to get Dad?" I asked.

Momma swept an arm around me, her grip strong and steady.

Mrs. Okocho was still gone when eleven-fifteen rolled around. "How far is it to Dad's house?" I asked Momma.

"From here? Twenty minutes, easy," she said. "When your team goes on, she will be here. Now go get 'em."

Momma kissed me on the head and the Jenkinses had me run past to give them each a high five—even Mrs. Jenkins, who practically stung my hand.

I took slow, full breaths as I joined the rest of the Talent Pool in the hall. Mr. Harvey was giving our team one last pep talk—how proud he was, how confident he felt about our chances. "You've already done the hard part," he told us. "You guys put together the funniest, most amazing, face-melting show in elementary world history. Now all you have to do is share it with everyone else."

Mr. Harvey held out his hand and we all put ours on top. The team did a cheer together, but I stayed quiet and made a wish. I probably don't have to say what it was.

We waited outside the gym doors for the team before us to clear out. I tried to peek through the small glass window, but I couldn't see the bleachers.

"Oh my gosh," Darla huffed, shifting the keyboard strap on her shoulder. "Take all day, please!"

"They're fine, we're fine," Mr. Harvey assured us.

When the last team had cleared away their props, a volunteer opened the doors for us. My eyes went straight for the bleachers. Momma and the Jenkinses were on their feet, and Mrs. Okocho was right there with them.

But no Dad.

I bit my lip to keep it from trembling. In the center of the floor, Donnie Yerba lined up a pair of easels from which he hung the backdrop we'd painted. Darla set up the keyboard and Russell took his place beside her to narrate. And I stood still, staring at Momma and Mrs. Okocho for an answer. Mrs. Okocho frowned and shook her head. Momma mouthed two words at me: *I'm sorry*.

"Come on," Gautam whispered, and he jostled me off to the sideline where the rest of the team had gathered.

The head judge, Miss Shapiro, read from a notecard to introduce us. "Presenting their original musical, *The Secret Lives of Pets*, I welcome, from the city of Pittsburgh, the students of Cedarville Elementary School!"

After a few seconds of cheering, Russell began his first lines. "On a day like today, in a house much like yours…"

When Russell finished, Darla struck a chord on the piano. Two girls wearing cat ears and matching black turtlenecks bounced out to sing the opening song, "Kitty Rock Anthem." They sang and danced, and the crowd cheered. But all I saw was the little gap between Momma and Mrs. Okocho where Dad should have been.

The show went on without a flaw. "Hamster" was a hit; Gautam managed to nail every word of "Pesky Pete the Parakeet"—and I couldn't have cared less.

Russell returned and spoke once again. "But not all of the pets had grand plans of mischief," he said. That was my cue. I gritted my teeth and went to my spot near the keyboard. "Tucked in a sad, little corner..." Russell said, "beneath a desk of solitude... lay a most loyal companion."

I knelt down beside Darla. I could see the keyboard case folded in half beneath Darla's chair. Staring up at me were those stitched-on words: *The Kidd on Keys*. I wanted to break my stupid dog-ear headband in half and run all the way home.

Russell held out his arms to the crowd. "A most loyal...and lonely...friend."

Darla played my song's little intro riff.

I couldn't remember a single word. I stared over at Darla, begging for help with my eyes.

She nodded a four count at me, and she played the intro one more time.

My mouth was so dry that it felt sealed shut. I could barely take a breath. I glimpsed my cheering section across from me—their smiles were fading as they watched me freeze. I wished I could just dissolve into the floor.

Darla played the intro once again. This time, though, I saw Ricky doing something. He was rifling through his coat. He pulled out a pair of drumsticks.

Darla played a fourth time, and Ricky tapped his legs on the two and the four. The intro played again, and this time Mr. Jenkins clapped along with his son.

My fear dropped away. But I didn't feel good underneath. I was furious. *They shouldn't be helping!* my brain screamed. *It shouldn't be them.*

Then something bizarre happened. In a flash, the words to my song came back, every single one. I began to sing.

No—I began to *roar.*

"*If you want to keep your smile,*

Then don't you look at me!"

I ripped through the song, swinging the notes as hard as I could, bending them like curveballs. The harder I pushed, though, the more it excited the crowd. The clapping spread to Mrs. Okocho and Momma, and then across the row, and then back to the top bleacher. Darla began to throw in more complicated note runs between each line.

"*Don't know where they went to be exact, but I just know they won't come back.*

I've got the left-me-all-alone-some, can't-even-pick-up-the-phone-some dog blues."

The bleachers exploded with applause. Ricky put his pinkies to his mouth and whistled. I hurried off to my teammates at the sidelines. "I feel sick..."

I whimpered, and I pushed straight past them and went into the hall.

I leaned against the lockers so I wouldn't fall over.

"Hey." I turned around and saw Ricky. "Are you okay?"

"Get away from me," I snapped.

Ricky looked totally puzzled. "What's going on?"

I stepped toward him. "Just go away, Ricky," I said, wiping my nose.

"Don't be embarrassed about freezing up," he said. "You were so awesome after."

Then I shoved him right in the chest.

"What is your problem?" he demanded.

"You are!" I yelled. "Go back to your perfect family and stay out of my life!"

Ricky's eyes got wet. Then he went back inside without another word. When the door closed, I sank down and scrunched against the lockers, and I bawled into my knees.

The gym doors reopened and I heard Momma rushing toward me. She wrapped her arms around me and I soaked her shoulder with my tears. "I'm here," she said.

And right then and there, she hooked an arm under my knees and lifted me off the ground like I was four years old again, like I was as light as a loaf of bread. “I’m taking you home,” she told me.

I didn’t argue. I couldn’t find any words to say. A single thought flickered through my head, before it was gone, too. *I have the strongest Momma in the world.*

The phone woke me up like an alarm. As usual, Ella sprung from the foot of my bed and hurtled toward the kitchen to investigate. I didn’t even shift under the covers. I just tilted my head and checked the clock—three in the afternoon. I couldn’t believe I’d only been home for two hours. I felt like I’d slept half a day.

I heard Momma answer the phone. After a moment, she came to my door with it in her hand. Ella wiggled back in and hopped onto my bed.

I pushed myself up with my elbows. “Is it him?”

Momma shook her head. “Mr. Harvey,” she replied. “He wanted to check on you.”

Momma passed the phone to me. “Hello?”

“Hey there, playwright,” Mr. Harvey said. “I hope your tummy’s a little better.”

Before we drove home from the Innovation Conversation, Mrs. Okocho had told him that I’d

gotten ill and needed to leave right away. Then she gathered Dad's keyboard for me as the team finished, and drove us straight home. Momma put the keyboard in her bedroom, because I couldn't stand to look at it.

"A little," I replied. Actually, my stomach felt grumbly—I'd skipped lunch and gone straight to bed when we got home.

"I'm glad," Mr. Harvey said. "Everybody was worried about you. Anyway, that's not the only reason I'm calling."

"What's the matter?" I asked.

"We just got our final score from the judges. Fourth place!"

I closed my eyes. We hadn't won. "Did we lose points because I left early?"

"What?" asked Mr. Harvey. "No way. Wait—this is *good* news! There were fifty-two teams there today. And the top five teams move on. We're going to the state round, Latasha!"

Different feelings rushed through me, too fast to even put them in order. I was proud, and excited, and energized…

"It's in Harrisburg, February ninth," Mr. Harvey continued. "We'll have plenty of time to make things perfect before then."

...And I was afraid. I couldn't go through another day like today. I just couldn't do it.

"What do you say?" he asked. "Are you ready to really buckle down?"

My answer shot out of me like it was trying to escape. "I quit."

Momma agreed to let me have alone time until dinner, on two conditions. The first: "After we eat, we're going to talk about Talent Pool." And the second: "You can't sleep the whole day away," she said. "Find something to do."

My usual choices were out. I didn't want to listen to music, and I couldn't find the right words to put in my journal. I tried writing an apology to Ricky for losing my temper, but everything I put down just seemed wrong. So instead, I did something I used to do a lot, which never failed to cheer me up—I read picture books to Ella.

Together, we caught up with our old friend Sam-I-Am; we learned what *really* happened between the Big Bad Wolf and the Three Little Pigs; and, of course, we did Ella's favorite thing—we let the wild rumpus start. But even though my bedroom door was wide open, my girl never ran out on me, not even for a second.

"You are the best, number one, A-plus little girl," I told her. She'd run out of gas and was now sprawled out, panting on my throw rug. Her surgery scar got itchy sometimes when she ran around, so I lightly swiped across the scar with my palm.

I heard a knock at our front door. Ella looked in its direction, but she didn't get up. "Uh-oh," I said, raising my eyebrows. "Okocho alert."

I didn't really mind, though. Story time had cheered me up and I owed her a thank you, anyway—she'd tried so hard to help. It wasn't her fault that Dad hadn't been home.

Momma opened the door and I waited for Mrs. Okocho's laugh. But that's not what I heard.

"You have a lot of nerve coming here," Momma hissed.

"I want to talk to her."

My face twisted and my stomach pulled tight.

I felt something rising inside me, but it wasn't tears this time. It was a fireball.

I sprung to my feet and went for my door. "You stay here," I told Ella. I closed her in the bedroom and charged for the kitchen.

"Do you realize what you did to her?" I heard

Momma say.

"I know, Steph. I know."

I turned the corner and saw Dad at the door. He and Momma looked at me.

"Where were you?" I growled.

"Kid," he began softly. "Things got really messed up, and—"

"—Where *were* you?"

"Latasha," Momma said, and she crossed toward me from the sink.

"I wasn't where I should have been," Dad replied. His gaze was so low that I could barely see his eyes. "I'm sorry."

"Apology not accepted!" I said. "Where were you?"

"I was—" Dad rubbed his cheeks. "I got kicked out of the band."

I opened my mouth, but I stayed silent. Dad grabbed a chair from the table and slumped onto it.

"Last night we had a gig," he said. "I missed part of the sound check. Joe lit into me, and I threw it right back at him. Maybe I crossed a line. I was stupid." He swallowed hard, his eyes flitting around the room until he settled back on Momma and me. "Joe tossed me. He sent me home. Except—I didn't go home, not until very late." He ran a hand through his wild hair.

"I lost my hat."

Dad looked like he'd shrunk a whole foot. "This morning," he continued, "nine-thirty, maybe? Your mother called me. I missed her, but it got me out of bed. I went to brush my teeth, and…I thought about Joe. And how I'd wrecked such a good thing." His lips smiled, but his eyes were dull. "So I hid. Turned off my phone, didn't answer my buzzer—not even when your landlady came by and tried to cuss the front door down. Because I couldn't think of facing you."

"I needed you there today," I said.

Dad nodded. "I know—and like I said, I'm sorry."

"But that doesn't fix it!" I shouted. "You made a promise. You promised you wouldn't forget me."

"I didn't forget," Dad insisted. "That's why I'm here. I didn't want you to think I up and forgot."

I folded my arms. "Oh, that's right," I said with a sharp scowl. "You thought really hard, and then you ditched me."

Dad tossed a hand up and let it fall. "What do you want me to say?" he asked, leaning toward me. "That I break my promises? That I'm a liar?"

I felt Momma grip my shoulders. "Don't talk to her that way," she warned.

Dad stood. "News flash, Latasha," he announced. "Your father is a loser. Okay? Are we clear? I mess things up. That's what I do."

I shrugged off Momma's hands. "But Daddy," I burst out, "if you keep messing up, how is Momma ever going to take you back?"

My words were a shock even to me. They'd just come out, before I could even think. Dad stared mutely. I heard Momma sniffle behind me.

"I..." Dad's eyes seemed foggy, like he'd been given a hard shake. "I don't want that."

The fire in me snuffed out and I went cold.

Dad looked at each of us. "I've got to..." He opened the door and rushed down the stairs. On the first floor, the front door slammed.

I finally knew my father. And all I could do was cry.

Chapter Eleven

The First Snow

"Only two more days until break," Momma said. "You're doing really well."

I closed my eyes so Momma couldn't see me rolling them. This was the fourth day straight that she'd given me a little pep talk out in front of my school, and all of her cheer was starting to annoy me. Only one person could make me feel better, and I hadn't heard a word from him since he'd run out of our kitchen. He hadn't even called about his keyboard.

"Just think," Momma went on. "Today and tomorrow here, and then you've got a whole eleven days off to play with Ella."

She brushed the fresh dusting of snow off my jacket. It was the first day we'd had snow on the ground, and Momma had been pointing out how beautiful everything looked the whole walk over. As if nothing was wrong at all.

"Remember the first time Ella went out in the snow?" she asked.

I remembered it perfectly. I'd taken her out back to go potty, but she was so confused by all the white on the ground. She'd done this goofy high-legged walk through it, like she was afraid of falling through—and she'd had no idea where she was allowed to pee.

That still wasn't enough to pull a smile out of me, though. I just wanted to disappear into the crowd of kids who were streaming in the front doors.

"Christmas, New Year's…" Momma said. "And then you've got a birthday right around the corner. Can you believe you'll be ten in a month?"

A month and a day, I thought with a sneer. *At least get the math right.*

But we'd argued enough times over the last few days. "Momma, I'm really cold," I said instead. "Can I go in now?"

"Oh! Sure thing," Momma said, adjusting the scarf around my neck. "I love you."

"You, too," I replied as I hurried off.

That morning, Miss Prooper kicked off social studies by reading a super-long list of Pennsylvania facts to us from a sheet of paper. I nodded along as she spoke, but really, I wasn't listening to a word. I was busy dreaming up a list of my own—a list about lunchtime and all the ways I could avoid it.

It was too bad, because Thursday was dinosaur chicken nugget day—but I couldn't deal with Darla or the other Talent Pool kids, and I *really* couldn't speak with Ricky. I was sure he hated me after how I'd treated him, and I was also pretty sure I deserved it.

For the first three days of the week, I'd used the same trick: I'd pretended I had a headache and got a cafeteria monitor to give me a pass to the nurse's office. That had worked out well—until the nurse mentioned calling Momma yesterday because of all of my headaches. So that was off the table.

It used to be that if I wanted a quiet lunch, I could go to Mr. Harvey's classroom. He always eats lunch at his desk so that students can use his classroom library—even past students, like me. But that was out now, too, for obvious reasons.

The library? I thought. *The band room?*

More than anything else, I wished that someone would just pick me up and take me out to lunch—that someone would pull up to the curb in their powder-blue station wagon and treat me one more time to the best french fries in the city. I screwed my eyes shut and hoped the idea would fade away.

"Miss Gandy?"

My eyes snapped open. Miss Prooper was peering at me over her reading glasses.

"Yes?" I replied, pasting a smile onto my face.

"Can you answer the question?" she asked.

I groaned to myself—this lady lived to catch kids who were zoning out. "Can..." I said. "Could you repeat it one more time?"

Miss Prooper sighed through her nose. "Can you tell us one nickname for the state of Pennsylvania?"

I gaped at Miss Prooper, unable to answer.

She arched a gray eyebrow. "The Blank State?"

I could feel all the eyes in the classroom shifting toward me. Finally Miss Prooper shook her head. "The Keystone State, the Quaker State, the Coal State, the Oil State...really, I just listed them five minutes ago."

Miss Prooper went to the chalkboard to write. Over her shoulder, she said, "Even our Gifted and Talented students need to pay attention, Miss Gandy."

A few kids around me snickered. I glowered at Miss Prooper's back. "I'm not Miss Gandy," I muttered. "That's my mother."

My teacher spun fiercely on her heel. "What was that?" she demanded.

I couldn't believe she'd heard me. "Nothing," I stammered.

Miss Prooper wedged her way down the aisle and stopped in front of me. "Are you absolutely sure?" she asked. I wanted to fold myself in half and hide inside my desk. "I'd love to hear—"

"Aw, come *on*!" someone interrupted.

I turned my chair with a screech. Dante was glaring at our teacher from the back row. "Leave her alone, Prooper-Scooper."

The whole room let out a long *ooooooh*.

"Quiet!" Miss Prooper barked.

I stared at Dante in disbelief, then back at her. Her mouth was open in a tiny little O. "Front office, now," she snarled. "The both of you."

I'd been to our In-School-Suspension room once before, last year. It wasn't like today, though. I'd just been taking something to a friend—I hadn't had to stay.

That was what Dr. DeSoto decided when Dante and I got to the office. She gave us a lecture about showing respect to our teachers and then she escorted us down to I.S.S.

At least I got out of lunch, I thought.

There were already two other kids in different corners of the room when we arrived. Dr. DeSoto gave instructions about us to Miss Schneider, who teaches gym and runs I.S.S. "They're here 'til the final bell," our principal said, and then she left.

Miss Schneider refolded her newspaper. “Have a seat,” she told us.

As soon as we'd sat, I asked Dante the question I'd had ever since his outburst. “What were you thinking?” I whispered.

“I said ‘have a seat,’” Miss Schneider reminded us, “not ‘have a chat.’”

I frowned. I didn't say anything more, but I looked at Dante for an answer.

Dante pulled a spiral notebook from his backpack. He wrote something on a page and turned it so I could see. His note read, *You've been sad.*

I glanced at Miss Schneider. She was hunched over her desk, working on the crossword page. I leaned over to Dante's notebook and wrote back. *Who says I'm sad?*

Dante tapped himself on the chest. Then he wrote, *I tried to help you.*

I snatched the notebook from him. *How is this help?* I scribbled.

Dante gently took it back. *My plan didn't work*, he wrote. *Sorry.*

What plan?

To get sent here, Dante wrote.

I scrunched my eyebrows—each thing that kid wrote was more confusing than the last.

He added on the next line: *I thought she'd just punish me. Not us.*

I closed my eyes in frustration. Who on Earth would actually *want* to get punished?

Dante noticed my expression and wrote some more. When he finished, he tore out the page and handed it to me. *If you get in trouble,* the note read, *your mom will be mad. But it's okay for me. My parents don't care.*

I tried to look Dante in the eye, but he just studied the scratches on the top of his desk.

When the final bell rang, we were free to go—and free to talk.

"Thanks again for sticking up for me," I told Dante as we zipped up our coats.

"Don't sweat it, Gandy," he replied. Then he turned to face me. "Actually, do me a favor. Talk to Jenkins, would you?"

My whole body tensed up. "I don't know," I said. I went out to the hallway, which was jammed with kids in bulky winter gear.

Dante hurried after me. "You have to," he pleaded. "For real, that dude has been bumming me out all week! Moping around like a little girl." He winced. "No offense."

"No offense," I agreed. We stopped in the front foyer. "You know, you're a good friend."

Dante just shrugged.

I was going to ask him if he needed a ride home, but I got interrupted by a loud voice.

"Latasha! Hey!"

I turned and my stomach dropped down to my knees. Darla and Gautam were running toward me with big smiles on their faces.

"Long time, no see!" Darla said. "Are you feeling better?"

I wasn't anymore, but Gautam chimed in before I could say anything. "We heard you cursed out Miss Prooper in class!"

"I didn't!" I protested. "Dante and I just got busted for talking back."

"Oh," Gautam said.

"And it was really just me," Dante added.

Darla glanced at the two boys with a smirk. "Anyway," she said, "we're getting Yoo-Hoos from the vending machine before Talent Pool. You want to come?"

I wondered for a second why they were even talking to me, but then realized: *They don't know that*

I quit. Then I realized something else: *I'm going to have to tell them I quit.* And that meant I'd have to tell them the whole messy story of *why* I quit.

Instead, I bolted out the front door.

"Hey!" Dante called after me.

Mrs. Okocho's Oldsmobile was already idling by the yellow curb. I jumped into her car and slammed the door shut. Instead of pulling away, Mrs. Okocho looked over at me with concern. "The principal called your mama," she said. "This is not like you."

"Please just drive," I huffed.

"Just this once," I moaned at Ella, "stay down!" I usually loved my pup's dancing hellos, but I'd had the worst day of a lousy week, and I was in for an awful night, too, once Momma got home. I didn't want to fight with Momma—but I didn't think I'd be able to stop myself, either.

I fumbled with Ella's leash, trying to clip it on. "I can't take you for potty 'til you settle," I grumbled.

My fingers hooked under her collar, but Ella spun in a circle and wrenched my wrist. "Ow!" I shouted, bolting to my feet. I gave the kitchen floor a room-rattling stomp. "Ella Fitzgerald Gandy!"

Her tail dropped and she galloped away to my bedroom. I chased after her, just in time to see her scramble under my bed. "Ella, you come out right now," I snapped.

The phone rang in the kitchen.

I turned my head toward the doorway, then back to Ella. She just watched me from the shadows. It made me feel like a monster.

The phone kept ringing. "This is not over, pup," I warned, and I stalked out of the room.

I yanked the phone off the receiver. "Hello."

"Latasha," Mrs. Okocho said on the other end.

"I know, I know," I replied. "I'm being loud up here. I'll stop."

"Latasha," she repeated in a sharp tone. "Will you please come join me for tea? I insist."

I knew that when Momma was at work, Mrs. Okocho was the boss. But I wasn't about to pretend that I liked it.

"I don't know," I told her. "I think I'd rather have *coffee*."

Mrs. Okocho set her silver tea tray on the dining room table. "Coffee is a drink for fun," she replied coolly. "Serious times call for tea."

Whatever, I thought.

Mrs. Okocho filled our cups from her teapot and sat down. "You know," she said, stirring in a lump of sugar, "you are right to be angry with him."

That made me pause. "Thank you," I said. I grabbed the plastic bear full of honey and dribbled some into my tea.

"For a long while," she said, "I was very angry with Mr. Okocho."

I waited for her to continue. Mrs. Okocho rarely mentioned her husband—all I really knew was that he had died some time before we moved in. "On the day he passed," she said, "he asked that I fry plantains for lunch. These are a fruit, like a banana. I did not have any in my kitchen, so I walked to the market. It was a beautiful day. A good day to start a garden. I bought the plantains, and hibiscus leaves as well, to make a punch. When I returned…he had gone to sleep."

I had no idea what I should say.

"My heart was shattered, of course," she said. "But I was angry as well. I hated him for leaving me without even a warning."

The story made me sad and frustrated at the same time. “But it’s not like he wanted to go,” I replied. “It’s not the same!”

“I know it is not the same,” Mrs. Okocho admitted.

I yanked a napkin from the holder on the table. “Then why’d you even tell me all that?” I asked, rubbing the corners of my eyes.

“Because, child,” she replied, “sometimes people we love very much…they leave us. And we do not get any choice in the matter.”

I snorted—as if I needed to be told that.

Mrs. Okocho clasped her hands and set them on the table. “But there is something we can choose,” she said. “How we treat those who are still here.”

I gave the ceiling a long look. “I think I owe some apologies,” I said.

Mrs. Okocho smiled. “Drink your tea first,” she told me. “Ella will wait for you.”

I obeyed and took a sip. “It’s not her I’m worried about.”

“What a pleasant surprise!” Mrs. Jenkins said. “Ricky’s out back.”

After I’d made up with Ella—which only took

about a dozen treats and five minutes of belly-rubs—it was time to get to the hard stuff. Mrs. Jenkins led me across the house toward the back door. "Your show was wonderful," she told me.

"Thank you," I replied. "I'm sorry that we disappeared after. That was my fault."

Mrs. Jenkins shook her head. "No," she said with a hint of a smile.

Outside, Ricky was bundled up in a dark blue snowsuit. "Let's run, Ham!" he shouted as he dove past his dog and slid across the frozen ground. If Hamlet was impressed, he sure didn't show it.

I opened the door and stepped out. "Don't break a drumstick," I called to them.

Ricky flopped on his back and looked at me. Hamlet, to my surprise, stood up and walked over. He went past me to the window, leaving smeary nose prints on the glass. I realized who he was looking for. "It's just me today," I told him, patting his head.

Ricky trudged over to me. I pointed out to the ground where he'd been sliding. "How'd you get it so icy?" I asked. "Garden hose?"

"What do you want, Latasha," he said flatly.

"I was really mean to you," I said.

"Yeah, you were," he agreed.

"And it wasn't fair."

"When are you going to tell me something I don't know?"

"I will, if you quit sassing me!" I snapped.

Ricky bit back a grin. "This is the worst apology ever," he said.

I nodded wearily. "Can we go inside?" I asked. "It might take a while."

We went back in, and once Ricky had changed into regular clothes, we sat in the living room near the fireplace. And I told him everything—even the embarrassing stuff, like how I'd been jealous of him, and how I thought my dad would fix everything, and how I couldn't have been more wrong. "He doesn't even want to be my dad," I whispered.

Ricky was leaning back against Hamlet on the floor, just listening. I don't think he knew what to say.

"Anyway," I went on. "I'm really sorry for how I treated you."

"Yeah," Ricky said. "I'm really sorry, too."

"What are you sorry for?" I asked.

Ricky furrowed his brow. "I don't really know," he replied. "I just feel sorry."

"You don't have to be sorry," I said. "You didn't do anything bad."

He sat up straight. "I didn't?"

I shook my head.

"Wow," he mused. "That's a first."

That made me chuckle. I pushed myself to my feet. "I'd better get going," I said.

"Do you have to?" asked Ricky.

"Momma will hit the roof if she comes home and I'm not there," I said. "I've got another long talk coming. And I know just how it's going to start, too."

"Latasha Esther Gandy?" asked Ricky.

"Big time."

When Momma got home, she sure didn't let me down. She practically bellowed my name, and then she went off with a bunch of those questions that weren't really questions. "What has gotten into you? What were you thinking?"

For the first few seconds of scolding, I was itching to raise my voice back. But I thought of Mrs. Okocho—and, weirdly enough, Dante—and waited it out. Once Momma had cooled off, I explained what had happened in school, and why.

I still had to write an apology to Miss Prooper, but Momma was more understanding than I'd expected. "You can come home and vent when you need to," she told me, "but you can't mouth off to your teachers, not ever."

I nodded. "Can we go in early tomorrow, then?" I asked. "I don't want to give my note to her in front of the whole class."

"Sure thing," she replied. "I'll even come in with you, if you want."

"Maybe," I said.

Momma smiled at me. "Everything will be fine," she told me. "You'll see."

That reminded me of something. "Momma," I began. "Don't take this the wrong way."

She tilted her head and waited.

"Please don't give me any more pep talks," I sighed. "They really get on my nerves."

Momma clutched my hand. "Deal."

Chapter Twelve

Family-Only

The next day, I skipped lunch again—but not to hide out.

"What can I do for you?" asked Mr. Harvey, sliding aside his carton of Chinese food.

I stepped into his classroom, ready to beg if I had to. "I don't want to let the Talent Pool down," I said. "Can I..." I was so nervous that I couldn't think of the right word. "Can I un-quit?"

Mr. Harvey gave me a knowing grin and jammed his chopsticks into the carton. "Un-quit?" he said. "What makes you think I ever let you quit in the first place?"

Then, just a couple of hours later, winter break began. And one by one, my days got better. I passed the time doing crafts with Mrs. Okocho and taking Ella across to Ricky's for play dates with Hamlet. And even though work tired her out, each night Momma stayed up with me to watch a movie, work on a puzzle, or have me read aloud to her.

I still stumbled sometimes when I felt extra-lonely—like on Christmas, when I got mad and tried to bend my *Tough Ladies* mix CD in half. I didn't realize that CDs don't bend—they shatter and leave a glittery mess all over the carpet. I was just lucky that Ella didn't try to eat any of it.

Mostly, though, I felt okay, as long as I stayed away from things that made me miss Dad. Some things were easy to avoid, like the Dirty O. Other things took more effort. The day school got back in session, I moved Dad's keyboard out of the house and into Mr. Harvey's supply closet so I'd never have to see it outside of Talent Pool practice.

But one thing was impossible to dodge.

"What do you mean, you don't want to do anything for your birthday?" asked Momma. "You're going into double digits!"

"I already said why," I answered. If there was any one day that made me think of Dad, it was my birthday. I could remember every card he'd sent me—before these past few months, my birthday had been the only day I felt like I had a father.

"I know," Momma said. "But...I want to throw you a real party. We can finally afford one."

Just before New Year's, Momma had done something huge—she'd made the final payment on Ella's surgery! We'd walked over to Dr. Vanderstam's and delivered it personally, then we'd stopped for a slice at Pizza Franco on the way home.

But even Momma's party offer couldn't sway me. "January twenty-first," I said testily, "is going to be a normal, boring day."

"Technically, this would be on the nineteenth," Momma said. "The Saturday before."

I lowered my brow at her.

"C'mon," she said, sliding closer to me on the couch. "We've got a week to plan the perfect party. I'll make sure you have a great time. Pizza, cake, games, all of your friends—"

"—Momma," I interrupted. "You're pep-talking."

"Well," she replied. "Forgive me for thinking that the day you came into the world is worth celebrating."

I sighed loudly.

"Look," Momma said. "You can't just pretend you don't have a birthday. How about we do something small? No streamers, no party hats...something family-only."

I closed one eye as I thought it over. "Can we have cookie cake?" I asked.

Momma's face lit up. "That's my girl."

The morning of our family-only party, I came out of the shower to find Momma fussing with something on Ella's head. "Relax, pup…"

"Momma!" I complained, yanking away the towel that was wrapped around my hair. "You said no party hats!"

Momma turned toward me. "Come on, she looks adorable."

Actually, with the party hat cocked forward on her brow, Ella looked a bit like a unicorn. That is, until she whipped the hat off her head, grabbed it in her teeth, and dashed for my room.

Momma and I shared a grin. "It was worth a try," she said.

Around eleven, we opened my presents. Momma only got me one thing, but it was the perfect thing—an e-reader!

"Now you can carry as many books as you want," she said.

"Thank you, thank you, thank you!" I squealed.

From Ella, I got a new notebook and a really nice fountain pen in a clear plastic case. But I liked the note that came with it best of all. It said, in handwriting that only looked a little like Momma's: *Please do not let me eat this pen. I know I will try.*

After Momma and I spent some time searching online for e-books, we heard a knock at the door. Ella scrambled off in an instant, but before Momma or I could get up, the door opened. "Hi, hello, good morning!" Mrs. Okocho shouted.

"You said we were doing family-only today," I told Momma with a grimace.

"What?" she asked. "Mrs. O isn't family?"

I opened my mouth to argue, but it was actually a pretty good point.

"Aiy! Down!" Mrs. Okocho cried. "Down, you fiend!"

Momma and I hustled to the kitchen and bribed Ella away before she could lick our landlady to death. Mrs. Okocho wiped her cheek with a shudder, and then approached me. She handed over a dense, box-shaped object wrapped in pink paper.

"I hope you will be surprised," she said. She leaned in close. "It is a thesaurus."

I hefted the heavy gift in my hands. "I'm very surprised," I told her.

Momma grilled mozzarella sandwiches for lunch, and then she pulled my cake out of the fridge. "The bakery said we should let it warm up a little first," she told us. She joined us at the table. "What do you want to do until then?"

"Latasha," Mrs. Okocho said excitedly, "now that you are ten years, I could teach to you my favorite card game. Have you ever heard of blackjack?"

I had! "Oh, I don't know about that," Momma cut in.

"We will not play for money!" Mrs. Okocho promised. Then, with a wink she added, "Well, no more than you can afford to lose, ha-ha!"

I grinned widely. Momma and Mrs. Okocho argued back and forth about blackjack until they were interrupted by another knock at the door.

"Latasha," Momma said over Ella's jumpy racket, "would you get that?"

I could tell she knew who it was. Like I was tearing off a bandage, I closed my eyes, gripped the doorknob, and yanked it open.

"Happy birthday!" yelled the Jenkinses.

Ella leaped into my back and knocked me right into them. Thankfully, Mr. and Mrs. Jenkins each caught one of my arms before I could totally topple over.

"Good gravy," Mr. Jenkins said as they filed into the apartment.

"Oh my gosh, Dad," Ricky scoffed. He handed me another box-shaped gift, this one lighter than Mrs. Okocho's. "This is from us, plus Ham."

I gripped the present firmly. My eyes drifted to Momma's smiling face. I didn't know what to say.

Mrs. Jenkins stepped beside me. "Your mother said you wanted a family-only day," she explained. "But I figured—well, you're part of our family. So here we are."

I looked around the kitchen. I'd never seen it so crowded. And I wanted to hug every person in it. But how would there ever be enough time to do it right?

Ricky's voice snapped me out of my trance. "You want to open that thing?" he asked.

"Ricardo," Mr. Jenkins warned.

"No worries," I said, shaking my head. I tore away the paper to reveal a photograph in a wood frame. It gave me a lump in my throat.

"What is it?" asked Mrs. Okocho.

I showed her the picture. It was a fall day on Graham Street. Ricky and I were standing on the sidewalk, flashing million-watt smiles. Hamlet sat, expressionless, at Ricky's side. At my feet, a panting tripod dog splayed out on the concrete. Inked in calligraphy on the mat holding the photo were two words: *Best Buddies*.

After Mrs. Okocho and the moms got their *awws* out of the way, it was time for cake. Everyone sang "Happy Birthday" and I blew out my candles in a single breath. Then Momma watched as I used a big knife to make the first cut.

"Did I surprise you?" she asked.

I turned to her. "I thought this was a no-secrets house," I replied.

She placed a hand on each of my cheeks and kissed my forehead. "Let's call today an exception."

Each guest took a cut of cake and moved into the

living room to sit.

After everyone had gotten a piece, I noticed there was still a quarter-cake left.

"We can freeze it," Momma assured me.

"Actually," I said, looking at the leftovers, "can I call someone else to come over? Another friend?"

Momma nodded, pleased. "Absolutely," she said.

"They might need a ride," I added.

"I'm sure someone will help."

I sprang to the living room doorway. "Hey, Ricky," I called in. "What's Dante's number?"

It turned out on Monday that Momma had one last surprise for me. When I walked out of school, I found her waiting for me at the curb. "I traded half a shift," she told me. "I wasn't about to let you spend the afternoon alone on your birthday. Get your earmuffs on and we'll start walking."

As we trekked home, I told Momma about how great the day had been. "Miss Prooper didn't mention my birthday," I explained, "but everybody else did. Darla and the Talent Pool kids sang to me at lunch, and Mr. Harvey came by and gave me a cupcake!"

"That was very thoughtful of him," Momma said.

"I saved it for dessert tonight. It's vanilla with strawberry icing."

"You might want to eat it now," she suggested. "Mrs. Okocho's been cooking today. A stew or something. It's very…"

"Malodorous?" I asked.

Momma's cheeks dimpled. "You've cracked your thesaurus, I see."

When we reached our porch, I noticed that the lid of our mailbox was open. When I gave it a closer look, my heart began to beat in double time.

A thick manila envelope was stuffed inside the box. I pulled it out and shook it to hear the coins rattle inside. Momma looked at it warily. "I could open that for you," she said, "if you want."

I flipped Dad's envelope in my hands. "I'll be okay," I said.

I rushed up the stairs. I was so eager to open the envelope that I barely noticed the weird aromas wafting from under Mrs. Okocho's door.

I unlocked our door and pushed past Ella to the kitchen table. I tore the envelope open and shook the change and Dad's note out onto the table. I looked at the note. My eyebrows creased in confusion.

Momma came in and knelt next to Ella, rubbing her belly to settle her down. Honestly, I could have used some of that. "What did he write?" she asked.

"'From the Kidd to his kid—happy tenth,'" I read. "'Here's to having one more chance.'"

"That's weird," Momma said.

I looked at the coins on the table. Ten pennies, ten nickels, ten dimes, ten quarters—no dollars. I shook the envelope again and realized it wasn't empty. I removed the paper hiding inside, but it wasn't cash. It was ten one-dollar scratch lottery tickets.

I tossed them onto the table. What was this supposed to mean? That he wanted another chance from me? That he wanted me to forgive him? Or was it just about the scratch tickets, and nothing more? I had half a mind to leave Dad's note and the tickets on my bedroom floor and let Ella "play" with them. I saw her near the corner now, sniffing at the heating vent. She must have caught scent of Mrs. Okocho's strange cooking.

I realized what I could do. "Momma, I'm running downstairs for a minute."

"Are you sure?" asked Mrs. Okocho.

I wasn't at all—but I didn't want time to change my mind. "You scratch," I said, "and I'll eat."

Mrs. Okocho sat at her table, my scratch tickets on her place mat, a silver dollar in hand. I sat across from her. And waiting in front of me was a steaming bowl of Mrs. Okocho's funky stew. It was a thick, globby red with vegetables and chunks of some kind of steak in it. It smelled like lemon and pepper—and gym class.

"We start together," Mrs. Okocho said. She set down the tickets and raised her silver dollar. "Do not worry. I took out the bones."

That almost sent me running out of the room. But then Mrs. Okocho scratched her first ticket, so I held my breath and spooned a bite into my mouth. I chewed the meat and vegetables, and when there was nothing left to chew, I swallowed it. The taste was—

"This is really...good?!" I exclaimed, completely baffled.

"Do you taste the garlic?" asked Mrs. Okocho, tossing a scratch ticket aside.

I took another bite. "Yeah, I do!" I said, licking my lips. "I couldn't smell it before."

I ate another few bites, searching for a nice chunk of that tasty steak. I actually thought I might have a second serving.

"Yes," she said, "the taste is much better than the smell. That is the trouble with goat stew."

I looked over at her. "With what now?"

"The goat meat," Mrs. Okocho said. "It has an odor."

My spoon clattered into my dish. "I just ate a goat?" I cried.

Mrs. Okocho chuckled. "Come now," she said, holding her fingers a few inches apart. "You ate that much of a goat."

"I just ate a cute little goat," I moaned. I couldn't even look at my bowl. Why had I gone through with this dopey idea?

"And, I might add, you loved it," Mrs. Okocho said.

I didn't look at her.

"Cows are cute," she said with a frown. "So are pigs…in the right light."

I peeked down at my bowl.

"It was good, no?" asked Mrs. Okocho.

"All right," I admitted. "It was."

"Then there is no problem," she said. She scratched her last ticket. "Bah! Not a winner in the bunch! This is why I prefer the blackjack."

I slowly ate another bite of my stew. It had no right to taste this good. "Can I…bring some of this up to Ella?"

"Oh, my stew is fit for a dog!" Mrs. Okocho

exclaimed. "What a compliment to the chef!"

"Sorry," I said.

"Why not share some with your mama instead?" she asked.

Mrs. Okocho made me a Tupperware of goat stew and I carried it up the stairs. "What's that you've got there?" asked Momma. She was spreading some peanut butter down a celery stalk.

"Early dinner!" I said. "It's from Mrs. Okocho. I tried it, and it is awesome."

Momma looked at me like I'd turned into a toad. "You tried her foot-stinky stew?" she asked.

"It tastes totally different," I insisted. I heard tapping at my feet. Ella had snuck up like a three-legged ninja and sat there, her happy tail whacking the floor. "Ella wants some."

"Ella eats dryer sheets," Momma retorted.

"Come on," I said. "Can't you be brave like me?"

Momma cracked a knowing grin. "Get me a spoon," she said.

I fetched one from the drawer while Momma opened the Tupperware. She ducked back at the smell and cried, "Good golly, Miss Molly!"

I crossed my arms.

"If it wasn't your birthday…" Momma said, and she took a bite.

I watched her face change just like mine had. “Wow,” she said.

She ate some more, nodding all the while. She picked out a piece of goat meat for Ella. “A treat for the pup!” she announced, and she fed it to her.

“Wasn’t I right?” I asked.

"You were," Momma admitted.

Ella circled around the table and sat beside her again.

"What do you know," Momma said, "a new dog!" She gave Ella a carrot slice and took another bite.

Momma tapped her spoon against the side of the Tupperware. "It's a little different," she said, "but this right here is the best beef stew that I have ever tried."

I watched Momma eat all the stew and scrape the very last spoonfuls of sauce. Once or twice, I came right up to the edge of telling her that she was not eating beef. We are, after all, a no-secrets family. But like Momma'd told me, there are exceptions. Sometimes, it's simply better not to know.

The End

Acknowledgements

Such little space, so many to thank—a lot of people have helped to keep wind in my literary sails. I'll start with Jane, Kellie, Evette, Ashley, and Kent, and all the people who've kept things rolling at Midlandia Press. Thank you to Amy and my Lincoln Interactive colleagues, who've been as supportive as can be as I wrote, traveled, and spoke to students.

Jenn, Debbie, Ang, Vinnie, and the rest of my draft readers: thanks for assuring me this book was going somewhere.

I had a big assist from my various online writing communities. Thanks to the members of #kidlitchat, #mglitchat, and, of course, the #nerdybookclub crew. Writing can be a solitary affair, but you all helped to keep it lively.

I'm grateful to many inspiring teachers—some from the past, and some whom I've only recently met. Thank you, Sharon, Milan, Jim, Hilary, Jane, Melissa, and Donalyn, and thanks especially to Colby, one of my biggest Latasha boosters, and who first planted the possibility that I should write this sequel.

Most important of all, thanks to every young person whose school I visited. Thank you, kids, for your boundless energy, your love of reading, and your audible excitement every time I mentioned this novel. If you hadn't wanted it, I might never have finished it.

About the Author

Michael Scotto is the author of the Tales of Midlandia picture book and iPad app series, as well as the middle-grade novels *Postcards from Pismo* and *Latasha and the Little Red Tornado.* He currently lives with his wife and their very naughty dog in Pittsburgh, PA, a mere three miles from Latasha's home. For his contributions as an advocate for youth literacy and creative thought, Michael was honored in 2011 by *Pittsburgh Magazine* and PUMP as one of the "Pittsburgh 40 Under 40." *Latasha and the Kidd on Keys* is his third novel.

About the Illustrator

Evette Gabriel is a contributing artist and the art director for the Tales of Midlandia picture book and iPad app series, as well as the illustrator of the middle-grade novel *Latasha and the Little Red Tornado.* Evette has worked at the *Pittsburgh Tribune-Review* as an editorial staff illustrator and continues to work in the editorial and children's markets. She currently lives with her husband and two feline companions in Pittsburgh, PA.